DEBATING P.C.

THE CONTROVERSY OVER POLITICAL CORRECTNESS ON COLLEGE CAMPUSES

DEBATING P.C.

THE CONTROVERSY OVER POLITICAL CORRECTNESS ON COLLEGE CAMPUSES

EDITED BY **Paul Berman**

ISBN: 0-440-50466-X

Printed in the United States of America

Published simultaneously in Canada

February 1992

10 9 8 7 6 5 4 3 2

The following selections in this anthology are reproduced by permission of the authors, their publishers, or their agents.

1. *The Big Chill? Interview with Dinesh D'Souza*
   by Dinesh D'Souza and Robert MacNeil. Courtesy MacNeil/Lehrer Productions © 1991 All Rights Reserved
2. *On Differences: Modern Language Association Presidential Address 1990*
   by Catharine R. Stimpson. Reprinted by permission of the Modern Language Association of America from *PMLA* 106 (1991)
3. *The Periphery v. the Center: The MLA in Chicago*
   by Roger Kimball. A version of this essay appeared in the February 1991 issue of *The New Criterion*. It is reprinted with permission of the author.
4. *The Storm over the University*
   by John Searle. Reprinted from *The New York Review of Books*, December 6, 1990, by permission of the author © John R. Searle 1990
5. *Public Image Limited: Political Correctness and the Media's Big Lie*

by Michael Berubé. Reprinted by permission of the author and *The Village Voice*

6. *The Value of the Canon*
   by Irving Howe. Reprinted by permission of *The New Republic,* © 1991, The New Republic, Inc.

7. *The Politics of Knowledge*
   by Edward W. Said. Reprinted from *Raritan,* Vol. XI, No. 1, Summer 1991, by permission of the author

8. *Whose Canon Is It, Anyway?*
   by Henry Louis Gates, Jr. "Whose Canon Is It, Anyway?" by Henry Louis Gates, Jr. Copyright © 1989 by Henry Louis Gates, Jr. Reprinted by permission of Brandt & Brandt Literary Agents, Inc.

9. *Why Do We Read?*
   by Katha Pollitt. Reprinted from *The Nation,* September 23, 1991, by permission of the author

10. *"Speech Codes" on the Campus and Problems of Free Speech*
    by Nat Hentoff. Reprinted from *Dissent,* Fall 1991, by permission of the author

11. *Freedom of Hate Speech*
    by Richard Perry and Patricia Williams. Reprinted from *Tikkun,* Vol. 6, No. 4, by permission of the authors

12. *There's No Such Thing as Free Speech and It's a Good Thing, Too*
    by Stanley Fish. Reprinted by permission of the author

13. *The Statement of the Black Faculty Caucus*
    by Ted Gordon and Wahneema Lubiano. Reprinted from *The Daily Texan,* The University of Texas at Austin.

14. *Radical English*
    by George F. Will. © 1991, Washington Post Writers Group. Reprinted with permission

15. *Critics of Attempts to Democratize the Curriculum Are Waging a Campaign to Misrepresent the Work of Responsible Professors*
    by Paula Rothenberg. Reprinted by permission of the author from *The Chronicle of Higher Education,* April 10, 1991, B1 and B3

16. *Multiculturalism: E Pluribus Plures*
    by Diane Ravitch. Reprinted by permission of the author from *The American Scholar,* Summer 1990

17. *Multiculturalism: An Exchange*
    by Molefi Kete Asante. Reprinted by permission of the author from *The American Scholar,* Spring 1991

18. *The Prospect Before Us*
    by Hilton Kramer. Reprinted from *The New Criterion,* copyright Hilton Kramer

19. *P. C. Rider*
    by Enrique Fernández. Reprinted by permission of the author and *The Village Voice*

20. *Diverse New World*
    by Cornel West. Reprinted by permission of the author from *Democratic Left,* July/August 1991, Vol. XIX, No. 4

21. *The Challenge for the Left*
    by Barbara Ehrenreich. Reprinted by permission of the author from
    Democratic Left, July/August 1991, Vol. XIX, No. 4

Special thanks are due Tony Kaye for his assistance and research.

Contents

PART TWO

POLITICS AND THE CANON

PART THREE

FREE SPEECH AND SPEECH CODES

PART FOUR

TEXAS SHOOT-OUT

PART FIVE

THE PUBLIC SCHOOLS

PART SIX

DIVERSE VIEWS

x *Contents*

INTRODUCTION: THE DEBATE
AND ITS ORIGINS

I.

The national debate over "political correctness" began in the fall of 1990 with a small, innocuous-seeming article in *The New York Times*—and within a few months was plastered across the covers of *Newsweek, The Atlantic, New York, The New Republic,* and *The Village Voice,* not to mention the TV news-talk shows and the newspaper op-ed pages. George Bush himself, not otherwise known as a university intellectual or a First Amendment hard-liner, weighed in with a speech at the University of Michigan defending campus freedoms against "politically correct" censors. Dinesh D'Souza's book *Illiberal Education: The Politics of Race and Sex on Campus* rose to the best seller list. The PEN American Center in New York held a major symposium, and the intellectual journal *Partisan Review*, a conference. Every ideology known on earth, plus a few others, was invoked in this debate, which made it hard to tell exactly what was under dispute. Yet at its heart, the debate consisted of only a few main points.

These points were by and large accusations, made at first by neoconservatives, later by liberals and a number of old-school leftists. According to the accusations, a new postmodern generation from the 1960s has come into power in the universities, mostly in the humanities departments but also in the central administrations. The postmodern professors promote a strange radical ideology that decries the United States and the West as hopelessly oppressive and that focuses on the reactionary prejudices of Western culture.

The new ideology tends toward nihilism, erasing any distinction between truth and falsity and between quality and lack of quality in art. Guided by these ideas, the postmodern professors have set out to undermine the traditional study of literature and the humanities. In the eyes of their accusers, they have reduced literary criticism to a silly obsession with political questions that don't belong to literature, and to a weird concern with sexual questions. In some cases they have gotten their students to study cheap products of Marxist and feminist propaganda instead of the masterpieces of world literature. They fan the flames of ethnic and sexual discontent among the students.

But the worst thing they do, according to the accusations, the thing that arouses so much angry resentment, is generate an atmosphere of campus repression. In the name of "sensitivity" to others and under pain of being denounced as a sexist or racist, the postmodern radicals require everyone around them to adhere to their own codes of speech and behavior. Professors and students who remain outside the new movement have to walk on eggshells, ever reminding themselves to say "high school women" instead of "high school girls" or a hundred other politically incorrect phrases. Already the zealots of political correctness have intimidated a handful of well-respected professors into dropping courses that touch on controversial topics. They have succeeded in imposing official speech codes on a large number of campuses. And the resulting atmosphere—the prissiness of it, the air of caution that many people in academic settings have adopted, the new habit of using one language in private and a different and euphemistic one in public—has finally come to resemble, according to the accusers, the odious McCarthy era of the 1950s. Except this time the intimidation originates on the left.

The main accusation is summed up by the title of a 1986 article from *Commentary* magazine: "The Campus: 'An Island of Repression in a Sea of Freedom' " (by Chester E. Finn, Jr.). But there are secondary accusations too. The repression, bad enough in the universities, is said to be spreading to the museums, where the political slant of the new ideas has a disastrous effect on art, and to the cultural journalism of a beleaguered politically correct city like Boston. And still worse, the same trends have made the fatal leap to the curriculum committees of public school education.

New curricular developments emphasizing hyperethnicity, Afrocentrism, and other notions of the avant-garde have been adopted in quite a few school districts around the country and are on the verge of being adopted in some of the major states, with effects that, in the view of the critics, can be predicted to be calamitous. There is going to be a deliberate miseducation of children from impoverished backgrounds. The educational emphasis on ethnic distinctions and the suspicion of American democratic institutions are going to wear down the bonds that hold the country together. And sooner or later, according to these accusations, problems that are political and social, not just educational, will come of all this, and the United States will break up into a swarm of warring Croatias and Serbias. "Deculturation prefigures disintegration," in James Atlas's sardonic phrase.

All in all, these were very exotic accusations, which made them interesting—but also easy to doubt, as some of P.C.'s severest critics have frankly acknowledged. Any number of liberal and left wing professors instantly stood up to challenge the entire complaint and to scoff at the alarmist tone. (In a moment I will mention some aspects of that response.) Yet the accusations were not without a historical background. In some respects they have been with us for a decade or longer—ever since the engagé art critic Hilton Kramer used to scandalize the readers of *The New York Times* with his thunderings against the radical counterculture and the left. Elements of the argument surfaced in the national political discussion as early as 1984, when William Bennett, at that time the chairman of the National Endowment for the Humanities, criticized the universities in a pamphlet called *To Reclaim a Legacy.*

Allan Bloom's oddball best seller of 1987, *The Closing of the American Mind,* brought the debate to a wider public. Bennett's conservative successor at the National Endowment for the Humanities, Lynne V. Cheney, produced a pamphlet of her own called *Humanities in America*—which was answered by the liberal members of the American Council of Learned Societies in their own pamphlet, *Speaking for the Humanities.* There was a national debate in 1988 about the curriculum at Stanford University and the merits of substituting "multiculturalism" for the traditional study of Western Civ. And the same argument took other forms—the debates over artists like Andres Serrano and Robert Mapplethorpe (accused respectively of blasphemy and obscenity) and over Yale University's literary theorist, the late Paul de Man, whose secret life turned out postmortem to include a stint as a pro-Nazi book critic in German-occupied Belgium.

Aspects of the debate turned up in other countries too. There was a battle at Cambridge University in 1981 when university authorities more or less declined to make room for some of the new literary theories. France saw the biggest arguments of all—measured in ink spilled and probable influence (once the news of these arguments begins to spread into other languages), with the subjects ranging from the influence and politics of the German philosopher Martin Heidegger to the new glass pyramid at the Louvre to the meaning of Third World revolution.

What was new, then, in the American controversy over political correctness in the early 1990s? A few things, certainly. The name was new. "Politically correct" was originally an approving phrase on the Leninist left to denote someone who steadfastly toed the party line. Then it evolved into "P.C.," an ironic phrase among wised-up leftists to denote someone whose line-toeing fervor was too much to bear. Only in conjunction with the P.C. debate itself did the phrase get picked up by people who had no fidelity to radicalism at all, but who relished the nasty syllables for their twist of irony. Apart from this phrase, some of the particulars had a fresh aspect: the focus on campus speech codes, and the amusing experience of watching people on the right argue for the First Amendment and people on the left against it. The way that certain liberals and old-school leftists joined the neoconservatives in making several of the arguments was also new, and perhaps quite significant, since previous debates tended to observe a chaste division of left and right.

Yet at bottom, the P.C. debate was just a continuation of an argument that is more than a decade old. And the longevity of this argument, the way it keeps reappearing in different forms, growing instead of shrinking, producing best-selling books about university education every couple of years, its international dimension, the heat and fury— all this should tell us that something big and important is under discussion. How to specify that big and important thing is not so easy, though. The closer you examine the argument over political correctness, the more it begins to look like one of Paul de Man's literary interpretations, where everything is a puzzle without a solution. No three people agree about the meaning of central terms like "deconstruction," "difference," "multiculturalism," or "poststructuralism." Every participant carries around his own definitions, the way that on certain American streets every person packs his own gun. And when you take these numberless definitions into consideration, the entire argument begins to look like . . . what?

I would say it looks like the Battle of Waterloo as described by Stendhal. A murky fog hangs over the field. Now and then a line of soldiers marches past. Who are they? Which army do they represent? They may be Belgian deconstructionists from Yale, or perhaps the followers of Lionel Trilling in exile from Columbia. Perhaps they are French mercenaries. It is impossible to tell. The fog thickens. Shots go off. The debate is unintelligible. But it is noisy!

II.

What explains the confusion? One explanation—there are others—lies in the peculiar history of certain very radical ideas that came out of the sixties' left, both in this country and in France. The left-wing uprisings of circa 1968 had two phases, which were in perfect discord, like two piano strings vibrating against each other. The first phase was an uprising on behalf of the ideals of liberal humanism— an uprising on behalf of the freedom of the individual against a soulless system. The second phase was the opposite, as least philosophically. It was a revolt *against* liberal humanism. It said, in effect: Liberal humanism is a deception. Western-style democracy, rationalism, objectivity, and the autonomy of the individual are slogans designed to convince the downtrodden that subordination is justice.

This second phase, the phase of ultra-radicalism, received a supremely sophisticated expression at the hands
of various Paris philosophers, in the theories that can be
called postmodern or poststructuralist. Or maybe it's better
(since everyone argues over what is the correct label) to
call these theories " '68 Philosophy," as suggested by two
of the younger Paris thinkers, Luc Ferry and Alain Renaut.
The theories were, in any case, something other than mild
doctrines of social reform. They were extravaganzas of
cynicism. They were angry theories (though coolly expressed), hard to read, tangled, more poetic than logical.
They were by no means internally consistent, one theory
with the next. But if they had a single gist, it was this:
Despite the claims of humanist thought, the individual is
not free to make his own decisions, nor is the world what it
appears to be. Instead, we and the world are permeated by
giant, hidden, impersonal structures, the way that human
forms in *Invasion of the Body Snatchers* are inhabited by
extraterrestrial beings.

What are these permeating structures? They can be
described every which way, mix-and-match style, according to the different versions of '68 Philosophy. There was,
thus, the version of the Paris Heideggerians, for instance
Jacques Derrida (we are permeated by the entire unfortunate tradition of Western thought). Or the Paris Nietz-
scheans, for instance Michel Foucault (we are permeated
by the will to power). Or the Paris Freudians, for instance
Jacques Lacan (we are permeated by the structures of the
unconscious). Or the Paris Marxists, for instance Pierre
Bourdieu (we are permeated by economic structures). Or
the Paris anthropologists who were influenced by Claude
Lévi-Strauss (we are permeated by unchanging cultural
structures).

Mostly there was the idea that regardless of how the
permeating structures are labeled, One Big Structure un-

derlies all the others—and if this deepest of all structures can be described, it is by means of the linguistic theories that derive from Ferdinand de Saussure. That is: We are permeated by the structures of language. We imagine that language is our tool, but it is we who are the tool and language is our master. Therefore we should stop deluding ourselves with foolish humanist ideas about the autonomy of the individual and the hope of making sense of the world. Or maybe—this is an implicit alternative possibility in several of the '68 theories—by recognizing the existence and power of the permeating structures, we will bring on a grand revolution, Marxist-style, or even grander. The theories rarely said anything specific about such a possibility, though a writer like Foucault might speak of "an Apocalyptic dream." But even without a direct invocation of the Apocalypse, there was an urgent tone in how these ideas were written, and the tone sometimes conveyed a touch of millenarian expectation.

Now, whatever else could be said about these theories, they were wonderfully expressive. The whole period from World War I through the end of the Cold War was (maybe still is) an era of ever-recurring catastrophe and mass death, with still greater catastrophes lurking in the future in the form of nuclear war or God knows what; and in such an era, to cast a cold eye on rationality and humanism seemed entirely sensible. It was a way of saying that a) things are out of control, and b) the effort to get them under control by looking to logical analysis or proposing a lofty view of mankind is like summoning a criminal to stop a crime. The theories evoked something about middle-class life in noncatastrophic conditions too—the emptiness of middle-class existence, the feeling of drift and purposelessness that seems to afflict the middle class everywhere and that makes some people susceptible to the idea of an impending catastrophe.

The theories were modern art's extension into philosophy. They were the equivalent of *Finnegans Wake* or canvases by Rothko, and in that respect they were artistically faithful to the bleak twentieth-century spirit. But there was no point in asking whether these theories were faithful to truth and reality in the ordinary sense of social science or conventional philosophy. Super-brilliance was their panache, and the more super the brilliance became, the murkier became the ideas. The prose was characteristically mud, as befitted a philosophy that regarded clarity and lucidity as engines of Western oppression. Sometimes the theories were put-ons or jokes. Or the theories were fictions that claimed to be nonfictions. They elevated puns into a literary genre. The truest class struggle in the '68 sense was always the struggle between the hip and the unhip, and these theories were, in short, the *Das Kapital* of hip. They were illegal thoughts, so to speak—"provocations, not programs," in Allan Megill's phrase. Of course that will always be the subversive appeal of '68 Philosophy.

Still, sooner or later the irritating flatfooted question about ordinary truth and reality and its relation to these ideas is bound to intrude. For what if, by unlucky chance, it turns out that everything in the world is *not* a language structure? In the field of politics, for instance, what if the difference between democratic societies and nondemocratic societies turns out to be real, not just rhetorical?

The many dazzlements of '68 Philosophy were never any use in addressing mundane questions like these. The great god of the Paris thinkers was Heidegger, who was second to none in holding Western rationalism and humanism responsible for all the unhappiness of modern life and for hinting at millenarian alternatives. But the alternative he ended up embracing was the Nazism of Adolf Hitler. Of course, the Paris ultra-radicals who imbibed the theories of '68 Philosophy were anything but right wing. Yet there was nothing in their leftism to prevent a substantial number of them from tilting to an opposite extreme and celebrating dictators like Mao Zedong, so long as the horrors of liberal civilization were being opposed. For the whole point of postmodern theorizing was, after all, to adopt positions that were so far out, so wild, as to blow your mind.

In Paris, the '68 theories had their day, which lasted well into the late seventies and beyond. Then a new generation of writers came along, the people who were students in '68 but came into adulthood only in the calmer years that followed—writers like Ferry, Renaut, Pascal Bruckner, Alain Finkielkraut (and writing in English, the late J. G. Merquior), who worried about the mind-blowing ultra-radicalism of the older generation. These younger writers began to suspect that '68 Philosophy, in turning so ferociously against liberalism, sometimes bore a closer relation to the old German romantic philosophies of the far right (the cult of irrationalism, the eagerness to disparage universal ideas of rights, etc.) than anyone seemed to imagine when the theories were in vogue. They worried that by carrying skepticism to extremes, the '68 Philosophers were turning into a species of idiot, the sort of people who can no longer make sensible judgments because they stumble around wondering: Is that a door? Is that a window? The younger writers raised an eyebrow at the muddy prose style, too, and suspected, as Merquior commented (citing Pope), that

> Much was believ'd, but little understood,
> and to be dull was constru'd to be good.

The younger writers set out to resurrect the very notions that '68 Philosophy was designed to debunk—an admiration for Enlightenment reason, clarity, lucidity, and Western-style freedoms. Their resurrections have sometimes leaned in a more leftish direction, sometimes in a more conservative direction (whatever those terms might mean in today's world). Either way, the drift toward humanism was unmistakable. Even a few of the elders of the sixties, disturbed by the implications of their own doctrines, pulled back over the course of the later seventies and the eighties. There were writers like Tzvetan Todorov, the Paris literary theorist, who shifted camp altogether. And in the realm of ideas a new liberal age, the era of human rights, was at hand—in Paris.

III.

The history of leftism's ultra-radical phase in America was very different. The sixties' revolt against liberalism in America was a matter more of action than of theory. Political liberalism seemed to have pushed America into Vietnam. Liberalism seemed incapable of redressing the grievances of black America. It seemed to have failed—and radicals responded simply by going outside the liberal way of doing things.

They turned away from the liberal civil rights movement, away from the liberal Democrats and the unions and the social democratic intellectuals, and they took actions and built organizations of their own. And among these ultra-radical efforts, the most important, the ones that made a permanent change in American life, were the sundry campaigns that arose at the end of the sixties and eventually came to be known as "identity politics"—the movements for women's rights, for gay and lesbian liberation, for various ethnic revivals, and for black nationalism (which had different origins but was related nonetheless).

The secret of these movements, their genius, was simply to invent alternative personalities and encourage people to adopt them. The radical left fell apart after a few years in

America just as in France, mostly because it became too extreme for its own good. But the identity-politics movements remained. They were useful, even indispensable, to their own adherents. And they were adaptable. They didn't stay forever locked in a war with political liberalism; they pushed their way into the Democratic party and the general culture, and they became permanent features of American life.

Radical leftism in the American sixties naturally made all kinds of efforts to work up some ambitious theories, too, and part of those efforts, no small part either, was to import ideas from France. But that was slow going, possibly because the original works in French were translated only gradually, and in several cases made it into print only after the radical spark from the sixties was gone. Or it was because the French ideas were too baroque for American tastes, and too cynical; or because writers like Herbert Marcuse and others from a German tradition of philosophy, who were already established in the United States, seemed to make it unnecessary to turn in French directions.

Still, the sixties Paris ideas did establish some footholds in the United States, in the art world, for instance, where radical posturing has a certain virtue—the more radical, the more virtuous, if you do it well. But the biggest and most important of the footholds, the foothold that has mattered most in the current debate, was in the humanities departments of a handful of universities. French ideas established themselves in waves of fashion in these departments during the course of the seventies and into the eighties. There was an early vogue for the anthropological/ Marxist/linguistic ideas of Roland Barthes. Next came a wave for the Heideggerian/linguistic ideas of Derrida, in the form of "deconstruction" (meaning, interpreting literature in order to show the impossibility of a definite interpretation). Then came a feminist wave for the Freudian/linguistic ideas of Lacan, and after that a wave for Foucault. But of all these waves, the one that finally sparked the P.C. debate of today didn't begin in Paris at all. It was an authentically American mutation of '68 Philosophy, something different, a New World spin on the Paris ideas—a novel variation to add to the already-established mix-and-match versions that drew from Heidegger, Nietzsche, Freud, Marx, linguistics, and anthropology.

The new variation drew from American identity politics. Its fundamental unit was the identity-politics idea that in cultural affairs, the single most important way to classify people is by race, ethnicity, and gender—the kind of thinking that leads us to define one person as a white male, someone else as an Asian female, a third person as a Latina lesbian, and so forth. With this idea firmly in place, the new American thinkers picked up the freshly translated volumes from Paris plus a few that were written over here and went rummaging through the already-existing varieties of '68 Philosophy, picking and choosing selected components, sometimes finding ideas that were already suited for the new version and bringing them into stronger American focus, other times making a few alterations.

From Derrida and '68 Philosophy as a whole came the idea that language and literature are the vast impersonal structures that, more than government or economics or politics, determine the nature of society. Likewise from Derrida and the linguists, who defined the meaning of words by their difference from one another, came the idea of defining people in the same way, thus offering the crucial analogy between identity politics and linguistic analysis. From Foucault and the Nietzschean theorists of culture (and from Antonio Gramsci, the Italian Marxist) came the idea of looking at culture as a field of struggle for achieving political power. Also from Foucault came a focus on marginal social groups. From Marxism came the idea of an impending beneficial social change. From Lacan and the Freudians came a focus on the erotic and on male domination. From the Third Worldist writers came an anti-imperialist variation on Heidegger's view of the regrettable intellectual tradition of Western civilization.

And *voilà*: the great new mélange, '68 Philosophy in its American mutation. Its name is, or ought to be, "race/class/gender-ism," since "race, class, and gender" is the phrase that dominates its analyses. There is no single author who has succeeded in giving the idea an authoritative definition, no one book or article that you can point to. But I will draw a caricature.

Race/class/gender-ism, in my caricature, pictures culture and language as the giant hidden structure that permeates life. But culture and language are themselves only reflections of various social groups, which are defined by race, gender, and sexual orientation. (The word "class" is invoked only for the purpose of conjuring a slight aura of Marxism.) Groups, not individuals, produce culture. Every group has its own culture, or would, if oppressors didn't get in the way. Thus we have the cultures of white men, of black men, of women, of black women, of homosexuals, of Hispanic women, and so forth. Categories that go beyond race, gender, and sexual orientation might also play a role—especially any trait that could put a person at a disadvantage, such as being handicapped.

The different cultures are engaged in a struggle for power. The culture of white males (specified sometimes as European males, other times as "whitemales," most popularly as Dead White European Males or DWEMs) has pretty much won this struggle, and thus has achieved domination over the rest of the world. The domination has succeeded by using terms like rationalism, humanism, universality, and literary merit to persuade other people of their own inferiority. But by shining the light of race/class/gender analysis upon it, this success can be revealed as the power play that it is.

Race/class/gender analysis will show the culture of white males to be a culture of domination and destruction, more or less the way Heidegger pictured Western philosophy, or the way anti-imperialists picture imperialism. By teaching everyone to appreciate the culture of all groups in equal measure and by discouraging the use of certain common phrases that convey racial and gender hierarchies, in short by altering the literature and the language, we will bring to an end the domination of this one small group. The name of this domination, "Eurocentrism," evokes the "ethnocentrism" that is criticized by the French followers of Lévi-Strauss as well as the "logocentrism" that is analyzed by the French Heidegerrians. (Logocentrism in this context means the intellectual tradition of Western civilization that has led to the errors of rationalism and humanism— and can be conflated with still another centrism, phallocentrism, to become phallogocentrism, meaning, more or less, the regrettable tradition of imposed masculine logic.) And in eliminating these various centrisms, in abandoning the idea of any kind of cultural "center" at all, a new and more egalitarian society will emerge, giving full rein to diverse cultures of every kind.

Race/class/gender-ism is, in short, a bit of the old ultra-radicalism. It is '68 Philosophy, American style, with certain virtues of the French original too—the impiety carried to eye-opening extremes, sometimes the wit, though the American version tends to be more earnest and less clever than the French. The American idea even offers something of the old Apocalyptic spirit, not openly but by implication—in the excitement that these ideas have aroused, the feeling that a new intellectual revolution is at hand, something monumental like the invention of modern physics at the beginning of the century. This is, by the way, an intriguing notion. For even if the theory that I've just described is utter nonsense, it is true that due to the social reforms in the Western countries during the last few decades, and due to the democratic revolutions around the world, the social basis for a global culture is far huger than it ever was before, and who can say what this will produce a hundred years hence?

Still, if the American doctrine has some of the appeal of '68 Philosophy, it is also vulnerable to all the criticisms and questions that were posed several years ago in Paris. For instance: Does race/class/gender-ism, in putting primary emphasis on a category like race as a factor in culture, offer a refreshingly candid view of influences that have always existed but are normally concealed? Or does the emphasis on race bring us back to the dubious theories of the European past, as Todorov has suggested? Is there a hint in these ideas of the old German romantic philosophies of the far right?

It pains the admirers of Yale deconstruction and of race/class/gender-ism when anyone mentions the early career of de Man, the Yale critic, on the grounds that a young person's early mistakes should not be used to hound his later achievements. Yet the controversy over de Man and his youthful errors has had one merit at least, which is to give everyone the opportunity to read some Nazi-style literary criticism, for instance de Man's collaborationist article from 1941, "The Jews in Contemporary Literature," which has been brought back into print. Now, here was an example of cultural analysis in which writers were categorized on the basis of racial "difference," the Jews on one hand and the Europeans on the other.

Exactly what makes de Man's early reactionary harping on race different from the postmodern, supposedly progressive harping on race today? It is argued that "race" in the postmodern, sociological, progressive usage has nothing to do with "race" in the old, reactionary, biological usage, and that only someone who is motivated by hostility or by a stubborn unwillingness to entertain new ideas would detect in these up-to-date progressive ideas a scent of old-fashioned reactionary rightism. Yet the distinction between the postmodern ideas and the reactionary ones is not necessarily so clear—if only because, among some of the deconstructionist masters of literary interpretation, there is a peculiar inability to detect any Nazism at all in de Man's Nazi articles, which raises doubts about the reliability of the new techniques. And because, in the movement for multiculturalism that has emerged out of race/class/gender-ism, a touch of the young de Man's Euro-style racial thinking does sometimes creep into the discussion, obviously not among the sophisticated thinkers, who are embarrassed by the problem, but on the margins of the movement. It was disturbing, for instance, but not terribly surprising, to discover a certain inappropriate fixation on the Jews in the thinking of a couple of the professors who helped draw up the proposed new multicultural public-school social-studies curriculum in New York State.

Of course someone might say about the several doubts and problems that hover over these new ideas: so what? Just because a doctrine is a bit dotty or has trouble fending off unattractive elements, valuable results might come of it anyway, in the right hands. "Saying absurd things," as Richard Rorty observes, "is perfectly compatible with being a force for good." Especially in America, I would add. In France, every educated person receives a pretty good schooling in philosophy, which has the evil effect of encouraging people to be logically consistent in their foolish ideas. But in America we tend to be suspicious of philosophy, unless it is something like John Dewey's mixture of see-if-it-works pragmatism and social democratic reform. We like ideas—but we water them down.

The natural instinct for most American intellectuals, when it comes to doctrines from France, is silently to demote the philosophies into methods—into techniques that you *apply,* the way you might apply a carpentry technique, when the occasion requires, and not on other occasions. Some of the professors who promote race/class/gender-ism are happy to embrace the idea in all its radical grandeur. But a far larger number have no interest in way-out implications. Working up a philosophical opposition to humanism and rationalism was never their idea, except maybe for rhetorical effect. On the contrary, these professors *are* humanists, and always were. They seek the further flowering of liberal democracy.

When they argue for multiculturalism, they don't mean to displace the culture of rationalism and humanism with a variety of nonrationalist and nonhumanist traditions. They merely wish to remind everyone not to allow the central culture that does exist to fall prey to habits of bigotry or smallmindedness. Fundamentally they wish us to be *more* rational, not less. Tolerance, that grandest of concepts from the Western Enlightenment, is the name blazoned across their jackets. They don't mean to overthrow the Western literary canon the way Heidegger wanted to overthrow the Western philosophical canon. They want to expand it. They mean to remind us to look around to see if, because of discrimination in the past or its persistence today, certain authors and works of art have been overlooked. And sure enough, certain authors and works and perspectives have indeed been overlooked, and today some of them have been rediscovered, which is a testimony to the new ideas. And it is good to look for still more writers and more traditions and variety of every sort, not in order to undermine the general culture, but to strengthen it.

The liberal professors who play with these ideas are not

revolutionaries against modernity. Mostly they mean to teach a good course—even if, here and there on the faculty, someone may like to keep the students and the state assembly on their toes by uttering a rattling enigmatic Paris slogan now and then or by railing against universal standards and the rule of white males.

IV.

To professors like these and their supporters, to the postmodern liberals who spice up their teaching and writing with a few sprinkles of race/class/gender-ism or a bit of world-weary deconstruction, something about the current debate is very chilling.

They see the *Newsweek* cover pointing a finger at the "Thought Police," which means themselves, and they see President Bush denounce them, and they look around for their own allies, who turn out not to be many. And they have reason to feel a pinch of fear. It is because of the disproportion between their own power and that of the hostile institutions arrayed against them.

They wonder: Isn't something overblown about the outrage over P.C. and the new theories and the curricular debate? There are silly panels at the MLA conventions, but do these merit a national crusade? The tales of P.C. power make them rub their eyes. And these charges of McCarthyism! The real-life McCarthyism of the fifties was a hysterical movement against a relatively small number of American Communists, but its real target, according to one very sound interpretation, was the heritage of New Deal liberalism from the thirties. Mightn't something similar be at work today, and mightn't the real target in the anti–P.C. campaign, as some writers have conjectured, be the heritage of democratic openness and social reform that dates from the radical sixties?

The feminist transformation of American universities has the look of irreversibility, if strictly on demographic grounds. But in the age of AIDS, it's hard to know what will be the eventual status of the freedoms that have lately attached to homosexuality—the freedom to speak about it openly, for instance. The future status of racial integretation in the universities is likewise hard to predict. Official segregation in American universities sounds like something out of the Middle Ages but was entirely common no more than thirty years ago. At a place like Duke University, today the home of some of the friskier literary theorists, black students were simply not admitted, as the literary critic Louis Menand has pointed out. The anti–P.C. argument leapfrogs sometimes from a criticism of P.C. obnoxiousness and the daffiness of the new literary theories to a criticism of affirmative action, in fact to an argument that affirmative action has turned into a fiasco, not just in its details but as a whole. But that may not be the case.

At the time when schools like Duke were barred to black students, the university-educated African-American middle class was small. Today that class has multiplied severalfold, partly because of affirmative action pressure on the universities, which suggests success, and on a grand scale. Yet the success could easily enough be rolled partway back, given the wrong confluence of political forces. The statistics on African-American admissions to universities seem to bob up and down for mysterious reasons, even without any effort to push them down, and the statistics on keeping the students in school are not good, and the entire situation seems to wobble.

Does the vehemence and enthusiasm of the campaign against P.C. threaten these shaky successes, possibly because of an extra anger that clings to the P.C. debate, some last lingering resentment from the long struggle to achieve campus desegregation? It may sound insulting to the fair-minded academic crusaders against P.C. even to ask that question. Yet the popular enthusiasm against P.C., the way the issue has seemed to appeal to a public far wider than the academy, raises the question all by itself. Even on campus, where life is supposed to be a little rosier than in the rest of the world, incidents of racist meanness against black students and other minorities are not exactly unknown. For a while in the late eighties, those incidents grew more common, sometimes with the encouragement of right wing campus journalists, who in turn were backed by conservative foundations and powerful political figures. Isn't *that* the biggest problem on the American campus?

The postmodern professors gaze at their accusers, and they see bad faith. They see conservatives who claim to be more liberal than the liberals, and cultural critics who talk about insulating culture from politics but who wield the literary canon like a club, knocking heads whenever their *own* political preferences come under attack. And the postmodern professors would laugh—if they weren't ducking under a table.

Are their responses foolish? Mostly they are incomplete, I would say. For there still remains what is, finally, the central issue—the intellectual atmosphere on the campuses (and in a few other places). The anti–P.C. professors' organization, the National Association of Scholars, has its share of well-regarded members, not all of them operatives of the conservative movement, who are eager to recount unpleasant memories in gory detail: the hazing they have undergone at the hands of politically correct university colleagues, the need they feel to bite their tongues or to move to a different department merely to get on with their conventional work. The N.A.S. journal, *Academic Questions,* publishes new complaints all the time. A spirit of hyperbole animates some of these complaints, just as it animates the debate as a whole, and doubtless the entire accusation against P.C. would sound more convincing stripped to essentials, without any of the entertaining references to Mao's Red Guards. But exaggeration does not make a complaint untrue.

Todd Gitlin writes: "A bitter intolerance emanates from much of the academic left." The thing exists—even if not everywhere. And if the intolerance is bitter among some of the professors, how much worse it is in the world of their own students—among the hard-pressed student leftists especially. Merely to hold a reasonably well-attended left-wing meeting at a campus today can turn into a nightmare when the politically correct requirements are insisted on, what with the demands for racial and gender balance and correct phrasing and the accusations about racism, sexism, homophobia, and Eurocentrism that fly at the drop of a hat. The leaders of the conventional adult left are always pulling their hair out over these things, looking for ways to offer a word of friendly advice to the self-persecuting student leftists. (Some of the friendly words appear in the following documents.) The very history of the term P.C. testifies to the left-wing awareness of a left-wing syndrome. But the syndrome doesn't disappear.

Here is the mystery in the debate over P.C. For if the professors and their students are as devoted to every kind of tolerant and humane idea as they say, and if their radical instincts are closer to Michael Harrington than to Martin Heidegger, and if pluralism is their utopia, how can they work up, some of them, so much zeal for small-time inquisitions? All sorts of explanations can be proposed—for instance, the explanation that points to a heritage of Hawthornean puritanism that is every bit as nasty and unconscious among liberals as among conservatives. Or there is the argument that liberals, too, have their share of bad faith. You could point to old habits of left-wing intolerance that persist long after they have been discredited. Or you could observe that if most of the postmodern professors have a liberal heart, the anti-liberals of the left sometimes end up determing the atmosphere.

But without slighting any of these explanations here is an additional one suitably based on structures of language, which I derive from Pierre Bourdieu's theory of academic jargon. In a polemic against Heidegger, Bourdieu observes that professors like to suppose that academic jargon can mean anything they want it to. If someone defines a word to denote ideas that are, say, strictly liberal and open-minded, the professors imagine that no other meanings will inhere. But Bourdieu (who was trying to show that Heidegger remained something of a Nazi even when he was merely an unpolitical academic) insists that words, even academic words, carry meanings of their own that can't be wished away, even by professors.

Currently we have a lot of academic terms like "difference," "diversity," "the Other," "logocentrism," and "theory," that are intended to be consonant with humanist traditions of the liberal left. But these words willy-nilly hark back to a cultural theory that has its roots in the anti-humanist intellectual currents of a generation ago, and buried within those terms may be certain definite ideas that are anything but liberal. There is the idea that we are living under a terrible oppression based on lies about liberal humanism, and that with proper analysis the hidden vast structure of domination can be revealed. There is the temptation to flirt with irrationalist and racial theories whose normal home is on the extreme right.

And there is the idea that, sparkling like jewels here and there, a millenarian alternative is somewhere lurking, that we can turn the world upside down—if we, the anti-bigot reformers, can only get hold of the dominating verbal structures. For if we can only command the school curric-ulum, or dictate the literary canon, or get everyone to abandon certain previously unanalyzed phrases that contain the entire structure of oppressive social domination, and replace these phrases with other phrases that contain a new, better society—if we can only do that, great results will occur, and the radiant new day will be at hand.

That is a wild notion, which consciously no one believes, at least not in full. Yet bits and pieces of that idea peek out from within the academic vocabulary. And wild or not, the bits and pieces have a popular appeal, if only because they promise that something can be done about the social inequalities and injustices in the United States that seem so intractable in a conservative age. Perhaps if America were experiencing right now a significant movement for radical social reform, the temptation to embark on verbal campaigns and to invest these campaigns with outlandish hopes would be less, and the students and younger professors would put their energy into real-life democratic movements instead, which might be a relief to their harassed colleagues. A peculiar sort of leftism is plainly an origin of the P.C. syndrome, but it's easy to imagine that another kind of turn to the left—to a conventional movement for social reform—would also be the solution.

Meanwhile here is a phenomenon that is weirder and less productive than any conventional movement for democracy. Dwight Macdonald defined 1930s fellow-traveling as the fog that arose when the warm ocean currents of American liberalism encountered the Soviet iceberg. Political correctness in the 1990s is a related syndrome. It is the fog that arises from American liberalism's encounter with the iceberg of French cynicism.

This book contains twenty-one of the most interesting statements that have been produced on the subject of political correctness—broadly defined to include not only the argument over speech habits and official codes but the related issues of the literary canon and the public school curriculum. There is even one comment on the art museums, by Hilton Kramer. I have selected writers and statements from every kind of journal—popular, academic, intellectual, and political—and even from a television show.

I have tried to balance the different views, so that here is Dinesh D'Souza, who writes for the conservative journals, but also, at the opposite end of the book, Cornel West and Barbara Ehrenreich, with perspectives from the democratic left. Here is Catharine R. Stimpson, 1990 president of the Modern Language Association, and here, too, is Roger Kimball, arch-critic of said association, and so on through the anthology. Diane Ravitch and Molefi Kete Asante debate the merits of Afrocentric public school curricula. And then one of the surprises in reading these pages is to discover writers who on political grounds ought to disagree (and with a grudge too), but who seem to harbor a secret point of agreement, out of mutual love for literature.

Some of the super-radical positions are without expression here, which is too bad—for instance, the position that views multiculturalism as itself a form of white male domination. On the other hand, readers will find three documents from one of the sharpest local disputes over P.C. and multiculturalism, the debate about curriculum at the University of Texas, Austin.

I regret to say that too many academic people will stumble across their own names in one or another article, cited in an unfriendly polemical spirit by their severest critics. And nowhere in the book will these criticized persons get the chance to rebut or reply. That is injust. I beg the forgiveness of every one of these people, the wronged leftists and the wronged rightists and the wronged in-betweenists, and I ask them to remember that injustice as well as incompleteness is always the outcome when large debates shrivel into small anthologies.

The literary critic Gerald Graff has argued for some time that the best possible response to the crisis in the universities is to "teach the conflict"—to make a study of the debate itself. This proposal strikes the most radical of the professors as a wishy-washy way to take a real debate and render it toothless, and it strikes other people as a misguided proposal to drag into the classroom arguments that should be conducted among the professors themselves, not in front of their students. But Graff's proposal seems to me the soul of sense. The debate over political correctness has managed to raise nearly every important question connected to culture and education—the proper relation of culture to a democratic society, the relation of literature to life, the purpose of higher education. Naturally to raise a question is not to settle it, which means the crisis in education goes on. But only in medicine are crises a sign of impending death. In intellectual matters, crises are signs of life.

PART ONE

DEBATING POLITICAL CORRECTNESS

THE BIG CHILL? INTERVIEW WITH DINESH D'SOUZA

Dinesh D'Souza
and
Robert MacNeil

No debate can truly be called national until it has appeared on television. One of the most prominent TV discussions of political correctness has been Robert MacNeil's interview with Dinesh D'Souza, which ran on *The MacNeil/Lehrer Newshour,* June 18, 1991. Mr. D'Souza, who was well-known in his student days at Dartmouth as a conservative firebrand, has written *Illiberal Education: The Politics of Race and Sex on Campus.* Here is a transcript of the interview.

MR. MACNEIL: Tonight we continue our week of conversations on political correctness, the trend on college campuses some see as having a chilling effect on free speech and traditional scholarship. Others see it as an effort to recognize the achievements of women and minorities. Tonight we're joined by one of the most provocative critics of political correctness, Dinesh D'Souza, whose book *Illiberal*

Education is a national best seller. In a recent conversation I asked what "illiberal education" meant.

MR. D'SOUZA: My basic argument is that the central principles of liberal education are being turned on their head. Liberal education should be about equality of opportunity, about giving everyone a fair chance. Instead, in many universities it is now quite routine to see the practice of racial preference, both in student admissions, as well as in faculty hiring. Second, liberal education should be about integration, about bringing groups together. Instead, we have a new separatism on campus, what some have called a new segregation on campus. And finally, liberal education should be about high standards and about free speech, free and open debate. Instead, many campuses are witnessing attack on academic standards as being the sole property of white males and, further, many campuses, more than a hundred, now have censorship regulations outlawing racially and sexually offensive speech. So we have gone from liberal education to its antithetical opposite, to illiberal education.

MR. MACNEIL: More than a hundred campuses have such regulations. That is still a fairly small percentage of the very large and diverse animal that is American higher education.

MR. D'SOUZA: That's true. On the other hand, these are campuses like Stanford, like the University of Michigan, some of the Ivy League colleges, campuses that set the pace for other colleges, both in the area of admissions and the area of life on campus and the curriculum. When these elite, private and state schools set policies, many others follow suit.

MR. MACNEIL: The curriculum, discuss the curriculum. Some of these are very large universities. How much of the curriculum is banned or tainted by this trend that you're talking about?

MR. D'SOUZA: Since the 1960s, the colleges have moved away from requirements. They have tended to require very little of their students, and until quite recently, a number of colleges had required courses in the classics of Western civilization so that if you were a physics major or a math major, you would still have to take these courses. Now what has happened is that we have seen an attack on these courses as being biased, as being Eurocentric, and the argument is that they should make way for non-Western requirements, so, for example, in a much publicized case, Stanford abolished its so-called Western culture requirement and replaced it with a multicultural requirement emphasizing the work by women, by persons of color, and by natives of the Third World.

MR. MACNEIL: You're not in favor of that?

MR. D'SOUZA: I'm in favor of a multicultural curriculum that emphasizes what Matthew Arnold called the best that has been thought and said. Non-Western cultures have produced great works that are worthy of study, and I think young people should know something about the rise of Islamic fundamentalism. To do so, it's helpful to be exposed to the Koran. Young people should know something about the rise of Japanese capitalism. Is there a Confucian ethic behind the success of Asian entrepreneurship in the same way we hear about Max Weber, the Protestant ethic, and the spirit of capitalism? These are legitimate questions. But they are not the questions routinely pursued in most multicultural courses, which instead have degenerated into a kind of ethnic cheerleading, a primitive romanticism about the Third World, combined with the systematic denunciation of the West.

MR. MACNEIL: And what proportion of the core curriculum do you think is now given over to such courses in great universities like Stanford or Berkeley, which we have seen at the beginning of this series?

MR. D'SOUZA: I think that it is currently the case that at places like Stanford you read Western classics in conjunction with non-Western works, but there is a movement of change, of transition, if you will, in which the Western classics are increasingly diminished and the non-Western works, very often polemical, ideological, anti-Western in tone, are being emphasized.

MR. MACNEIL: And why is it not a good thing to stimulate thinking about the multiculturalism that is increasingly becoming a fact in this country through works which raise the consciousness of those people themselves—black, Asian, whatever, or the sensitivity of people like me who are white? What is wrong with doing that?

MR. D'SOUZA: There's nothing wrong with a critical examination. In fact, my argument is that this critical examination does not, in fact, take place. The reason is that non-Western classics are, to put it bluntly, politically incorrect. If you look at the Koran, for example, it embodies a notion of male superiority. The *Tale of Genji*, the Japanese classic, for example, celebrates a hierarchical version of society, and the Indian classics, such as the *Bhagavad* and *Gitanjali,* are rejections of Western materialism and atheism. The activists who want to study other cultures want to find an alternative to what they consider to be the racist, sexist, and homophobic West. Yet, when they look abroad, they find that non-Western cultures are often inhospitable to their political prejudices. So they ignore the non-Western classics and instead, they find a Third World revolutionary who is advocating a neo-Marxist revolution and they teach him, they pass him off as an authentic voice of the Third

World. But, in fact, Frantz Fanon, for example, does not represent the people of the Third World. He represents the politics and the prejudices of Stanford professors and Stanford students.

MR. MACNEIL: But that is not all that students at Stanford are learning.

MR. D'SOUZA: It's not. But when you examine in detail the specific currents of multiculturalism, you realize that they operate to the effect of distorting non-Western cultures. You must have heard about this trend called Afrocentricity, which is common both in the high schools as well as in the colleges. Well, Afrocentricity is basically an effort to trace the lineage of American blacks to the country of Egypt, which is said to be an African culture, and it is further said that the Pharaohs were black, that Cleopatra was black, that Hannibal was black, and so on. These things are taught not even as controversial but as true. Now, Egypt is in the continent of Africa, yet Egypt has never been considered an African civilization, but instead a distinctive Egyptian civilization. The Egyptians went into the deep south, but very often to capture slaves. And slavery persisted in the Arab world long after it was abolished in the West.

MR. MACNEIL: But the teaching of Afrocentric courses is not confined to teaching that Egypt was one of the ingredients of African culture. That isn't the only content.

MR. D'SOUZA: The teaching springs from a desire to say that each ethnic group, in this case blacks, have a civilization that constitutes their cultural property, and there's a desire to say that this civilization is just as great, if not greater, as what the white guys did. Egypt is the country in Africa which can, in fact, boast of considerable historical achievement, and this is why a lot of focus is on the country of Egypt. Now I don't mean to suggest that there is not a legitimate examination of slavery, of Frederick Douglass, of the Civil War, of W. E. B. Du Bois, of Booker T. Washington. This is the intellectual enterprise in which not just black Americans but whites too should be part.

MR. MACNEIL: Come to the other part of political correctness which is much talked about today, and that is the effort of some universities to limit what people of one race or sex or sexual persuasion can say about another one. Give me your feelings about that.

MR. D'SOUZA: Well, the argument is that we are witnessing a terrible rise of hateful speech and incidents on campus and we need censorship as a means to curtail these. But the fact is anybody who is close to or on an American campus knows that there is no epidemic of hundreds of thousands of American students yelling "nigger" at each other. That is simply not the problem.

The problem is that students are beginning to talk among themselves about the taboo topics surrounding racial preference, surrounding racial separatism, surrounding activism, homosexuality, homosexual rights activism, and so on, and the university is seeking to regulate the students' discussion of these topics so as not to give offense. To take a fairly typical example, at the University of Michigan, a student was hauled before a disciplinary committee and accused of making the statement that homosexuality is immoral. The student pleaded guilty. This, in fact, was his view, based, I suppose, on religious or aesthetic preference, and the university administrators told him: your punishment is that you will have to write a forced apology titled "Learned My Lesson" to be published in the campus newspaper, and we want to enroll you in sensitivity education to raise your consciousness on this issue. So a subject that is a matter of legitimate discussion is, instead, settled not by reference to persuasion but by reference to force.

MR. MACNEIL: Do you think there should be any restriction on what students say about other students on campus, the terms they use?

MR. D'SOUZA: I'm not a free speech absolutist. I might part company here with the ACLU. I don't believe that people should be able to say anything they want, whenever they want, wherever they want. But you could have a code on a campus that simply had one line in it: A student shall not yell racial epithets at each other. None of the codes say this because, as I said, that's not the problem. The universities are trying to outlaw and suppress a different kind of discussion.

MR. MACNEIL: What is your motive in raising all this?

MR. D'SOUZA: I'm a native of India. I was raised in Bombay. I came to this country in 1978. I became a citizen last year. I'm a first-generation immigrant to the United States. I think that America is becoming a multiracial society and the whole issue is transcending black and white. We are going to have four or more groups, whites, blacks, Hispanics, and Asians in this diverse culture. It's very important to have a fair set of rules to arbitrate the differences among these groups. And the problem is that universities and to some extent society at large are moving away from a fair or neutral set of principles and are engaging in a politics of expediency, of racial rationing, of racial preference. I think this is a formula for division, for Balkanization, and ultimately for racial hostility.

MR. MACNEIL: When you were at Dartmouth College and you edited the *Review*, you were notorious for a while—I guess I could safely say you were the enfant terrible of the conservatives for a number of articles that the *Review* published that appeared to exacerbate racial tensions there. You were trying to stir it up a bit then, were you?

MR. D'SOUZA: I think that some of the more flamboyant controversies involving the *Review* have occurred long after I graduated. I've been out since '83, and some of the more recent upsurges in tension have occurred subsequently. I think it is the case that universities tend to enforce a kind of political or liberal etiquette on a campus. And what the *Review* does is challenge those orthodoxies. You can describe it as America's original politically incorrect institution. And so that created tension. That created a skirmish not so much with other students as with the administration.

MR. MACNEIL: But the motive was to stir it up and to get people talking about things that were considered impermissible up to that time.

MR. D'SOUZA: I think that's right, that the topics of race and to a lesser extent gender have been taboo in our society, particularly in the universities. What people say in public is not the same as what they believe in private. I think the *Review* sometimes in an adolescent and sophomoric way was trying to open up the discussion on those topics.

MR. MACNEIL: What should universities do to encourage appreciation of multiculturalism and sensitivity to people of different races and different sexes and points of view, actually? What should universities do if what they're doing now, in your view, is wrong?

MR. D'SOUZA: I think universities should encourage the freedom of mind that is going to draw students to that which is different, to that which is unusual. We have a natural curiosity about those who are not like us, and this is why we're interested, for example, not just in other cultures but in the past. I heard a wonderful line the other day which said that the past is another country. It's really true that if you go into fifth-century B.C. Greece, you are in a different civilization, one that is in a historical sense connected to our own but which operated in very different ways. And this natural sense of wonder, this imagination, can be imaginatively cultivated by colleges, but they have to do so in a manner that respects difference and that respects freedom.

MR. MACNEIL: People of my generation who are still on campuses and in faculties make the point that the past is a different country to people of your generation or a bit younger who weren't around during the civil rights struggles of the sixties and, therefore, don't appreciate the history of that and are, therefore, more insensitive than is the older generation to what blacks of that generation and this generation have gone through.

MR. D'SOUZA: I don't think it's true.

MR. MACNEIL: You don't think that's true.

MR. D'SOUZA: In fact, I think survey data show that Americans have become consistently more tolerant on racial issues. I do think that there was a civil rights consensus in this country built in the late '50s and the 1960s which emphasized two principles: first, the principle of integration or desegregation, which began with *Brown* v. *Board of Education,* the famous Supreme Court case; and second, the principle of equality of opportunity, giving everyone a fair chance. Martin Luther King put it best—Judge us by the content of our character, not the color of our skins. The problem is that those two principles have collapsed. In fact, they have been to some extent abandoned by the civil rights leadership itself, so that integration has given way to racial separatism and the affirmation of ethnic difference, and equality of opportunity has given way to racial preference.

MR. MACNEIL: What do you say to the argument which one hears that raising the issue of political correctness is another way now of attacking affirmative action, which is in itself another way of keeping white racial fears or fears of reverse discrimination on the poltical agenda?

MR. D'SOUZA: Well, the central paradox is that affirmative action or racial preference policies that are now routinely practiced by colleges are saying to students that the best way to fight discrimination in America is to practice discrimination. This is to say the least a paradoxical assertion, one that at the very least needs to be publicly stated and defended. Maybe there are good arguments for affirmative action, but they need to be named. Look at the case of Georgetown University, where the kid released partial data about the subject and the university responded not by releasing full information, not by debating the issue, but by punishing the student. Critics of political correctness are not saying get rid of affirmative action, but (a) let's talk about it and (b) let's discuss some possible alternatives.

MR. MACNEIL: But are not some critics of political correctness, to return to my question, particularly on the conservative end of the political spectrum—and there are critics on the liberal end as well—are not some critics raising the issue so as to keep the question of affirmative action at the top of the political agenda?

MR. D'SOUZA: Well, I suppose that's true. Everyone makes arguments that have some political connotation and you like to make arguments favorable to your own point of view. But what's striking about this whole debate is the broad spectrum of opinion and criticism that's emerged. I mean—David Duke has not emerged as a primary commentator on political correctness. We're talking about historians and scholars within the university and without, ranging from conservatives to Marxists who are taking these positions.

MR. MACNEIL: Since this was first raised within the last year or so, first raised in a large way, do you think that the original wave has already begun to pass and that, due to the publicity given to it, and with some of the sillier examples of political correctness having been exposed, it's already declining?

MR. D'SOUZA: I think we might start to see a change this fall. I do think that some of the more repressive and authoritarian forces in the universities are somewhat on the defensive and we might see some constructive change over time. But it's a slow process, because many of the people we're talking about have tenure. They are institutionalized, they are heads of major academic organizations. We are not criticizing a handful of student radicals, but really people who are deans and college presidents, the academic establishment.

ON DIFFERENCES: MODERN LANGUAGE ASSOCIATION PRESIDENTIAL ADDRESS 1990

Catharine R. Stimpson

Catharine R. Stimpson, University Professor and dean of the Graduate School at Rutgers University, was the 1990 president of the Modern Language Association. At the 1990 convention of the MLA in Chicago, she delivered the following address, which takes up some of the salient topics in the debate. The speech ran in *PMLA*, May 1991, where the full scholarly citations can be found.

I dedicate this address to our colleagues who have met AIDS with exemplary rage, gallantry, and courage.

I begin by quoting two canonical figures. They were born within 130 years of each other, a span roughly comparable to that between Anne Bradstreet and Thomas Paine, Aphra Behn and Edward Gibbon, Phillis Wheatley and W. E. B. Du Bois. The first figure is a lyric poet. She writes:

He is more than a hero

He is a god in my eyes—
the man who is allowed
to sit beside you—
                    (Sappho, fragment 39, 1–4)

The second is a historian and anthropologist. He announces:

In this book, the result of my inquiries into history,
I hope to do two things: to preserve the memory of
the past by putting on record the astonishing
achievements both of our own and of the Asiatic
peoples; secondly, and more particularly, to show
how the two races came into conflict.
                                    (Herodotus 13)

Like all canonical writings, this stanza by Sappho and
paragraph by Herodotus mean innumerable things. I now
engage them as dramas of difference. These dramas have
many stages: between speaker and subject, among trans-
lators, among men and women, among peoples, about the
meaning of difference. In Sappho, differences are the condition of passion; in Herodotus, the condition of group
definitions and death. Like every other reading, mine is
partial and incomplete. It is, however, a road sign to my
address. For my subject is the study of the modern languages and literatures as a drama of difference. If we
perform this drama wisely, our actions will be the condition
of our increase. Although I speak of differences, I also
mirror the wish of Louise Pound. In 1955, during my
earliest years in college, she served as the first woman
president of the Modern Language Association. In her
address, she said wryly:

I hope this microphone works. If you have to listen to me I hope you can hear me. Once before at a gathering of a learned society, seeing an upright gadget before me, I talked with extreme care directly into it for half an hour, moving neither to the right nor to the left, only to find as I went down from the platform that it was a *lamp*.

Today the word *difference* has almost as many entries in our dictionary of culture as the middle of the road has cracks and holes, as the pronoun *we* has splits and fissures, as a convention hotel has rooms. Indeed, the entries so proliferate that some of us predict that we will disappear into our differences. Simultaneously we are suspicious of indifference. In our thinking and teaching, we hope to make a difference. This desire is part of the ethics of our profession. We want to read a novel more cogently than others, write a page persuasively, teach a language successfully.

Of our several dictionary entries for *difference,* one is philosophical and linguistic, a reference to the deep, sophisticated interrogations of differences within language. A second entry concerns another form of literary criticism, a method that compares books, genres, traditions, and tongues in order to analyze the distinctive features of each. A third entry is psychoanalytic, the exploration of the drastic consequences that ensue when the difference between subject and other is recognized. A fourth is at once psychological and sociological, a picture of the heterogeneous, divided subject, the legatee of membership in several groups, each with its own defining characteristic. The profuse workshop of history has stamped out and stacked up the templates of group membership: age, class, ethnicity, institution, gender, nation, tribe, race, rank, religion, sexuality. For good reason, many of our vital inquiries today ask what happens to culture when such differentiation means strength for some, subordination for many—when the grammar of power is hypotactic. In *Omeros,* Derek Walcott's epic interweaving of Homer and the "New Worlds" of the Atlantic and the Caribbean, a father tells his poet son:

> I was raised in this obscure Caribbean port,
> where my bastard father christened me for his shire:
> Warwick. . . . But never felt part

> of the foreign machinery known as Literature.

For equally good reason, many of our vital inquiries also ask what happens to culture when we write openly about our diversities—when the grammar of power is paratactic. Then a poet like Marilyn Hacker can grasp the nettle of the sonnet to compose a sequence about motherhood and sexual difference. Then, like Václav Havel, we can treasure a life that moves toward "plurality, diversity, independent self-constitution" and fears a "post-totalitarian system that demands conformity, uniformity, and discipline."

In the last few years, several terms have evolved to denote a pluralistic, diverse culture. Among them are *rhizome, multiculturalism,* and *cultural democracy.* Prominent within literary and cultural theory, the rhizome of Gilles Deleuze and Félix Guattari is a figure for forms of knowing that stem out and burrow underground, for points of awareness that connect everywhere and anywhere, for a linguistics that must be a pragmatics. Multiculturalism has broader currency. Most often it means treating society as the home of several equally valuable but distinct racial and ethnic groups. For me, multiculturalism is also the necessary recognition that we cannot think of culture unless we think of many cultures at the same time—whether we define culture broadly as a shared set of values, attitudes, beliefs, and practices or more narrowly as the most valued aesthetic objects. Perhaps the literature of exile is a painful strain of involuntary multiculturalism.

As anthropology, history, cultural studies, and literary history show, the relations among various cultures are manifold. Cultures have destroyed other cultures; resisted destruction; exploited other cultures; resisted exploitation; competed with one another; influenced, accommodated, and created one another. Part of the sweep of Walcott's *Omeros* is that this poem—its seven books, its triplets, its subtle, supple, and rugged metrics—embodies every one of these possibilities. Indeed, literature demonstrates how frequently, even how compulsively, texts emerge when cultural, linguistic, and formal border crossings take place. Some of our greatest writers have urged the vernacular into literature. Our most intricate traditions demand cultural collisions and allegiances. In *The Signifying Monkey,* Henry Louis Gates, Jr., demonstrates the interplay between black vernacular and black literature, between African and African American traditions, among black writers, and among "black texts" and "Western texts." Our traditions, even when they seem nationally and racially coherent, show a mingling of cultural borrowings and blanknesses. "You inquire my Books," wrote Emily Dickinson to T. W. Higginson on 25 April 1862.

> For Poets—I have Keats—and Mr and Mrs Browning.
> For Prose—Mr Ruskin—Sir Thomas Browne—and
> the Revelations. I went to school—but in your man-
> ner of the phrase—had no education. . . . You speak

of Mr Whitman—I never read his Book—but was told he was disgraceful.

Given the conflicts and passions of our moment, multiculturalism has inevitably provoked a spectrum of responses. For some, it connotes an effort to substitute emotion for reason, a thin many-other-worldism for a deep grasp of Western history, philosophy, literature, and art. Others, although they find the concept of multiculturalism important, fear that its practitioners will satisfy themselves with academic reform and not take on the harder task of social change. For still others, with whom I am in much sympathy, multiculturalism promises to bring dignity to the dispossessed and self-empowerment to the disempowered, to recuperate the texts and traditions of ignored groups, to broaden cultural history.

I am baffled why we cannot be students of Western culture and of multiculturalism at the same time, why we cannot show the historical and present-day relations among many cultures. As literary critics, we can also read and teach both the Western and the multicultural text. Surely some Western texts are also multicultural. Because this job of reading demands that readers move out of their everyday worlds, it has some similarities to teaching many contemporary students any text written before the Age of Rock and Roll. The process of reading the multicultural text begins with questions. If we do not share the writer's space, however defined, do we ask the text to dramatize "universals" that transcend that space, that apparently offer a vast mirror in which to glimpse our own image? If the text is macaronic, can we rightly demand translation of its various languages? If the text's strategy is to appeal only to a single community, a closed circle, a centricity, are we to feel excluded? If so, are we to respond forgivingly? resentfully?

One good critic answers no to all these questions. When we first encounter the multicultural text, we will find it strange. We will apply our familiar categories and definitions to make this new world intelligible. If our only references are Western, we will, for example, think of the ghosts in Maxine Hong Kingston in the same way that we think of the ghost of Hamlet's father. Our categories and definitions, however, will not work. Their sudden impotence will then defamiliarize them. Moreover, our reading itself will offer "an experience of multiculturalism, in which not everything is likely to be wholly understood by every reader. The texts often only mirror the misunderstandings and failures of intelligibility in . . . multicultural situations." In its duplicitious, masquerading way, reading will permit us to enter other worlds. However, a multicultural reading will keep us on guard against pretending to be natives, colonial administrators, or tourists on sun-swept isles.

The third concept, cultural democracy, has a family resemblance to multiculturalism. A definition of cultural democracy emerged in the early 1970s in formal European debates about cultural policy. Cultural democracy, too, respects a multiplicity of cultures and subcultures. They are "communication patterns . . . mythologies and interdicts." Citizens work actively to sustain and invigorate their individual cultures, which are all connected and supported by cultural institutions. These institutions break up hegemony rather than nurture it, an ironic mandate for the state-supported ones. "There is no room," one paper about cultural democracy states, "for any transcendental or other reason—nationalist, racial, religious or ethical—which could justify a cultural policy dealing only with activities which affect merely a small fraction of the population."

The advocates of cultural democracy self-consciously contrast it with two other forces: mass culture and the democratization of culture. The democratization of culture is the effort to bring high culture to a mass audience through schools, government agencies, concerts, museums, inexpensive publishing, libraries, records, and tapes. In part, the argument in the United States in the 1980s about the National Endowment for the Humanities was over the comparable worths of cultural democracy, which the endowment seemed to question, and of the democratization of culture, which it seemed to practice. Crucially, for the earlier advocates of cultural democracy and for me, both concepts had merits, which had to be weighed and balanced. However, the democratization of culture brought "something good" to people at the expense of ignoring the goods they already possessed and could create. It threatened to transform a people into a public.

Mass culture and the democratization of culture travel together even more uneasily. They sit side by side most comfortably in a paperback edition of *The Odyssey* or in a serious television show about Homer. Cultural democracy and mass culture also have a fragile truce. Some cultural democrats were less confident than many of us are now about crossing back and forth over "the great divide" between culture and mass culture. Of course, mass culture is as much a part of contemporary life as winds are of the earth's environment. One proof of its pervasiveness is a recent cartoon showing two academics in a bar. Both are men. They otherwise bear little physical resemblance to the late, unlamented twosome Milli Vanilli, but one is saying to the other—ironically, I hope—"I've decided to lip sync my next MLA paper." Cultural democrats fault mass culture for transmogrifying the individual from a producer of meaning into a consumer, or, more idiomatically, from a flourishing tree of knowledge into a couch potato.

The earlier cultural democrats warily labeled television the most influential instrument of mass culture. They were aware that the massive ovens of television baked the bread of our daily narratives. In the early 1970s, their studies found that each day 74 percent of the children in France between the ages of eight and eleven discussed the television programs they had watched the day before, and that these children derived 70 percent of their knowledge from television. In California, secondary school pupils each week averaged twenty-seven hours attending classes and thirty hours watching television. In Poland, children seven to eighteen watched for about twenty-two hours a week. Cultural democrats recognized the virtues of television. For example, it conveys powerful images of differences to comparatively homogeneous communities. Such technologies as videotape can be widely available. Nevertheless, television was replacing a people, or communal clusters of people, with a mass-media audience.

Rhizomatics, multiculturalism, cultural democracy: These words become a part of our dictionary because differences are a part of our lives. No wild-eyed czar spewed these words out and then sold them to a bunch of wide-eyed academics. I am no mistress of ceremonies bringing on a master narrative, no village explainer expounding the Big Global Picture, no friendly local apocalyptist finding rupture and crisis in every decade. Still, I will note that we live in a rush of history. We have a congeries of names for this volatile moment, especially as it is experienced in the West: *postindustrial, postmodern, poststructuralist, postcolonial, postfeminist, post-Marxist, post-Gutenberg.* Commentators have mocked the repetitive use of *post-* as if these terms were Post-it notes from the pads of melodramatic, ineffectual intellectuals. On the contrary, these rubics will be useful to the future archivists of a deep, unruly period of historical transition that is, at its most decorous, mixing up the relations of the general to the particular and of the same to the different.

In simple, we are establishing new patterns of a common culture, new global economic and communications systems. Simultaneously we are creating a counterforce, a variety of particular identities. For example, "[l]iterature in English is . . . increasingly international, even global." Yet literary English will differ if the writer is from the Pacific Rim, Asia, Africa, the Middle East, the British Isles, the Republic of Ireland, the Caribbean, the United States, Canada. Intensifying this bifurcation between globe and place is the decay of other global systems, the modern empires. This has released and strengthened the local cultures imperial structures had repressed. For painful economic and political reasons, migrants, many of whom once inhabited the regions of these empires, travel within and between continents, carrying local cultures to new places. Ironically, the modern commitment to equality has also contributed to the growth of our perception of differences. If and when we attempt to translate the principles of equality into action, we see how dependent we have been on differences, on the other, for our well-being. Not without its own strategies for survival, literature permits the other, Hegel's slave, to speak. The modern commitment to education encourages such speech. For education both imposes standards and gives us the equipment to cut our own. Vitally, figures as diverse as Gertrude Stein and postcolonial writers take Shakespeare's Caliban from canonical English literature as an emblem—of the task of writing in a mode that differs from the standard English tradition in which they were instructed.

The question of literacy helps to capture the cultural complexities and some of the cultural differences of our period. First, we have no common definition of what literacy is. The concept is another of our contested zones. One of our dividing lines is whether we measure literacy by looking first at the use of languages themselves or at the use of written texts. Next, no matter what the measure, we must be deeply troubled by the inability of many people to read or write, mostly through no fault of their own. There are have-nots of the written word. They live in "developed" and "developing" countries alike. They are more likely to be women than to be men. If the erosion of soil would concern an agronomist, if the flickering out of all the stars would concern an astronomer, so we must care acutely about the fate of literacy.

Our anxiety about literacy issues from several sources. One is our concern about the distress of the person who needs to read and cannot, who needs to write and cannot. A second source is our recognition of the obvious: literature and books need readers and writers in order to survive. It is equally obvious that literature is not dead, or in intensive care, or even in the hospital. We seem to me, however, to share the worry that we are marginal, that too few people today care about languages, literature, and literary criticism unless a foreign language is going to beef up economic competitiveness, that we demonstrate Walter Benjamin's dictum "The greater the decrease in the social significance of an art form, the sharper the distinction between criticism and enjoyment by the public."

A scene in the Marx Brothers' movie *A Day at the Races* might be a parable for a set of common, if conflicting, perceptions about books: that they are only instrumental, that they endlessly interpret one another, that they are a bit of a scam. Tony (Chico Marx) is selling ice cream at the races. He needs money in order to bet. When a sucker, Hackenbush, appears, Tony sells him books that putatively provide inside knowledge. Tony begins with an optician's eye test; moves to a code book with which to interpret the block letters on the eye chart, then to a breeder's guide, then to a set of guidebooks; gives Hackenbush nine books in lieu of change; and finally offers a bookcase. At the end,

Tony has his money and a winning horse. Hackenbush has nothing except the books.

Two different but compatible elements of our culture promise to invigorate literacy and our belief in the word. The first is multiculturalism itself. The 24 December 1990 issue of *The New Yorker* can serve as a symbol. Its cover depicts Santa Claus rampaging along in an emergency truck. The magazine's listing of cultural events in New York gives five pages to the movies, three to art, two to theater, almost one to dance, two to nightlife, one to music; there is one column for photography and a bit of sports. No books, I thought, my holiday joy marred. Then I read a list of events without categories that included a reading of Zora Neale Hurston—a multicultural writer, I thought more cheerfully, recharging literature for audiences across a range of subcultures.

A second element is the computer. More than a word processor or a hard disk for storing data, the computer may be altering rhetoric—without destroying it. One of our most visionary scholars, Richard Lanham, describes a change "falling for the most part outside the academic study of rhetoric but affecting and illuminating it at every point . . . the coming of the electronic word, the movement from letters printed on paper to digitized images projected onto a phosphorous screen." Enjoying the power and credentials of the newly rewritten word, we watch "[t]he fixed printed surface [as it] becomes volatile and interactive."

We are, then, unable to table the multiplication of differences in our culture, educational institutions, and ideas. Our historical arithmetic guarantees that faculties are expanding. Ever more women of all races and minority men have PhDs and academic jobs—a tribute to their merit and persistence and to our ability to see merit where we were blind before. A changing faculty is teaching students who are changing even more rapidly. Although most

United States campuses are still predominantly white, they are far more racially diverse than they were. At the University of California, Berkeley, in 1980, 66 percent of the undergraduate population was white. In 1989, 45 percent was. In 1990, the freshman class was 34 percent white, and 30 percent of the remainder were of Asian descent, 22 percent of Mexican or Latin American, and 7 percent of African. At Stanford University, over 40 percent of the entering undergraduates are Native American or of Asian, African, or Mexican descent. Across the curriculum, among educational theorists, in women's studies, teachers are asking how to establish a community of learning for diverse participants, how to promote a "safe atmosphere for open discussion" that nevertheless avoids specious generalizations about group behavior, how to foster a collaboration among strangers who know too little about one another and suspect too much.

Yet these changes are also demographic inflections of Feste's speech in *Twelfth Night*: "Anything that's mended is but patch'd; virtue that transgresses is but patch'd with sin, and sin that amends is but patch'd with virtue." One report tells us that between 1976 and 1986, college enrollment among middle-income African-Americans fell 17 percent. Between 1976 and 1988, the equivalent numbers for Hispanic students declined 7 percent. Students speak of the isolation of campus ethnic and racial groups from one another. All of us speak of "incidents," using our euphemism for events that are anti-Semitic, racist, sexist, homophobic. Our graduate programs badly need a far larger absolute number of minority students, our faculties a larger absolute number of minority scholars. In the modern languages and literatures, the percentage of Ph.D.s with tenure is still highest among white men, who are followed, in descending order, by minority men, minority women, and white women.

On the good campus, the rooms in which we think and teach provide our sense of common purpose. If hospitals are for healing, if courtrooms are for adjudicating legal guilt and innocence, our institutions of learning are for thinking and teaching. Today, in newer and traditional fields, our scholarship is responsible. The footnote has not gone the way of the dodo. Our curriculum committees vote for both continuity and change. In a 1984–85 survey of English departments, the MLA found that the requirements for the major had remained stable. During the early 1980s, however, 34 percent of the departments had added courses on women writers; 25 percent on ethnic or minority literatures; 26 percent on film studies; 39 percent on professional or technical writing; 30 percent in upper-level composition or rhetoric; 25 percent in rhetorical or composition theory; 16 percent in genres. These figures reflect not only our students' needs but intense intellectual interest in the definition of literary culture, in its relations with visual languages, and in rhetoric, a subject that has pulled anthropology, history, literature, and other disciplines together in the study of discourse.

In part because of these additions, our thinking is heterogeneous. Theories grapple with one another. No matter how vehemently some of us say that we hate theory, each of us has a theory about language and literature, a perspective, an interpretative method. In books, articles, and conferences, we correct one another. Our regime of signs is not a tyranny but an argumentative parliament. What Henry James said of the novel we might say of criticism: It "lives upon exercise, and the very meaning of exercise is freedom. The only obligation to which in advance we may hold a novel, without incurring the accusation of being arbitrary, is that it be interesting."

As Gerald Graff has taught us, our intellectual diversity is symptomatic of a multicultural society in which we realistically expect controversy rather than quick consensus. Graff also warns us that we are handling our conflicts badly. First, we prefer stressing our divisions over admitting that our academic culture puts us closer to one another than we are to most of our students. To them,

> a Roland Barthes and an Allan Bloom would seem far more similar to one another than to people like themselves, their parents, and friends. In their eyes, a Barthes and a Bloom would be just a couple of intellectuals speaking a very different language from their own about problems they have a hard time regarding as problems.

Next, we are responding timidly to a situation we admit exists. Clinging to an outworn pluralism, we add a course here and a method there, which we teach in not so splendid isolation in our individual classrooms. Graff plausibly encourages us to teach the conflict. If we do, we will show our students that it is possible to live openly with differences in a dialogic community, or, to borrow from Stanley Fish, an interpretative community. Graff knows as well as I do that our conversations have limits. A hungry child cannot eat our words. A battered woman cannot tape her broken ribs with our interpretations. Nevertheless, a community of discourse can give us community in discourse. We can create the moral equivalent of cultural border skirmishes.

All this is delicate and demanding. The rapidity of change in our communities and concepts can fatigue even our mettle. We have developed wonderful new methods, yet we want to retain some of the old. As humanists, we think most carefully if we have a repertoire of methods, if we refuse to parody bad science—to march from method to method, discarding one as we pick up another, treating literary studies as if it were a form of serial monogamy. Some of our most original voices are asking those most classical of questions. What is the literary? What is literature? Think, Richard Poirier tells us, of literature as an activity, a "troping," the turning of a word in and by other words "like the twisting or coiling of a strand or thread within and through the other strands that make up a piece of rope." This turning or troping "is in itself an act of power over meanings already in place." Some of our most scrupulous voices remind us to remember the "question of the formal arrangements in which language materials appear," to remember the "aesthetic—not beauty but . . . the secular attention to an inalienable element of sensuality and its *jouissance*." Some careful voices ask us to recall that *discrimination* has at least two meanings. The first is socioeconomic, legal, cultural, and psychological. Here discrimination is bias, a repugnant and murderous treatment of groups and individuals. *This* discrimination we must despise and end. The second meaning, however, is aesthetic. Here discrimination is the codification of criteria with which to judge works of art. We must, these voices thoughtfully suggest, be able to discriminate in this way as well. Surely, I agree, but surely too our judgments about art will bear more moral weight if a parallel struggle for justice accompanies them.

We work hard to carry on, keep up, and keep going. Faculty members in the humanities at four-year institutions put in an average of forty-eight hours a week on campus, more hours at home. We spend more time teaching than faculty members in any other field. Our rewards include a sense of professionalism, of doing dignified and valuable work. They do not include an opulent paycheck. In 1989–90, the average annual salary for a full-time member of the professorial ranks in the modern languages was $35,500, excluding fringe benefits.

Despite our work, self-interrogations, and thrift, the merry sounds of jingling bells and hosannas have not consistently accompanied our evolution. Instead, we are under booming rhetorical guns, some of them our own. For a few commentators during the 1980s, diversification was splendid for corporations but not for the modern languages and literatures. Companies could indulge in acquisitions but not the guardians of the canon. A free market was a historic blessing but not for literary studies. The most systematic censure claims that the profession is decadent, both bad in itself and a symptom of the corruption of criticism. In September 1982, the first issue of *The New Criterion* spoke plainly. Critical writing is "hopelessly ignorant, deliberately obscurantist, commercially compromised, or politically motivated." It is unable to distinguish among an independent high culture, popular culture, and commercial entertainment. In turn, the condition of criticism is a symptom of a more general corruption of culture, for which the 1960s are largely to blame. An "invidious assault on mind . . . was one of the most repulsive features of the radical movement of the Sixties." Hating both democracy and capitalism, though willing to enjoy their fruits, such radicals of the 1960s have found the university a home and haven. During the 1980s, these arguments included the more specific charge that the MLA was rigidly orthodox, powerful, "smug . . . and intolerant."

If they are rigorous and self-reflective, if they serve no hard partisan cause, such critiques keep the parliament of our discourse alive, even kicking, especially when we discuss the nature of rationalism, the definitions of culture, and the structure of education in a democracy. To my regret, these critiques often lack the objectivity they claim to defend. Respectful of tradition, they trot on certain rhetorical traditions. For lamenting the decline of culture is an old theme, railing at academics an old sport. The

Satyricon begins with an exuberant attack on rhetoricians and their "huge flatulent rhetoric." Gulliver has little truck with the higher learning of Laputa and Lagado. We who have been mocked by Petronius and Swift need not fear a Charles Sykes.

My sharpest regret is this: History is too labyrinthian, the modern languages and literatures are too important, our intellectual differences are too intricate, and our social differences are at once too tough, too sensitive, and too susceptible to manipulation for us to allow public debate about these subjects to be corroded and transported down into stupidity. No "side" is immune from stupidity. Together, as guardians of discourse, we must refuse to reduce complex intellectual movements to single persons and then to belittle the movements through ad hominem attacks. Similarly, we must refuse to reduce complex intellectual movements to single words and then to belittle the movements through ritualistic evocations of the words. Obvious examples now are the misuse of *feminist* and *theory*. Once the example might have been *comp*.

We must also resist the indulgence of romanticizing one's own group and demonizing the other. I teach Virginia Woolf's Judith Shakespeare as a fiction of great artfulness and as a parable about women's creativity in early modern England. I cannot claim, however, that all women have had a vivid literary talent that cruel patriarchs stifled and silenced. I am, as well, a Ph.D. from the 1960s. They were my salad days. They were also a decade that bore bitter fruit, a bad war and domestic strife that the nation had to overcome to bring simple justices home. No responsible historian can dress this decade in horns and forked tail in a Halloween charade.

Romanticizing one thing while demonizing another is a bad performance of an old two-step of language: the binary opposition. A common representation of contemporary differences about the humanities repeats the dance of polarization in slow-brain motion. Supposedly we wish either to restore a literary tradition or to reconstruct it, to reclaim a legacy or to renovate it, to draw up a list of great Western books or to devise a multicultural curriculum. Those who might wish to pursue both polar goals, while conscious of the epistemological difficulties of each, get lost in the wide-open territory between them. Supposedly we either support the "representation" of various groups— on faculties, for example, or in syllabi—or we support "merit." We are either "political" or "disinterested scholars." The repulsive logic of the last two speech acts is that when an Asian American scholar gets hired or a Latin American writer gets recognized, it is only because "political forces" have muscled their way into the house of cultural excellence, bringing their shabby baggage and braying mules with them.

In 1990, these rhetorical oppositions linked up into a single two-footed trope, the conflict between being "politically correct" and being "politically incorrect." The "P.C." phenomenon is an obvious response to two developments. The first is the formidable body of contemporary humanistic scholarship about the relations between power and culture. These analyses are far more systematic and disquieting than a discussion of Antigone's rebellion against Creon. Some scholars who do such studies go public with their politics and its relation to their academic work. This, in turn, has led to charges that their academic work is "only" political, especially if their politics are "left." The second development is the linkages between the social changes on our campuses and the intellectual ones. For the greater presence of women has helped to build women's studies. The open presence of gays and lesbians has made gay and lesbian studies possible. The brief against P.C.ers is that they insist on a single attitude toward diversity, a monolithic celebration of differences. The tone of this brief varies from the wry, ironic bemusement of the cartoon character Politically Correct Person to vitriolic accusations that our campuses are the equivalent of totalitarian reeducation camps.

I welcome the refreshments of satire and suspect the excesses of rage. So situated, I predict that the P.C. phenomenon, now hyped up, will eventually dry up. Our many differences will persist. My address has oscillated between anatomizing differences and bridging them. I have one more bridge to make. I hesitate to murmur it because it seems too obvious a reenactment of the feminine scene of heartfelt sentimentality. Nevertheless, we do all think about and teach languages and literature. We like, even love, what we do. This is at once a shared temperament and a motive for choosing our vocation. We know that no one can live without some language, that we cannot thrive without literature. We may not love one another. Indeed, Freud tells us that the commandment to love thy neighbor, let alone thy colleague, is impossible to obey. We do, however, love our languages and literature. None of us wishes to be left out of them—and rightly so.

In another fragment, Sappho promises and warns:

> You may forget but
> Let me tell you
> this: someone in
> some future time
> will think of us

With what technology will they think of us? Writing? Video or audio recording? Data-storage techniques we can neither predict nor imagine except in speculative fiction? Despite my love for textuality, despite my message that the medium is half the message, I neither know nor really care. I want the Herodotus we might have, no matter what the technology, to inscribe this: we erred, grumbled, had our conflicts. We were neither gods nor heroes. We were men and women of different races, sexualities, nations, and groups who all cared for culture. If we were greedy, we were greedy for knowledge, insight, imagination, irony, complexities, texts, verbal structures, textures. We had the freedom, with generosity, and courage to see the differences among texts and among ourselves. We erased the damaging differences. We typed out the differences that promised to renew us. We refused to destroy one another. For this, and for other reasons, we had our astonishing achievements.

I am grateful to have had the opportunity to serve as a president of the Modern Language Association.

THE PERIPHERY V. THE CENTER: THE MLA IN CHICAGO

Roger Kimball

Roger Kimball is the author of *Tenured Radicals: How Politics Has Corrupted Our Higher Education,* which is a criticism of new trends in the universities. The following article, adapted from *The New Criterion* (February 1991), the neoconservative journal, discusses the Modern Language Association convention of 1990, which was the setting also for Catharine R. Stimpson's speech "On Differences."

[M]ost of what is written in [today's] journals is either hopelessly ignorant, deliberately obscurantist, commercially compromised, or politically motivated. . . . As a result, the very notion of an independent high culture and the distinctions that separate it from popular culture and commercial entertainment have been radically eroded. . . . This fateful collapse in critical standards . . . and in the very idea of critical disinterestedness . . . has changed, and changed very much for the worse, the way the arts and humanities are now studied in our universities. . . . We are

*still living in the aftermath of the insidious assault on the
mind that was one of the most repulsive features of the
radical movement of the Sixties. . . . In everything from the
writing of textbooks to the reviewing of trade books, from
the introduction of kitsch into the museums to the decline
of literacy in the schools to the corruption of scholarly
research, the effect on the life of culture has been ongoing
and catastrophic.*
　　　　　—"A Note on *The New Criterion*," September 1982

Chicago's sobriquet, "the Windy City," seemed doubly
appropriate at the end of December 1990. In addition to
the frigid winter blasts, the snow, the icy rain, and the
other seasonal vagaries that contribute to the city's festive
spirit at that time of year, the Modern Language Association convoked its 106th annual convention, filling (or shall
we say "colonizing"?) the halls and meeting rooms of the
Hyatt Regency and other downtown hotels with gusts as
chilling and impenetrable in their own way as any north
wind barrelling in off Lake Michigan. From December 27
through 30, more than 10,000 members of the largest and
most influential academic organization in the United States
congregated in ritual displays of professional activity.
Fledgling members came seeking jobs or contacts; the
tenured elite interviewed and passed judgment on sup-
pliants; young and old alike browsed among the publishers'
exhibitions, delivered papers, and sampled the nearly 700
panels and social events that were crowded into the four-
day meeting.

　　For several years now, the annual meeting of the MLA
has provided observers of the academic scene with a spectacle as appalling as it is rich in unintended comedy. The
full range of barbarous jargon, intellectual posturing, and
aggressive politicization that has infected the academic
study of the humanities in this country is in full, florid

bloom at the MLA. To be sure, not all who flock to these meetings are happy about the recent assaults on the humanities. Because the annual meeting of the MLA also functions as the major clearing house for jobs in the modern languages and literatures, many academics come simply because they are looking for employment, or for employees, and have themselves little or no sympathy with the radical agenda that governs the activities and policies of the MLA.

Nor are all the sessions at the MLA devoted to esoteric trivia or politicized prosyletizing. Among the thousands of papers delivered at the convention in 1990, some dealt straightforwardly with technical matters—using new research tools, for example, or "Teaching and Learning German"—and some were traditional exercises in scholarship or literary criticism. Thus two of the three papers in the General Session on John Milton that I attended were clearly written, incisive efforts to come to terms with legitimate issues in Milton interpretation or scholarship, while the third—a vaguely deconstructivist performance entitled "Writing the Inside Out: Shakespeare, Milton, and the Supplement of Publication"—was merely tedious.

Nevertheless, the tenor of the convention—as, indeed, the tenor of the profession as a whole—is established not by the politically disengaged rank and file but by tenured or soon-to-be-tenured radicals who view the teaching of literature primarily as a species of ideological activism. It is true that the precise components of that activism will vary depending on the nature of the politics involved. Radical feminists have their issues and controversies, which tend to differ from issues and controversies that preoccupy the deconstructionists; champions of ethnic studies generally pursue an agenda quite distinct from that pursued by their feminist or deconstructionist colleagues; and proponents of homosexual studies busy themselves with yet other figures, commitments, and problems.

Despite the various issues that distinguish these and other groups, however, they are in many ways united. All reject the ideal of scholarly disinterestedness; all exhibit a pervasive animus against the achievements and values of Western culture; all systematically subjugate the teaching and study of literature to political imperatives; and all are extraordinarily intolerant of dissent. As I noted in the epilogue to my book *Tenured Radicals,* the rise of multiculturalism as an omnibus term for the new academic orthodoxy has provided common cause and something of a common vocabulary for a profession otherwise riven by an allegiance to competing radicalisms. At the center of the multiculturalist ethos is the contention that all cultures are equally valuable and, therefore, that preferring one culture, intellectual heritage, or moral and social order to another is to be guilty of ethnocentricism and racism. Preferring Western culture and its heritage to others is held to be especially ethnocentric and racist. The thoughtless egalitarianism behind these ideas helps to explain the current academic obsession with the notion of "difference" and the widespread insistence that the differences that separate us—preeminently, differences of race, class, sexuality, and ethnic heritage—must be given priority over our common humanity.

This celebration of "difference" may sound like a prescription for tolerance and genuine pluralism. But in fact it has fostered a positively Orwellian situation in which "diversity" really means strict intellectual conformity, and "tolerance" is reserved exclusively for those who subscribe to one's own perspective. As has been widely reported in the press recently, attempts to enforce the ethic of "difference" have led to egregious violations of academic freedom and have poisoned the atmosphere for honest intellectual exchange at campuses across the country. Deviation from the multiculturalist orthodoxy on any number of issues is punished by social ostracism, mandatory "consciousness-raising" classes, or even suspension or expulsion.

It is precisely this cluster of phenomena that is summed up in the phrase "political correctness." It goes without saying that the new academic elite controlling our most prestigious humanities departments will tell you not to worry, that nothing has happened that need concern parents, trustees, alumni, government or private funding sources. On the issue of enforcing politically correct behavior on campus, for example, they will assure you that the whole thing has been overblown by "conservative" journalists who can't appreciate that the free exchange of ideas must sometimes be curtailed for the higher virtue of protecting the feelings of designated victim groups. And the curriculum, they will say, has not been politicized, it has merely been democratized: opened up to reflect the differing needs and standards of groups and ideas hitherto insufficiently represented in the academy. You are not against democracy, are you?

While the cynical and self-justifying arguments oozing out of the academy seem to satisfy those making them, the truth is far more dismaying than our new academic mandarins let on. What we are facing is nothing less than the destruction of the fundamental premises that underlie both our conception of liberal education and a liberal democratic polity. Respect for rationality and the rights of the individual, a commitment to the ideals of disinterested criticism, color-blind justice, and advancement according to merit, not according to sex, race, or ethnic origin: these quintessentially Western ideas are bedrocks of our political as well as our educational system. And they are precisely the ideas that are now under attack by *bien pensants* academics intoxicated with the thought of their own virtue. Whatever demurrals some individual members of the MLA may voice, it has been obvious for some time that this organization represents the epicenter of academic political correctness in the humanities. Because the rise of political correctness signals both intellectual intolerance and a politically motivated betrayal of literature, it is worth taking a critical look at the controversies and proceedings of the 106th convention of the Modern Language Association.

How, specifically, do the multiculturalist imperatives of political correctness manifest themselves in the subjects addressed at a major academic convention on literature? For one thing, literature itself takes a distant back seat to a wide variety of currently fashionable ideological concerns. While there were still some panels that devoted themselves to dealing with literary subjects as, well, as *literature,* this was in fact quite rare. In most of the popular and high-powered panels, both the traditional idea of literature and the concept of literary quality, insofar as they came up at all, were dismissed as "naïve," "elitist," "hegemonic," etc., etc. The chief substitutes for literature on display at the year's MLA were Marxism, feminism, what we might call homosexualism, "cultural studies," ethnic studies, and any of a number of indeterminate mixtures of the above leavened with dollops of deconstructivist or poststructuralist theory—in other words, multiculturalism *de luxe.*

There was, for example, session number 40, "Revolting Acts: Gay Performance in the Sixties," in which one could hear Michael Moon from Duke University, that veritable Hippocrene of political correctness, wax rhapsodic over Andy Warhol's "truly dangerously experimental" relationship with Valerie Solanas, the woman who shot Warhol in 1968. The same session—which like many of the panels devoted to homosexual themes attracted many more people than the room could accommodate—offered us Eve Kosofsky Sedgwick, Professor Moon's colleague at Duke, on the subject of "Gay Vanguardism." Professor Sedgwick spoke in glowing terms about the liberation movement of the '60s—she mentioned in particular movements on behalf of peace, mental patients, prisoners, and children—and expressed an interest in exploring "the pedagogical pederastic model" and in "denaturalizing or destabilizing gender assignment."

Then there was session 692, arranged by the Marxist Literary Group, devoted to "Gender, Race, and 'Othering' in the Narrative Arts." This panel was not, however, to be confused with number 26, "The Poetics of 'Othering': Gender, Class, and Cultural Identity in the Literature of Africa and its Diaspora," or with number 588, "Reinventing Gender." Other attractive sessions included number 62, "The Other Captives: American Indian Oral Captivity Narratives," and number 590, "The Ties that Bound: Homophobia and Relations among Males in Early America," in which one could hear papers on "Sodomy in the New World," "The Prurient Origins of the American Self," "New English Sodom," and "The Sodomitical Tourist." As far as I know, none of the sessions was X-rated.

John Milton, as I mentioned, got off rather lightly in the session devoted to his work that I attended. Not so poor Shakespeare. Session number 356, "Tactical Shakespeare: Resistance and the Economy of the Early Modern Subject," included a paper on "Early Modern Characters and Post-modern Subjects: Counterhegemonic Discourse in *The Comedy of Errors* and *The Winter's Tale*"—not exactly the kind of thing to increase the Bard's readership, one would have thought. And then there was session number 158, which was devoted to "Women's Responses to Shakespeare Today: Gender, Race, and Colonialism": precisely the subjects, of course, that leap to mind when one thinks of Shakespeare.

In fact, Shakespeare's work was not really the issue here at all. "Miranda's Canadian Metamorphoses: A Study in Postcolonial Resistance" and "The Racial Politics of Intertextuality: Gloria Naylor's Deconstruction of Shakespeare" dealt with some contemporary fiction based loosely on Shakespearean themes, while "Contemporary Indian Uses of Shakespeare: Issues of Gender and Race" dealt with the mesmerizing influence *Hamlet* had had on a certain Indian village. True, we heard about the "patriarchal bias of Shakespeare's tragedy," Miranda's "white liberal guilt," and Caliban's status as an oppressed Third World victim of white, patriarchal, imperialism; but none of that was particularly new.

In "Canon Revision and the Question of Shakespeare's Status," another contribution to "Women's Responses to Shakespeare Today," Peter B. Erikson from the Clark Art Institute in Williamstown, Massachusetts, provided the audience with a passionate brief for multiculturalism. While he wound up recommending that Shakespeare's status be downgraded (a process he referred to as the "unfetishizing of Shakespeare"), his main text was not Shakespeare but "The Storm over the University," an essay by the Berkeley philosopher John Searle that appeared in *The New York Review of Books* in December 1990. Since my book *Tenured Radicals* was the subject of a good part of Professor Searle's essay, I feel confident disputing Professor Erikson's claim that "[Searle's] treatment of Roger Kimball's articulation of *The New Criterion*'s vision is accommodating if not cozy."

In fact, Professor Searle was sharply critical of *Tenured Radicals* on several counts. But he also dared both to criticize some of the academy's reigning idols and—what was perhaps even more unforgivable—to refuse to declare himself a wholehearted champion of multiculturalism. Instead, he articulated what Professor Erikson accurately called a "sophisticated" version of the "traditionalist position." That is, while Professor Searle gladly acknowledged that the canon could and should change over time, he continued to endorse the idea that the work of some writers—Shakespeare, for example—is "of very high intellectual and artistic quality, to the point of being of universal human interest."

The thought that *anything* could be of "universal human interest" is one thing a card-carrying multiculturalist like Professor Erikson simply cannot abide. And indeed his often confused arguments about the "intellectual deficiencies" in what he took to be Professor Searle's "traditionalist model" turned mostly on his—Professor Erikson's—commitment to "identity politics" and the idea of "cultural difference" as opposed to "universalism." When he reads a work by a black woman author, he explained, "I do not enter into a transcendent human interaction but instead become more aware of my whiteness and maleness, social categories that shape my being." In other words, he repudiates precisely that quality which makes literature so valuable: its ability to speak to us *across* the barriers of time, geography, social system, religious belief, to say nothing of the currently favored barriers of sex, class, race, and ethnic origin. "Transcendent," like "universalist," is a naughty word for the politically correct multiculturalist largely because, if taken seriously, it suggests that the qualities that unite us as human beings are more important than the contingencies that separate us as social and political agents.

Citing ridiculous or repellent titles from academic conferences is a journalistic occupation that irritates politically correct academics almost as much as calling them politically correct. Several speakers took time out to sneer at "the media's" reporting on the phenomenon of political correctness: After all, who are these journalists if not middle-class hegemonists still beholden to the accommo-dationist politics of a universalist model of pluralism that is insufficiently blah, blah, blah. In only one of the more than a dozen sessions that I visited was there no mention of the subject. Indeed, I believe that the MLA may have to be credited with spawning a new sub-variety of political cor-rectness that consists in subscribing to all the politically correct pieties while loudly denying that such a thing exists. On the subject of titles, the issue is simply this: Either they mean something or they don't. If they're mean-ingless, they're superfluous, an insult to one's audience, and oughtn't to have been used in the first place; if they *do* mean something, then they are naturally to be taken as a clue to the subject of the paper or the session they an-nounce and are legitimately open to comment and criti-cism. After all, if a title is deliberately provocative, its author should not blame people for being provoked.

Which brings us to "Lesbianism, Heterosexuality, and Feminist Theory," an extremely popular session presided over by Biddy Martin from Cornell University. The papers presented in this session, especially the second—"The Lesbian Phallus: Or, Does Heterosexuality Exist?"—were criticized and ridiculed as soon as the program for the MLA convention was published. Was this fair? Given the topic and the paper titles—the other two were "Mapping the Frontier of the Black Hole: Toward a Black Feminist Theory" and "Perverse Desire, the Lure of the Mannish Lesbian"— I think we can be sure that the assembled scholars were not there to discuss *Little Women*.

The "black hole" contributor was Sue E. Hutchins from Scripps College, where she teaches English and Black Studies and Women's Studies and Religion. Professor

Hutchins used the metaphor of the black hole to describe "black lesbians' profound exclusion from dominant discourse." If, she explained, white heterosexual women can be said to occupy the "center" of cultural space" and black heterosexual women the margins, then black lesbians belong to the margin of the margins: hence, you see, the black hole. But all this, together with such ritual assertions as "black women loving black women is a revolutionary act," was merely a kind of throat-clearing for Professor Hutchins's real subject: the quest for a black lesbian in Africa. "Is there," she asked, "an individual who is both indigenous to the continent and who is a lesbian?"—that is, in case we didn't get it, "a lesbian in the conservative and severely literal Catharine Stimpson sense of the word: a woman who finds other women erotically attractive and gratifying."

Professor Hutchins's problem, of course, is that lesbianism is deeply frowned upon and exceedingly rare in black Africa. She tried to help herself out of this difficulty by announcing that she was willing to make do with a black African lesbian "in representation"—i.e., in fiction or myth—as well as "corporeally." And apparently she did finally dig up some anthropological evidence of African lesbian sexuality "in the Stimpson sense." Even so, it seems that the pickings were disappointingly slim. Professor Hutchins's response to her findings was revealing. It tells us, among much else, a good deal about our multiculturalists's habits of interpretation and how we should judge their use of evidence. Professor Hutchins solemnly informed us that her effort "is an attempt to show sensitivity to the text and the culture that produces it"—"I am suing for permission to read," she added in a gratuitous gesture toward victimhood. But what did Professor Hutchins do when faced with a dearth of black African lesbians? As she explained in one dramatic moment: "I either 'out' an author or I 'out' a character (it takes one to know one, you know), or . . . I 'out' language." In other words, she shows "sensitivity to the text and the culture that produces it" by inventing lesbian characters where there are none.

Such "inventiveness" was good preparation for the next contribution, Judith Butler's paper on the "lesbian phallus" and the question of the existence of heterosexuality. I regret to say that Professor Butler, who teaches in the Humanities Center at Johns Hopkins University, was a bit of a let-down on both subjects. Her main point, at which she arrived after a tortuous Lacanian reading of Freud's 1914 essay on narcissism, was that "erotogenicity" was not the privileged property of the genitals—and most especially not the male genitals—but was essentially "plastic" and "transferable." Voicing her "wariness with respect to the phallic ideal," she explained that her "task is not merely to disjoin the phallus [i.e., an idealized source of erotic gratification] from the penis but to underscore the phallus as transferable property." "The phallus," she concluded, is "always already plastic" (an observation that brought much knowing laughter from the assembled teachers and scholars). About the question of the existence of heterosexuality, she merely professed to having "lost interest along the way."

What was most notable about Professor Butler's paper was not her conclusions—these were an expected smorgasbord of politically correct attitudes current in radical lesbian feminism—but the sophistication of her arguments. It was clear that Professor Butler is gifted with a keen and methodical philosophical mind. While her presentation was needlessly prolix and her conclusions debatable, to say the least, hers was the most rigorously argued paper I heard at the MLA. One could not but lament that these gifts are wasted on political posturing and on pondering such subjects as "the lesbian phallus."

Professor Butler concluded her talk by making the politically correct gesture of announcing that she was not politically correct, criticizing what she described as the "current conservative media blitz" and deploring "homophobic discourse on AIDS." Now "homophobia"—that is, fear or dislike or intolerance of homosexuals—has recently joined the pantheon of things it is politically incorrect to seem to be. (Whether one actually *is* racist or sexist or homophobic is in some ways a secondary matter.) Because I have cited and skeptically described some of the panels at the MLA devoted to homosexual themes, I will doubtless be accused of being "homophobic." But then it is precisely on the subjects that are most difficult to debate in public— such as race or homosexuality—that the demand for political correctness exercises its greatest tyranny: there is one politically correct position and then there is everything else. In any event, it is important to stress that the issue raised by these panels has nothing to do with "homophobia." It has to do first of all with the kinds of things that are appropriate subjects for a public scholarly discussion of literature. I submit that neither "The Sodomitical Tourist" nor "The Lesbian Phallus" is appropriate. This is not because I suffer from "homophobia" but because I believe that the chief attraction of such topics is prurient. Panels devoted to homosexual themes often have the air of rallies for the initiate; "sexual orientation"—like race, ethnic origin, and so on in other contexts—is deliberately politicized and hailed as another mark of cultural "difference" that renders "universality" or "transcendence" impossible.

The more general issue, however, concerns the glorified place that has been allotted to sexuality and questions of "sexual orientation" in the academic study of the humanities. Why should the details of one's sexual interests— hetero-, homo-, or otherwise—be featured in panels and classes supposedly devoted to the study of literature? And of course mention of "literature" reminds us how far panels devoted to homosexual themes tend to stray from any concern with literature. They are hardly alone in this. The whole tendency of the multiculturalist imperative that has invaded the study of literature is to politicize teaching and scholarship from the ground up. The effect is not to make one more politically "sensitive" but to transform a concern with literature into an obsession with one's race, one's sex, one's sexual preferences, one's ethnic origin. What one gains is a political cause; what one loses is the freedom of disinterested appreciation.

Indeed, the substitution of certain political causes for disinterested appreciation may be said to have become the raison d'être of the Modern Language Association. In the session on "Ideology and/in the Teaching of Literature," for example, one could hear Ellen Rooney, who was recently granted tenure at Brown University, deliver a paper called "Assume the Position: Pluralist Ideology and Gynocriticism." Professor Rooney argued strenuously against the traditional idea that literature was "an object that we recognize and respond to in some immediate way," explaining that the attempt to separate ideology from literature was itself a misguided ideological effort. She also explained that pluralism—an ideal that, as she correctly noted, "imagines a universal community"—was a bad thing because it "excludes exclusion" and because, horror of horrors, it attempts to distinguish between "ideology and reading."

Then there was the session on anthologies of American literature. Here one could listen to Paul Lauter, chief editor of the multiculturalist potpourri known as *The Heath Anthology of American Literature*, natter on about Reaganism, social inequality, and other "literary" topics. In case one hadn't already guessed, Professor Lauter explained how the impetus for the anthology was "directly linked" to the "movement for social change" of the sixties. One might, he admits, wonder whether the editors of *The Heath Anthology* were "attempting to reconstitute the shape of our discipline—of higher education generally—on the basis of political as distinct from traditionally accepted aesthetic standards." Answer: "Of course we are. For I know of no standard of judgment . . . which transcends the particularities of time and place. . . . of politics in short." Never mind that it was not so long ago that an inability to distinguish between aesthetic judgment and political propagandizing would have disqualified someone from teaching. Nowadays, the inability to make such distinctions is taken as a sign of superior insight.

Blatantly reductive as Professor Lauter was, the MLA's annual award for political fantasy must go to the session entitled "After Glasnost: Whither Marxist Criticism?", one of many panels devoted to Marxist or Marxist-inspired themes. It would be difficult to imagine a more graphic illustration of how politically correct thinking effectively inoculates its adherents against anything so inconvenient as historical reality. Sitting among the hundred or so auditors assembled to discover the fate of contemporary Marxist criticism, one might have been forgiven for believing that the year was 1969—if not, indeed, 1935. The session began with Neil Larsen from Northeastern University, who spoke about "Negation of the Abnegation: Dialectical Criticism in the 1960s." Western Marxism, he told us, has recently become "noncommittal and perplexed" about the class struggle and has taken refuge in theoretical and cultural disputes instead of forging ahead with revolutionary fervor. Take the well-known British Marxist Terry Eagleton: According to Professor Larsen, the problem is that Professor Eagleton "draws back from the prospect of actively and consciously impelling these contradictions [of power in society] toward a revolutionary outcome." Moreover, it was "blindness to socialist class struggle" that recently provided openings for "neo-capitalist interests"—that is, for what most of us would call democracy—in Eastern Europe. This was very bad. The disintegration of Communism—what Professor Larsen called "socialist institutions"—in Eastern Europe has replicated "the worst mechanical and non-dialectical aspects of its socialist other."

The one novelty in Professor Larsen's paper was his insinuation that contemporary Marxist theory was guilty of "vulgar Marxism." Remember "vulgar Marxism"? That was the straw man that some Marxists invented when they wanted to castigate other Marxists for being insufficiently sophisticated. Vulgar Marxists believed that culture (the "superstructure") was a direct reflection of economic relations (the "base"). Sophisticated Marxists were not so naïve. They had read the writings of the Frankfurt School. They knew that the relation between culture and the productive forces of a society was a complicated affair. They still believed—"finally," "ultimately"—in economic determinism, but they were too cautious to say so outright. The determinism they believed in was "mediated." It was "dialectical." For the Sophisticated Marxist (a category that for our purposes may be said to consist largely of those who identify themselves as Marxists and who possess a Ph.D.) being "dialectical" is a little like what the adolescent mind sums up in the adjective "cool." It is good to be as dialectical as possible. Lenin was dialectical; Stalin (mostly) was not. Marx of course was highly dialectical. Being a member of the bourgeoisie is by definition undialectical—unless, that is, one happens to be a Sophisticated Marxist engaged in that paradigmatically bourgeois activity, teaching at a university, in which case one may be eligible for an exemption. How very dialectical, then, that Professor Larsen should suggest that the likes of Terry Eagleton and even that nonpareil of Sophisticated Marxists, the Duke professor Fredric Jameson, were in some deep dialectical sense insufficiently . . . dialectical and guilty, yes, of vulgar Marxism.

There was something almost quaint about Professor Larsen's paper. He loved talking about things like the relation between "base" and "superstructure," "Lenin's key dialectical insight," and "the internal contradictions of capitalism." He even appeared to believe that such exploded clichés *meant* something, much as scientists of an earlier era genuinely believed in such hypothetical entities as phlogiston or ether.

Less quaint, and considerably more fantastic, was the following presentation on the subject of the "construction of class in contemporary neo-Marxist theory" by Barbara Clare Foley from Rutgers University at Newark. Professor Foley first made herself notorious in 1985 when she was teaching at Northwestern University and helped organize a demonstration to prevent Adolfo Calero—at that time the head of the Nicaraguan Democratic Forces fighting against the Sandinista government—from speaking on campus. Professor Foley's politically correct behavior at Northwestern included taking the podium just before Mr. Calero was to speak and announcing—among other things—that "we are not going to let him speak" and that he "should feel lucky to get out of [here] alive." In the event, Mr. Calero was prevented from speaking. As Joseph Epstein reported in a vivid account of the incident, when Mr. Calero arrived there was a great deal of shouting and chanting, and before he could begin someone "rushed to the stage and threw a red liquid at him," spattering his clothes with a substance variously identified as red ink and animal blood. Mr. Calero was then led from the hall by security men.

In any event, it appears that Professor Foley is among those who admire Stalin and perhaps even consider him

appropriately "dialectical." As she warned at the beginning
of her talk, Professor Foley did not say much that was
relevant to anyone's work as a literary scholar. Instead, she
began by ridiculing the way Western "TV pundits" have
presented the disintegration of Communist regimes in
Eastern Europe. These misguided commentators, she ob-
served with biting sarcasm, believe that

> socialism—sometimes called Communism—has
> failed. First, because it did not recognize that the
> free market accords with human nature much better
> than a planned economy [this was met by laughter
> and applause from the audience]; and second, be-
> cause political pluralism as embodied in Western-
> style electoral politics makes for far more genuine
> mass political participation than does a one-party
> state.

One marveled to hear this middle-class beneficiary of a
free-market economy and Western political pluralism—and
a graduate of Radcliffe and the University of Chicago to
boot—go on to argue that the movement toward "repressive
state socialism became irreversible only in the Khrushchev-
era in the USSR and only after the defeat of the Cultural
Revolution in China." Perhaps neither Stalin nor Mao were
sufficiently repressive for Professor Foley's taste. In any
event, in her view "twentieth-century Communist-led
movements" represent "the greatest advance in history
toward human emancipation." Whatever mistakes or excesses may have been committed along the way, the efforts
to establish Communism in this century have been, she
insisted, "mainly good" from the point of view of the
working class and its "allies." (Tell that to the Ukrainians
and the Chinese peasants.)

Professor Foley was not without a long list of particulars. For example, we were told that in the United States the movements for racial justice and unionization were spearheaded "by reds in the 1930s." President Roosevelt, you see, instituted his New Deal programs only because he feared a Communist revolution. Furthermore—still dilating on the glorious record of Communism in this century and correcting the history books along the way—Professor Foley informed us that the Nazis were defeated "primarily by the Soviets." It's not clear what she thought generals Eisenhower, Patton, and Bradley and Field Marshall Montgomery were doing in 1944 and 1945. Nor did she dwell on the warm alliance between Stalin and Hitler that persisted until the Nazis invaded the Soviet Union in 1941. Rather, she proceeded to remind us that the Soviets have also been in the vanguard of human emancipation by aiding and abetting "dozens of post-War national liberation movements"—you know, the movements that have led to all those beneficient regimes in Africa, Cuba, Central America, and the Middle East.

Professor Foley wasn't done yet. Among the truly magnificent accomplishments of Communism in this century, she said, were the Soviet Five-Year Plan, the Chinese Great Leap Forward, and the Cultural Revolution. All were said to

> attest to the uncoerced [!] enthusiasm with which masses of workers and peasants have thrown themselves into the process of materially constructing a new infrastructure that they thought they would control . . . [and] to the dramatic transformation in human relationships and values that were enabled by the movement toward egalitarianism.

As examples of this miraculous transformation, Professor Foley described scenes of peasant women "making bonfires of their veils" and "Moscow bus riders performing citizen's arrests of fellow Russians who voiced racist insults to visiting black Americans." Of course, a more thorough "transformation in human relationships and values" was achieved by the nine to twelve *million* victims of Stalin's first Five-Year Plan from 1928 to 1933, to say nothing of the three million or so who perished in his Great Purge of the preceding years, the millions who disappeared into the Gulag, or still other millions who died in his subsequent experiments with a "one-party state." Mao's efforts at totalitarian social engineering met with a similar success. But these were incidents that Professor Foley did not have occasion to mention. For her, the problem was that the noble movements toward human freedom and an "egalitarian society" represented by Communism had been "arrested and reversed" by the imperialistic forces of the West. It is consoling, is it not, to know that literature students at Rutgers University, Newark, are in such responsible hands?

After Barbara Foley's performance, almost anything might have seemed tame. But in some respects, Catharine Stimpson's Presidential Address, "On Differences," epitomized to perfection the coy but thoroughly politicized spirit that now pervades the MLA and indeed the profession generally. In its breathtaking exhibition of politically correct attitudes, it managed to touch gently upon nearly every piety dear to the contemporary academic humanist while at the same time displaying appropriate contempt for a stunning array of "incorrect" opinions. Anyone who has seen Professor Stimpson in action knows that, while possessing a limited repertoire, she is an exceptionally able orator. Her most histrionically effective role is as defender of wounded virtue. She has also mastered the art of speaking almost entirely in clichés. This means that, unless one is paying close attention, she will often seem merely to be defending the status quo when in fact she is proposing radical change.

Professor Stimpson managed to add noticeably to the heady atmosphere of political rectitude wafting about the Hyatt Regency before even beginning her address by the simple device of dedicating it to colleagues "who have met AIDS with exemplary rage, gallantry, and courage." This gesture elicited somber, heartfelt applause. Everyone knows that AIDS is a horrible disease. But not all horrible diseases manage to transform themselves into signs of political election. AIDS has done so primarily because of the activism it has fostered among homosexuals. Many, many more people die each year from breast cancer, from heart attacks, and from other diseases than die from AIDS. But only AIDS enjoys the privileged status of being politically correct. Thus it is that AIDS is widely invoked as a token of political orthodoxy. For example, Martha Nussbaum, a professor of philosophy at Brown, noted not once but twice in her recent collection of essays that she was donating a portion of the royalties she received from the book to "The AIDS Action Committee of Boston." Now what are the royalties on a book of academic philosophical essay likely to be? $37.50? $78.95? The ritual invocation of AIDS is a superb example of the politically correct gesture: It costs nothing yet nonetheless imparts a warm glow of superior virtue.

While she, too, took time out to lambast the notion of political correctness and the way it had been used to criticize the MLA, Professor Stimpson devoted the body of her talk to the quintessential politically correct idea of 1991: "difference." Along the way she managed to get in praise for Václav Havel and several other exquisitely P.C. figures and themes. At one point, for example, she paused solemnly to note that there were limits to what even the most socially concerned literary criticism could do: "A hungry child cannot eat our words. A battered woman cannot tape her broken ribs with our interpretations," as if hungry children or battered women were the issue. Describing the study of modern literature as a "drama of difference," an effort to teach us to live "openly with difference," she devoted most of her address to contrasting the traditional view of the humanities unfavorably to multiculturalism, "cultural democracy," and their supporting ideologies. The former is elitist, hierarchical, and insufficiently sensitive to differences like "age, class, ethnicity, institution, gender, nation, tribe, race, rank, religion, sexuality," while the latter involve "treating society as the home of several equally valuable but distinct racial and ethnic groups," as she put it in one anodyne phrase.

Professor Stimpson acknowledged that not everyone in her flock was so enthusiastic about the prospect of multiculturalism "invigorating" the study of literature. She therefore proclaimed herself "baffled, baffled as to why we cannot be students of Western culture and multiculturalism at the same time." What she did not say, of course, was that multiculturalism implied a complete politicization of teaching and learning, that its radically egalitarian conception of culture ruled out not only the notion of literary quality but downgraded the very idea of literature as a distinct realm of endeavor and experience; she did not mention that multiculturalism, far from being a means of securing ethnic and racial equality, was an instrument for promoting ideological separatism based on all those differences she enjoyed enumerating: "age, class, ethnicity, institution, gender, nation, tribe, race, rank, religion, sexuality"; she did not dwell on the fact that the multiculturalist imperative explicitly denies the intellectual and moral foundations of Western culture—preeminently its commitment to rationality and the ideal of objectivity—and that consequently the idea of being "students of Western culture and multiculturalism at the same time" is either an empty rhetorical gesture or a contradiction in terms.

As it happens, one prominent focus of Professor Stimpson's attack was the passage from the inaugural issue of *The New Criterion* that serves as the epigraph for this essay. She read most of it aloud, suggesting that it represents a prime instance of the "booming rhetorical guns" under which the MLA has suffered so unfairly. Consider: "[M]ost of what is written . . . is either hopelessly ignorant, deliberately obscurantist, commercially compromised, or politically motivated." Could it be that the academy, that the MLA, is guilty of such things as deliberate obscurantism or politicizing the study of literature? "[T]he very notion of an independent high culture and the distinctions that separate it from popular culture and commercial entertainment have been radically eroded." Would anyone in the academy today really challenge the distinction between high culture and popular entertainment? "This fateful collapse in critical standards . . . and in the very idea of critical disinterestedness . . . has changed, and changed very much for the worse, the way the arts and humanities are now studied in our universities." Surely there was nothing at the MLA to suggest that academic standards had suffered or that well-known scholars have jettisoned the idea of critical disinterestedness? And as for "the radical movement of the sixties," well, Professor Stimpson called them her "salad days," Professors Lauter, Foley, and Larsen seem still to be living them, but who would say that the academy was influenced for the worse by a sixties radicalism—by drugs, promiscuity, a destruction of academic standards, an importation of politics into the classroom?

Professor Stimpson presents herself as the champion of the downtrodden and disempowered. Yet the multiculturalist conception of education she champions would bring not victory but profound defeat for genuine intellectual emancipation. In a recent essay entitled "Our Universal Civilization," the novelist V. S. Naipaul described his vocation as a writer as a journey from the periphery to the center: from his native Trinidad—the periphery of universal civilization—to London, its center. All true education traces some such movement from the periphery to the center, from our isolated selves to something larger. The multiculturalist imperative holds that there is no center, only a series of equally valid peripheries. As the 106th annual meeting of the MLA showed in unsettling detail, this doctrine has established itself as the reigning orthodoxy in literature departments in colleges and universities across the country. It is an insidious doctrine, spelling new forms of intellectual and moral separatism, and it is a tragedy that it should have found so warm a reception in the American academy.

THE STORM OVER THE UNIVERSITY

John Searle

John Searle, a philosopher at the University of California, Berkeley, wrote this article in *The New York Review of Books* (December 6, 1990) as a review-essay on three books: *Tenured Radicals: How Politics Has Corrupted Our Higher Education*, by Roger Kimball; *The Politics of Liberal Education*, edited by Darryl L. Gless and Barbara Herrnstein Smith; and *The Voice of Liberal Learning: Michael Oakeshott on Education*, edited by Timothy Fuller.

1.

I cannot recall a time when American education was not in a "crisis." We have lived through Sputnik (when we were "falling behind the Russians"), through the era of "Johnny can't read," and through the upheavals of the sixties. Now a good many books are telling us that the university is going to hell in several different directions at once. I believe that, at least in part, the crisis rhetoric has a structural explanation: Since we do not have a national consensus on what success in higher education would consist of, no matter what happens, some sizable part of the population is going to regard the situation as a disaster. As with taxation and relations between the sexes, higher education is essentially and continuously contested territory. Given the history of that crisis rhetoric, one's natural response to the current cries of desperation might reasonably be one of boredom.

A few years ago the literature of educational crises was changed by a previously little-known professor of philosophy at the University of Chicago in a book implausibly entitled *The Closing of the American Mind: How Higher Education has Failed Democracy and Impoverished the Souls of Today's Students*. To me, the amazing thing about Allan Bloom's book was not just its prodigious commercial success—more than half a year at the top of *The New York Times*'s best-seller list—but the depth of the hostility and even hatred that it inspired among a large number of professors. Most of Bloom's book is not about higher education as such, but consists of an idiosyncratic, often original, and even sometimes profound—as well as quirky and cranky—analysis of contemporary American intellectual culture, with an emphasis on the unacknowledged and largely unconscious influence of certain German thinkers, especially Weber and Nietzsche.

Why did Bloom's book arouse such passion? I will suggest an explanation later in this article, but it is worth noting that Bloom demonstrated to publishers and potential authors one thesis beyond doubt: It is possible to write an alarmist book about the state of higher education with a long-winded title and make a great deal of money. This consequence appears to provide at least part of the inspiration for a number of other books, equally alarmist and with almost equally heavy-duty titles, for example *The Moral Collapse of the University, Professionalism, Purity and Alienation,* by Bruce Wilshire; *Killing the Spirit, Higher Education in America,* by Page Smith; *Tenured Radicals: How Politics Has Corrupted Our Higher Education,* by Roger Kimball; and *The Moral and Spiritual Crisis in Education: A Curriculum for Justice and Compassion in Education,* by David E. Purpel.

One difficulty with the more alarmist of these books is that though they agree that the universities are in a desperate state, they do not agree on what is wrong or what to do about it. When there is no agreement not only on the cure but on the diagnosis itself, it is very hard to treat the patient. Another weakness of such books is their sometimes hysterical tone. There are, indeed, many problems in the universities, but for the most part, they tend to produce silliness rather than catastrophe. The spread of "poststructuralist" literary theory is perhaps the best known example of a silly but noncatastrophic phenomenon. Several of these books try to describe current threats to intellectual values. How serious are these threats? Right now we can't tell with any certainty because we can't yet know to what extent we are dealing with temporary fads and fashions or with long-term assaults on the integrity of the intellectual enterprise.

I think the best way to enter this discussion is by examining at least briefly the current debate about the status of what is called the "canon" of the best works in our civilization, and what part the canon should play in the education of undergraduates. I have selected two books from the current flood, because they take such strong and opposing stands on just this issue. On the side of tradition is Roger Kimball's *Tenured Radicals,* and opposed are most of the articles included in *The Politics of Liberal Education,* a collection of essays originally given at a conference sponsored by Duke and the University of North Carolina on the subject "Liberal Arts Education in the Late Twentieth Century: Emerging Conditions, Responsive Practices."

Consider what would have been taken to be a platitude a couple of decades ago, and is not regarded in many places as a wildly reactionary view. Here it is: There is a certain Western intellectual tradition that goes from, say, Socrates to Wittgenstein in philosophy, and from Homer to James Joyce in literature, and it is essential to the liberal education of young men and women in the United States that they should receive some exposure to at least some of the great works in this intellectual tradition; they should, in Matthew Arnold's overquoted words, "know the best that is known and thought in the world." The arguments given for this view—on the rare occasions when it was felt that arguments were even needed—were that knowledge of the tradition was essential to the self-understanding of educated Americans since the country, in an important sense, is the product of that tradition; that many of these works are historically important because of their influence; and that most of them, for example several works by Plato and Shakespeare, are of very high intellectual and artistic quality, to the point of being of universal human interest.

Until recently such views were not controversial. What exactly is the debate about? The question is more complex than one might think because of the variety of different objections to the tradition and the lack of any succinct statement of these objections. For example, many African Americans and Hispanic Americans feel left out of the "canon," and want to be included. Just as a few years ago they were demanding the creation of ethnic studies departments, so now they are demanding some representation of their experiences and their point of view as part of the general education of all undergraduates. This looks like a standard political demand for "representation" of the sort we are familiar with in higher education. If the objection to the "canon" is that it consists almost entirely of works by white males, specifically white males of European (including North American) origin, then there would appear to be an easy and common-sense solution to the problem: Simply open the doors to admit the work of talented writers who are not white, or not male, or not European. If, for example, the contribution of women in literature has been neglected, there are plenty of writers of similar stature to Jane Austen, George Eliot, and Virginia Woolf who can be added.

Some of the opponents of the tradition will accept this reform, but most the authors of *The Politics of Liberal Education* would not, and you will have misunderstood the nature of the dispute if you think that it can be resolved so simply. The central objections to the tradition are deeper and more radical, and they go far beyond the mere demand for increased representation. What are these objections?

To approach this question, I have selected the proceedings of the North Carolina conference not because they contain any notable or original ideas—such conferences seldom do—but because they express a mode of literary and political sensibility that has become fairly widespread in some university departments in the humanities and is characterized approvingly by some of the participants at the conference as "the cultural left." I doubt that "the cultural left" is a well-defined notion because it includes so many altogether different points of view. It includes 1960s-style radicals, feminists, deconstructionists, Marxists, people active in "gay studies" and "ethnic studies," and people of left-wing political persuasion who happen to teach in universities. But on certain basic issues of education these groups tend to agree. In describing the North Carolina conference in his concluding statement Richard Rorty writes:

Our conference has been in large part a rally of this cultural left. The audience responded readily and favorably to notions like "subversive readings," "hegemonic discourse," "the breaking down of traditional logocentric hierarchies," and so on. It chortled derisively at mentions of William Bennett, Allan Bloom, and E. D. Hirsch, Jr., and nodded respectfully at the names of Nietzsche, Derrida, Gramsci, or Foucault.

Whether or not Rorty is justified in using the label, the views expressed show a remarkable consensus in their opposition to the educational tradition and in their hostility to those who, like Bloom, have supported a version of the tradition. Here are some typical passages:

Mary Louise Pratt, a professor of comparative literature at Stanford, writes.

Bloom, Bennett, Bellow, and the rest (known by now in some quarters as the Killer B's) are advocating [the creation of] a narrowly specific cultural capital that will be the normative *referent* for everyone, but will remain the *property* of a small and powerful caste that is linguistically and ethnically unified. It is this caste that is referred to by the "we" in Saul Bellow's astoundingly racist remark that "when the Zulus have a Tolstoy, *we* will read him." Few doubt that behind the Bennett-Bloom program is a desire to close not the American mind, but the American university, to all but a narrow and highly uniform elite with no commitment to either multiculturalism or educatinal democracy. Thus while the Killer B's (plus a C—Lynne Cheney, the Bennett mouthpiece now heading the National Endowment for the Humanities) depict themselves as returning to the orthodoxies of yesteryear, their project must not be reduced to nostalgia or conservatism. Neither of these explain the blanket contempt they express for the country's universities. They are fueled not by reverence for the past, but by an aggressive desire to lay hold of the present and future. The B's act as they do not because they are unaware of the cultural and demographic diversification underway in the country; they are utterly aware. That is what they are trying to shape; that is why they are seeking, and using, national offices and founding national foundations.

Pratt laments "the West's relentless imperial expansion" and the "monumentalist cultural hierarchy that is historically as well as morally distortive" and goes on to characterize Bloom's book as "intellectually deplorable" and Bennett's *To Reclaim a Legacy* as "intellectually more deplorable." In the same vein, Henry A. Giroux, a professor of education at Miami University of Ohio, writes:

In the most general sense, Bloom and Hirsch represent the latest cultural offensive by the new elitists to rewrite the past and construct the present from the perspective of the privileged and the powerful. They disdain the democratic implications of pluralism and argue for a form of cultural uniformity in which difference is consigned to the margins of history or to the museum of the disadvantaged.

And according to Henry Louis Gates, Jr., a professor of English at Duke:

The teaching of literature [has become] the teaching of an aesthetic and political order, in which no women and people of color were ever able to discover the reflection or representation of their images, or hear the resonance of their cultural voices. The return of "the" canon, the high canon of Western masterpieces, represents the return of an order in which my people were the subjugated, the voiceless, the invisible, the unrepresented, and the unrepresentable. Who would return us to that medieval never-never land?

Anybody who has been to such a conference will recognize the atmosphere. It is only within such a setting that Bloom and Hirsch (one a professor of philosophy in Chicago, the other a professor of English in Virginia) can seem (to people who are themselves professors somewhere) to exemplify "the privileged and the powerful."

One of the conferees, Gerald Graff of Northwestern, writes:

Speaking as a leftist, I too find it tempting to try to turn the curriculum into an instrument of social transformation.

He goes on to resist the temptation with the following (italics mine):

But I doubt whether the curriculum (*as opposed to my particular courses*) can or should become an extension of the politics of the left.

It turns out that he objects to politicizing the entire curriculum not because there might be something immoral about using the classroom to impose a specific ideology on students, but because of the unfortunate fact that universities also contain professors who are not "leftists" and who do not want their courses to become "an extension of the politics of the left"; and there seems to be no answer to the question, "What is to be done with those constituencies which do not happen to agree . . . that social transformation is the primary goal of education." What indeed?

I said earlier that it was difficult to find a succinct statement of the objections to the educational tradition made by the so-called cultural left, but this is largely because the objections are taken for granted. If you read enough material of the sort I have quoted, and, more importantly, if you attend enough of these conferences, it is easy to extract the central objection. It runs something like this: The history of "Western Civilization" is in large part a history of oppression. Internally, Western civilization oppressed women, various slave and serf populations, and ethnic and cultural minorities generally. In foreign affairs, the history of Western civilization is one of imperialism and colonialism. The so-called canon of Western civilization consists in the official publications of this system of oppression, and it is no accident that the authors in the "canon" are almost exclusively Western white males, because the civilization itself is ruled by a caste consisting almost entirely of Western white males. So you cannot reform education by admitting new members to the club, by opening up the canon; the whole idea of "the canon" has to be abolished. It has to be abolished in favor of something that is "multicultural" and "nonhierarchical."

The word "nonhierarchical" in the last sentence is important and I will come back to it. In the meantime I hope I have given enough of the arguments from those who oppose the traditional conceptions of liberal education to make it clear why the dispute cannot be resolved just by opening up the club to new members, and why it seems so intractable. Even if the canon is opened up, even if membership in the club is thrown open to all comers, even after you have admitted every first-rate woman writer from Sappho to Elizabeth Bishop, the various groups that feel that they have been excluded are still going to feel excluded, or marginalized. At present there are still going to be too many Western white males.

The actual arguments given often speak of improving education, but the central presuppositions of each side are seldom explicitly stated. With few exceptions, those who defend the traditional conception of a liberal education with a core curriculum think that Western civilization in general, and the United States in particular, have on the whole been the source of valuable institutions that should be preserved and of traditions that should be transmitted, emphatically including the intellectual tradition of skeptical critical analysis. Those who think that the traditional canon should be abandoned believe that Western civilization in general, and the United States in particular, are in large part oppressive, imperialist, patriarchal, hegemonic, and in need of replacement, or at least of transformation. So the passionate objections that are made by the critics to Allan Bloom often have rather little to do with a theory of higher education as such. (This is unfortunate, because there is plenty to object to in Bloom's book on purely educational grounds—for example, its failure to give sufficient attention or value to the study of history and its blindness to the achievements of contemporary analytic philosophy.) Their objection to the educational tradition is intended to make a political point about the nature of American society.

There is a certain irony in this in that earlier student generations, my own for example, found the critical tradition that runs from Socrates through the *Federalist Papers,* through the writings of Mill and Marx, down to the twentieth century, to be liberating from the stuffy conventions of traditional American politics and pieties. Precisely by in-

culating a critical attitude, the "canon" served to demythologize the conventional pieties of the American bourgeoisie
and provided the student with a perspective from which to
critically analyze American culture and institutions. Ironically, the same tradition is now regarded as oppressive.
The texts once served an unmasking function; now we are
told that it is the texts which must be unmasked.

More puzzling than the hatred of Bloom is the hostility
shown to E. D. Hirsch, Jr. After all, Hirsch's central idea is
that it would be desirable for American schoolchildren to
be taught a common body of knowledge, a set of elementary facts and concepts that Hirsch calls "cultural literacy."
(Among the texts and ideas he believes should be "explained in depth" are, for example, the Bill of Rights, *Don
Quixote*, and ecology.) It is hard to imagine how anybody
could object to such an innocuous proposal for improving
education in the grade schools and high schools. However,
even this is greeted with rage; indeed, only Bloom and
Bennett arouse more anger than Hirsch in these polemics.
In a savage attack, Barbara Herrnstein Smith quotes Hirsch
as saying that his project of cultural literacy will result in

> breaking the cycle of illiteracy for deprived children;
> raising the living standards of families who have
> been illiterate; making our country more competitive
> in international markets; achieving greater social
> justice; enabling all citizens to participate in the
> political process; bringing us that much closer to the
> Ciceronian ideal of universal public discourse—in
> short, achieving the fundamental goals of the
> Founders at the birth of the republic.

To this project, she responds:

Wild applause; fireworks; music—*America the Beautiful;* all together, now: *Calvin Coolidge, Gunga Din, Peter Pan, spontaneous combustion.* Hurrah for America and the national culture! Hurrah!

Why the hysterical tone of opposition? Herrnstein Smith reveals her own preoccupations when she says that Hirsch is "promoting a *deeply conservative view of American society and culture* through a rousing populist rhetoric" (my italics). But of course there is no reason at all why students who become familiar with the range of facts and ideas compiled by Hirsch should not arrive at "radical" or "liberal" or other positions.

But what about the question of intellectual excellence? The very ideal of excellence implied in the canon is itself perceived as a threat. It is considered "elitist" and "hierarchical" to suppose that "intellectual excellence" should take precedence over such considerations as fairness, representativeness, the expression of the experiences of previously underrepresented minorities, etc. Indeed, in the recent debate at Stanford about the course of Western civilization, one of the arguments against the traditional curriculum (quoted with approval by Pratt) went as follows:

A course with such readings creates two sets of books, those privileged by being on the list and those not worthy of inclusion. Regardless of the good intentions of those who create such lists, the students have not viewed and will not view these separate categories as equal.

I find this an amazing argument. One obvious difficulty with it is that if it were valid, it would argue against any set of required readings whatever; indeed, any list you care to make about anything automatically creates two categories, those that are on the list and those that are not.

One curious feature of the entire debate about what is "hegemonic," "patriarchal," or "exclusionary" is that it is largely about the study of literature. No one seems to complain that the great ideas in physics, mathematics, chemistry, and biology, for example, also come in large part from dead white European males. Historians of science have been showing how talented women were discouraged throughout modern history from pursuing scientific careers. But I have not heard any complaints from physics departments that the ideas of Newton, Einstein, Rutherford, Bohr, Schrödinger, etc., were deficient because of the scientists' origins or gender. Even in history of philosophy courses—as opposed to general education courses—there is little or no objection to the fact that the great philosophers taught in these courses are mostly white Western males, from Socrates, Plato, and Aristotle through Frege, Russell, and Wittgenstein.

No doubt literature articulates the variety of human experience in ways that are unlike those of the sciences, but that is not enough by itself to explain the selective attitude that causes the humanities to be treated so differently from the sciences. To understand this difference you have to understand a second fundamental, but usually unstated, feature of the debate; in addition to having political objections to the United States and Europe, many members of the cultural left think that the primary function of teaching the humanities is political; they do not really believe that the humanities are valuable in their own except as a means of achieving "social transformation." They (apparently) accept that in subjects like physics and mathematics there may be objective and socially independent criteria of excellence (though they do not say much about the sciences at all), but where the humanities are concerned they think that the criteria that matter are essentially political.* The argument goes: Since any policy in the humanities will inevitably have a political dimension, courses in the humanities might as well be explicitly and beneficially political, instead of being disguised vehicles of oppression. These points are often stated in a kind of code. (In the code, to be "monumentalist" is to treat some works as if they were monuments, and to be "hierarchical" is to think that some works are better than others; I think "critical" used to mean vaguely Marxist as in some versions of "critical legal studies" but now it appears just to mean politically radical, as "critical pedagogy.")

For example, after having told us that "the most important questions facing both the liberal arts and higher education in general are moral and political" and that the university "is a place that is deeply political" Henry Giroux tells us the following about how we should teach "the canon":

> How we read or define a "canonical" work may not be as important as challenging the overall function and social uses the notion of the canon has served. Within this type of discourse, the canon can be analyzed as part of a wider set of relations that connect the academic disciplines, teaching, and power to considerations defined through broader, intersecting political and cultural concerns such as race, class, gender, ethnicity, and nationalism. What is in question here is not merely a defense of a particular canon, but the issue of struggle and empowerment. In other words, the liberal arts should

---

*Indeed, by "humanities" they do not mean everything that goes on under a Dean of Humanities but rather literature and cultural history.

be defended in the interest of creating critical rather than "good" citizens. The notion of the liberal arts has to be reconstituted around a knowledge-power relationship in which the question of curriculum is seen as a form of cultural and political production grounded in a radical conception of citizenship and public wisdom.

He concludes that this transformation of our attitudes toward the tradition will link the liberal arts to "the imperatives of a critical democracy."

Nothwithstanding its opaque prose, Giroux's message should be clear; the aim of a liberal education is to create political radicals, and the main point of reading the "canon" is to demythologize it by showing how it is used as a tool by the existing system of oppression. The traditional argument that the humanities are the core of a liberal education because of the intrinsic intellectual and aesthetic merits and importance of the works of Plato, Shakespeare, or Dante is regarded with scorn. Giroux again:

The liberal arts cannot be defended either as a self-contained discourse legitimating the humanistic goal of broadly improving the so-called "life of the mind" or as a rigorous science that can lead students to indubitable truths.

So the frustrating feature of the recent debate is that the underlying issues seldom come out into the open. Unless you accept two assumptions, that the Western tradition is oppressive, and that the main purpose of teaching the humanities is political transformation, the explicit arguments given against the canon will seem weak; that the canon is unrepresentative, inherently elitist, and, in a disguised form, political. Indeed if these arguments were strong ones, you could apply them against physics, chemistry, or mathematics.

From the point of view of the tradition, the answers to each argument are fairly obvious. First, it is not the aim of education to provide a representation or sample of everything that has been thought and written, but to give students access to works of high quality. Second, for that very reason, education is by its very nature "elitist" and "hierarchical" because it is designed to enable and encourage the student to discriminate between what is good and what is bad, what is intelligent and what is stupid, what is true and what is false. Third, the "tradition" is by no means a unified phenomenon, and properly taught, it should impart a critical attitude to the student, precisely because of the variety and intellectual independence of the works being taught, and the disagreements among them. Fourth, of course the humanities have a political dimension at least in the sense that they have political consequences; so does everything else. But it does not follow from the fact that there is a political dimension to the humanities—as there is to music, art, gastronomy, and sex, as well as mathematics, philosophy, and physics—that the only, or even the principal, criteria for assessing these efforts should be political ones.

2.

Of the books I have read on the current "crisis" in education, the one I found the most fun to read is Kimball's *Tenured Radicals*. Kimball's announced aim is "to expose these recent developments in the academic study of humanities for what they are: ideologically motivated assaults on the intellectual and moral substance of our culture." One may doubt that he is right to characterize the current problems in the vocabulary of "crisis" and "corruption," but from my own experience it seems to me that he is right to say that "the situation is far worse than they [his readers, mostly outside of universities] are ever likely to have imagined." Mr. Kimball has attended a number of what would appear to be rather tedious academic conferences, and read a large number of books and articles in which many strange claims are made. He describes these patiently and often hilariously. He was not at the conference in North Carolina, but it seems unlikely that anything that happened there would have surprised him, because he recounts what happened at several other, similar conferences.

Kimball's method is to quote and paraphrase some of the more extreme views he encountered. For example, reporting a speech by Professor Barbara Johnson, he writes:

> Blending a deconstructionist's obsession with language and a feminist's obsession with male dominance, she summed up Professor Riffaterre's paper as a "masterful demonstration of "the fact" that "gynophobia [i.e., the fear of women] is structured like a language" and, conversely, that "language is structured like gynophobia."
> . . . Women themselves conspire in perpetuating this unhappy situation, she told us, for "the collective linguistic psyche exists in symbiotic relation to the fallen woman." We also learned, by a similarly elusive logic, that the "literary canon is a defense against its own femininity," a defense "against the woman within." What any of this could possibly mean was never revealed, but no one seemed to mind: it all sounded so exquisitely chic.

Such a method will seem unfair if readers get the impression that in quoting extreme passages, Kimball is quoting only unusual or eccentric views. To judge by my own experience he is not being unfair; the sorts of things that he finds objectionable are, in fact, quite common. In fact, as Kimball knows, the audience at such a session will recognize Johnson's theses, at least in the sense that they know what ideas and authors she is invoking. The phrase about "structured like a language" is borrowed from Lacan; the reference to defending against the "woman within" derives from psychoanalysis, etc.

Kimball summarizes some of his general conclusions as follows:

> It is one of the clearest symptoms of the decadence besetting the academy that the ideals that once informed the humanities have been corrupted, will-fully misunderstood, or simply ignored by the new sophistries that have triumphed on our campuses. We know something is gravely amiss when teachers of the humanities confess—or, as is more often the case, when they boast—that they are no longer able to distinguish between truth and falsity. We know something is wrong when scholars assure us—and their pupils—that there is no essential difference between the disinterested pursuit of knowledge and partisan proselytizing, or when academic literary critics abandon the effort to identify and elucidate works of lasting achievement as a reactionary enter-prise unworthy of their calling. And indeed, the most troubling development of all is that such contentions are no longer the exceptional pronouncements of a radical elite, but have increasingly become the con-ventional wisdom in humanities departments of our major colleges and universities.

Kimball is himself a journalist, an editor of *The New Criterion*, and his book is intended as polemical journalism, not scholarship. Nonetheless, it seems to me, even judged as such it has certain weaknesses. First, Kimball offers no coherent alternative vision of what higher education in the humanities should consist in. He simply takes it for granted that there is a single, unified, coherent tradition, just as his opponents do, and he differs from them in supposing that all we need to do to rescue higher education is to return to the standards of that tradition. But the situation is not that simple. In my experience there never was, in fact, a fixed "canon"; there was rather a certain set of tentative judgments about what had importance and quality. Such judgments are always subject to revision, and in fact they were constantly being revised.

Furthermore both the composition of our student bodies and the relation of the United States to the rest of the world have undergone some enormous changes in the past generation. For example, in my own university more than 50 percent of the freshman class are nonwhites. And we are all aware that countries like Japan, China, and those of Latin America play a much larger part in our relations to the rest of the world than they did in the 1950s. It is an interesting question what influence these facts should have on our conception of the education of undergraduates. Perhaps in the end we will say they should have no effect, but it is not obvious.

Worse yet, the debate over college curriculum mainly concerns only a tiny fraction of undergraduate education, usually a single required freshman course in the humanities, together with other courses in literature which the scholars who describe themselves as the "cultural left" may seek to control, and which may (or may not) therefore be vehicles for promoting ideologies of "social transformation." Most undergraduate education—as well as our lack of any coherent theory of what we are trying to achieve in undergraduate education—is largely untouched by this discussion. Neither side has much to say about what actually happens in most college classrooms.

However, the debate about the freshman "core" course remains at the center of attention; the debate tends to be shallow because it is presented as a conflict between the cultural left, on the one hand, and the somewhat oversimplified views held by Bloom and Kimball, on the other. Why should one accept these as the only choices?

A second difficulty with Kimball's analysis is the thinness of his diagnosis. He argues that the radicals of the sixties have now become tenured professors, and are carrying on, within the university, the same ideology that they espoused as student radicals a quarter of a century ago. This analysis seems superficial. One difficulty with it is that many of the people he cites most prominently, such as Paul de Man and Jacques Derrida, were not active as student radicals in the sixties. Indeed, most of the heroes of the cultural left had little to do with the sit-ins and the demonstrations against the Vietnam War or with any of the causes that concerned radicals in the 1960s.

Furthermore, the diagnosis still leaves too many questions unanswered. Why do the radical critics attack mostly the humanities? After all, tenured faculty in the humanities comes from the same generation as the current faculty in the natural sciences, in philosophy, and in the social sciences, but—leaving out such newly created departments as "Ethnic Studies"—the "cultural left" is not heavily influential outside the departments of French, English, and comparative literature and a few history departments and law schools. More pressingly, why should literature have become the academic home of radical left-wing politics? It ought to astonish us that the current university centers of activist radical political views are not in sociology, political science, or economics but in English, French, and comparative literature. We can all learn much about the nature of politics, culture, and history from Shakespeare, Balzac, and Conrad; but the study of poetry, plays, and novels is hardly the ideal basis for understanding modern structures of power or the mechanisms of revolutionary change.

Kimball has nothing to tell us about these questions. I think the issues are complex, but several factors help to explain the migration of radical politics from the social sciences to the humanities. First, as empirical theories of society or blueprints for social change, Marxism and other such theories have been discredited by recent events. The collapse of the Soviet empire only marks officially something that most intellectuals have know quietly for a long time. The standard versions of radical leftist ideology in the form of theories of society and social change, such as Marxism, Leninism, Stalinism, Maoism, and Castroism, are all in disrepute. The most congenial home left for Marxism, now that it has been largely discredited as a theory of economics and politics, is in departments of literary criticism.

Secondly, for reasons I do not fully understand, many professors of literature no longer care about literature in the ways that seemed satisfactory to earlier generations. It seems pointless to many of them to teach literature as it was understood by such very different critics as Edmund Wilson, John Crowe Ransom, or I. A. Richards; so they teach it as a means of achieving left-wing political goals or as an occasion for exercises in deconstruction, etc. The absence of an accepted educational mission in many literary studies has created a vacuum waiting to be filled. Perhaps the original mistake was in supposing that there is a well-defined academic discipline of "literary criticism"—as opposed to literary scholarship—capable of accommodating Ph.D. programs, research projects, and careers for the ambitious. When such a discipline fails to be "scientific" or rigorous, or even well defined, the field is left wide open for various fashions, such as deconstruction, or for the current political enthusiasms.

Still, there is a fair amount of truth to Kimball's diagnosis. It is not simply that some of the people he quotes have a history of student radicalism, for many others do as well, but rather that often the sensibility they express is much in accord with some of the simplistic rhetoric of twenty-five years ago. As Gates puts it:

> Ours was the generation that took over buildings in the late sixties and demanded the creation of black and women's studies programs, and now, like the return of the repressed, has come back to challenge the traditional curriculum.

Suppose that one is dissatisfied with the low intellectual level of the "cultural left," but that one feels at the same time that much undergraduate education should be improved. This question was faced in an acute form in the debate at Stanford, concerning the reform of the curriculum in Western culture. Both the debate and its results are instructive. Stanford had a required one-year course in Western culture that had to be taken by all incoming students. This course was given in eight different "tracks," corresponding roughly to different departments and schools. Among the tracks, for example, were history, literature and the arts, philosophy, and Western thought and technology. But all shared a required reading list, containing the Bible, Plato's *Republic*. Homer, several medieval and Renaissance readings, including Augustine,

Dante, Thomas More, Machiavelli, Luther, and Galileo, and of the moderns, Voltaire, Marx, Freud, and Darwin. In addition, a list of writers ranging from Thucydides to Nietzsche was "strongly recommended."

Many of the objections made to this course were predictable, reflecting the views of the cultural left I have mentioned, as were the defenses. What emerged appears to have been a kind of compromise arrived at after many months of debate. Unfortunately, the controversy became so fogged by political polemics and by partial and inaccurate reports in the press that the central issues, and what actually occurred, were not made clear to the general public.

The title of the course was changed to "Culture, Ideas, Values." ("CIV" for short, with "Western" left out). The readings required for all tracks now include the Bible, "a Classical Greek philosopher, an early Christian thinker, a Renaissance dramatist, an Enlightenment thinker," and readings from Marx and Freud. At least one non-European work must be studied and at some point in each academic quarter "substantial attention" must be given to "the issues of *race, gender,* and *class.*"

What was the upshot of these reforms in educational practice? It is too early to tell what the long-term results will be, but at present, of the eight tracks, seven are quite similar to the originals. To the required readings have been added such texts as Confucius and the Koran, but I would guess that about 80 percent of the readings are by writers who are the same as, or comparable to, those in the previous program, though the texts used are not exactly the same. If anything, these seven tracks look to me like a slight improvement on the original course in Western culture, because they retain enough of the core readings so that the educational purpose of the original is not lost, and at the same time they enrich course work with readings from outside the European tradition.

The new plan also offered members of the faculty the possibility of formulating a completely revised course and some teachers have done so, with the result that the eighth track is a course called "Europe and the Americas." In this course, the required elements of the European canon remain, but they are read along with works of Spanish-American, American-Indian, and African-American authors. This eighth track presents a genuinely radical change from the earlier program, and it arouses the most objections from Kimball and other commentators.

However, it seems to me one can make a fairly strong case for the new course on purely educational grounds. Of eight tracks, it is not necessarily a bad thing to have one optional track where European civilization is taught as simply one civilization among others, and it does not seem to me at all worrying that Aristotle and Tocqueville are taught along with Frantz Fanon. Of course, as with all courses it all depends on how the course is taught. Yet even if we assume that the organizers have political goals, as I suppose they do, one of the most liberating effects of "liberal education" is in coming to see one's own culture as one possible form of life and sensibility among others; and the reading lists for the new course suggest that such an outcome is likely. Also, it is important to keep reminding ourselves that students are not just passive receptacles. In my experience, students are good at arguing back at professors, and indeed that is in large part what professors are for: to argue with. So my general impresssion from observing events at Stanford is that reports of the demise of "culture," Western or otherwise, in the required freshman course at Stanford are grossly exaggerated. If I were a freshman at Stanford, I might well be tempted to take "Europe and the Americas."

3.

One of the most ominous charges made in Kimball's book is that the cultural left in the humanities today has lost its traditional commitment to the search for truth. Indeed, according to Kimball, many no longer believe in the enterprise of an objective and disinterested search for truth, because they do not believe that such a thing is even possible. The claim is not that it is difficult and perhaps impossible to attain complete disinterest and objectivity, but rather that the very enterprise of trying to attain such things is misconceived from the beginning, because there is no objective reality for our objectivist methodology to attain. In short, many academics who make up the cultural left, according to Kimball, reject the "correspondence theory of truth"; they reject the idea that true statements are ever made true by virtue of the fact that there is an independently existing set of objects and features of the world to which such statements correspond.

Kimball's favorite target is a pamphlet produced by the American Council of Learned Societies, called *Speaking for the Humanities*. It is the product of a committee of six professors, five professors of English, and one professor of French and comparative literature. The pamphlet was explicitly designed to answer such critics as Bloom and Bennett, and it is written in a bland, academic prose. Its central sections, starting with "Ideology and Objectivity," begin somewhat condescendingly with the following: "Perhaps the most difficult aspect of modern thought, even for many humanities professors and certainly for society at large, is its challenge to the positivist ideal of objectivity and disinterest." But we learn after several pages that in fact this "positivist ideal" has been decisively replaced by something they call "theory," and that there are an overwhelming number of—unidentified—authorities who agree about this:

Over the past two decades, traditional assumptions about ways of studying the humanities have been contested, in large measure because a number of related disciplines—cultural anthropology, linguistics, psychoanalysis, the philosophy of language— were undergoing major changes that inevitably forced humanists to ask basic questions about their methods and the very definition of their fields.

Furthermore,

The challenge to claims of intellectual authority alluded to in the introduction of this report issues from almost all areas of modern thought—*science, psychology, feminism, linguistics, semiotics,* and *anthropology* [my italics].

And again,

As *the most powerful modern philosophies* and theories have been demonstrating, claims of disinterest, objectivity, and universality are not to be trusted and themselves tend to reflect local historical conditions [my italics].

As someone who takes more than a passing interest in "the most powerful modern philosophies," I know none of which it would be said that it "demonstrates" that such claims are "not to be trusted." Unfortunately the authors do not tell us exactly what results in these disciplines they have in mind. They also confidently quote "relativity and quantum mechanics" as supporting their new conception of the humanities. One wishes they had told us in some detail how the study of, say, inertial frames in relativity theory or the collapse of the wave function in quantum mechanics support their peculiar conception of the study of literature.

On first reading Kimball, it may appear that he is too hard on this pamphlet, but a close reading of the pamphlet makes it clear that he is not nearly hard enough. I do not here have the space to convey the smugness of its tone, the feebleness of its argument, or the weakness of its constant appeals to authority. Typical passages claim support from, "the most distinguished philosophers of science of our time," or tell us that, "the consensus of most of the dominant theories is. . . ."

One recurring fallacy deserves special mention. There is throughout the pamphlet a persistent confusion between epistemology and ontology; between how we know and what it is that we know when we know. It is an obvious fact that our epistemological efforts are undertaken by historically situated people, subject to all the usual imperfections, not merely of prejudice but of intellect. All investigations are relative to investigators. But it does not follow, nor is it indeed true, that all the matters investigated are relative to investigators.

Kimball sees that something very important is at stake in the debate concerning *Speaking for the Humanities*. He quotes Tzvetan Todorov's review of the pamphlet in the *New Republic* pointing out that its claim that most of the "dominant theories" reject the idea of disinterest and objectivity is "awkwardly reminiscent" of O'Brien's speech to Winston Smith in Orwell's *1984*:

> You believe that reality is something objective, external, existing in its own right. . . . But I tell you, Winston, that reality is not external. Reality exists in the human mind and nowhere else.

Kimball is mostly concerned with the political implications of this denial of an independently existing reality, but
I would like to stress its purely intellectual implications. If
you think there is no reality that words could possibly
correspond to, then obviously it will be a waste of time to
engage in an "objective and disinterested search for truth,"
because there is no such thing as truth. There are just
various forms of discourse engaged in by various groups of
people. Philosophers have a name for the view that there
exists a reality independent of our representations of it. It
is called "realism" or sometimes "metaphysical realism" or
"scientific realism." An immediate difficulty with denials
of metaphysical realism is that they remove the rational
constraints that are supposed to shape discourse, when
that discourse aims at something beyond itself. To paraphrase Dostoevsky, without metaphysical realism, anything is permissible.

Many arguments have been made against metaphysical
realism, all of them in my view inadequate. This is not the
place to go through each argument, but one can at least
cite some of the texts. As a matter of the sociology of
contemporary studies in the humanities, the two most
influential attacks on metaphysical realism are supposed
to have come from Thomas Kuhn's *The Structure of Scientific Revolutions* and Richard Rorty's *Philosophy and the
Mirror of Nature*. Kuhn is supposed to have shown that
science does not consist in the detached search for the
truth, but that scientists instead are an irrational community, who grasp hold of one "paradigm" until they find it
dissatisfying; then they have another "scientific revolution"
and rush to another paradigm.

I do not for a moment believe that this is the correct
interpretation of Kuhn's book, although he could have been
clearer about whether he was referring to the sociology of

scientific communities or the epistemology of scientific discovery. But whatever Kuhn's intentions, the effect has been to demythologize science in the eyes of people in literary studies, many of whom think that the claim of science to represent any independently existing reality has been discredited. When the authors of *Speaking for the Humanities* refer to "the most distinguished philosophers of science of our time," they clearly have Kuhn in mind.

What Kuhn did for science, Rorty did for philosophy. Rorty is supposed to have shown that philosophical claims do not correspond to an independently existing reality either. Both Kuhn and Rorty are supposed, oddly enough, to be supported by the deconstructive works of Jacques Derrida, who is alleged to have shown that the very idea of truth can be deconstructed, that the opposition between truth and falsity, between fact and fiction, is an illusory one, and that it is a "logocentric" prejudice to suppose that there is an independent reality that exists beyond texts. In fact, according to the literary theorists influenced by Derrida, there is nothing beyond or outside texts. So O'Brien is supposed to have triumphed over Winston after all.

Are there convincing arguments for metaphysical realism? The demand for a proof of the existence of a reality that is independent of our representations of reality is a puzzling one, because it looks like making the demand itself already presupposes what is demanded to be proved. The situation is a bit like those challenges one used to hear in the 1960s, when students would ask for a proof of rationality, "What is your argument for rationality?" But any demand for an "argument" or "proof" already presupposes standards of rationality, the applicability of which is constitutive of something's being an argument or proof. You cannot in the same breath appeal to argument and proof and deny rationality.

A similar point applies, but even more radically, to metaphysical realism. The person who denies metaphysical realism presupposes the existence of a public language, a language in which he or she communicates with other people. But what are the conditions of possibility of communication in a public language? What do I have to assume when I ask a question or make a claim that is supposed to be understood by others? At least this much: If we are using words to talk about something, in a way that we expect to be understood by others, then there must be at least the possibility of something those words can be used to talk about. Consider any claim, from particular statements such as "my dog has fleas," to theoretical claims such as "water is made of hydrogen and oxygen," to grand theories such as evolution or relativity, and you will see that they presuppose for their intelligibility that we are taking metaphysical realism for granted.

I am not claiming that one can prove metaphysical realism to be true from some standpoint that exists apart from our human linguistic practices. What I am arguing, rather, is that those practices themselves presuppose metaphysical realism. So one cannot within those practices intelligibly deny metaphysical realism, because the meaningfulness of our public utterances already presupposes an independently existing reality to which expressions in those utterances can refer. Metaphysical realism is thus not a thesis or a theory; it is rather the condition of having theses or theories or even of denying theses or theories. This is not an epistemic point about how we come to know truth as opposed to falsehood, rather it is a point about the conditions of possibility of communicating intelligibly. Falsehood stands as much in need of the real world as does truth.

4.

I said earlier that we lack a coherent theory of undergraduate education. Is such a theory in *The Voice of Liberal Learning,* by the English philosopher Michael Oakeshott? In his book we are in an altogether different intellectual atmosphere from the debate about the "canon." The book is a collection of elegantly written essays, usually lectures delivered for a particular occasion or other. Both the elegance of the prose and the occasional nature of the articles sometimes get in the way of the presentation of a coherent, overall philosophy of education. Also Oakeshott uses certain words in special ways. He apparently thinks it is important that he does not say much about "education," "tradition," or "subjects," but talks instead of "learning," "inheritance," "voices," and "conversation." However, it is possible to extract from these essays something of Oakeshott's conception of the relationships between human beings and culture, and the consequences these have for what he likes to call "learning." Oakeshott is usually characterized as a "conservative," but if that is true it is more in the sense in which Hume and Burke are conservatives, rather than in the sense of contemporary American or British politics.

Human beings, Oakeshott argues, are what they understand themselves to be; and the world that human beings inhabit is not a world of things, but of meanings. The understandings of these meanings requires an understanding of that understanding itself. It is a consequence of the relation between human beings and understanding that their inherited culture is not an addition to human beings, but is essentially what makes human beings human. "A man is his culture," and "What he is, he has had to learn to become."

A culture for Oakeshott is not a set of beliefs or perceptions or attitudes—and certainly not a body of knowledge or a "canon"—but a variety of distinct "languages" of understanding, including self-understanding. It is important for Oakeshott that culture does not consist in a set of "Great Books," but rather, as one learns and reads, in conversations that one continues to have with one's inheritance. In a "culture" there are a number of different "voices," and in "learning" one acquires access to these voices. There is a language of politics, of economics, of art, literature, philosophy; and learning consists in acquiring the ability to join these conversations. Liberal learning, especially at the university level, is therefore an introduction to this conversation, or rather to these series of conversations.

In learning, the teacher initiates the pupil into the inheritance of human achievements, but this inheritance consists of a variety of abilities. Each of these abilities combines "information" and "judgment." There are thus two components to knowledge, information and judgment, but judgment does not consist in a set of statements. It cannot be summarized in a set of explicit propositions, and it can only be acquired in conjunction with "information." Information can be "instructed," but judgment can only be imparted.

> "Judgement," then, is that which, when united with information, generates knowledge or 'ability' to do, to make, or to understand and explain. It is being able to think—not to think in no manner in particular, but to think with an appreciation of the considerations which belong to different modes of thought.

It is at this point that Oakeshott departs dramatically from the debate about the canon that we considered earlier. In that debate, both sides tend to think of education as a matter of acquiring a certain body of knowledge, together with the appropriate attitudes. This is emphatically not Oakeshott's view. He thinks that what he calls "judgment" is more a kind of intellectual know-how than it is a set of beliefs or attitudes.

Universities should not be thought of as "artifacts" with a "purpose," but rather as a "manner" of human activity. The university is a place in which the various conversations go on, and it imparts the manners of the conversations. Such places of education have three essential characteristics: they are serious; they are places of study; and they are detached, apart from the rest of the society. It follows, according to Oakeshott, that concern with contemporary political and social issues is the very opposite of education.

Does all this amount to a coherent vision of education? The best way to approach this question is to see if we can extract from Oakeshott's overall vision a description of what he would regard as a well-educated person. The abstractness of Oakeshott's account leads to a certain vagueness in the conception of how we might carry it out in an actual program in a real university; however, we can at least discern the outlines of Oakeshott's person of learning. He or she is likely to be a person profoundly respectful of the "intellectual inheritance." He or she will have good intellectual "manners," and will have what Oakeshott calls "judgment." Such a person will also have a great deal of information, most of it about the past of human culture and achievements. In short, Oakeshott's educated person looks a lot like the ideal of a First Class Honours B.A. in Classics or History from my undergraduate days in the fifties at Oxford. It is an attractive picture, but there are certain real weaknesses in it. First, Oakeshott does not have much to say about the critical purpose of education. His educated person does not look as if he would produce any intellectual revolutions, or even upset very many intellectual apple carts. What Oakeshott implies is not exactly conformity, but a kind of acceptance of the rules of the various discourses.

But perhaps the biggest single weakness of his conception of education is in the peripheral status it assigns to the natural sciences. The natural sciences do not fit his model, because, for the most part, the world of the natural sciences is not a world of meanings. It is a world of things; it is a world of entities, such as molecules or quarks, and forces, such as gravitational attraction or electromagnetic radiation. All of which are meaningless by Oakeshott's criterion. But, like it or not, the natural sciences are perhaps our greatest single intellectual achievement as human beings, and any education that neglects this fact is to that extent defective.

Because Oakeshott fails to allow for the ontology of the natural sciences as part of the world of our experience, he also cannot account for one of the great tensions in contemporary intellectual life, namely that between the modes of explanation that we have come to accept in the natural sciences, and the modes of explanation that are appropriate to mentalistic phenomena, such as those found in history, sociology, economics, and large parts of psychology. He correctly sees that it is bogus of the so-called "social sciences" to try to ape the explanatory apparatus of the natural sciences, but he fails to appreciate the power or even the nature of the model they are trying to ape.

The strength of his account is in perceiving that one of the great contributions of education lies not in what is explicitly said, but in the kind of sensibility that is imparted. What is said, by way of conveying information, is no more important than what is left unsaid. But the unsaid, as Oakeshott points out, can be imparted only by way of actually saying something.

Oakeshott overstates his pessimism about the possibilities of educating the new sorts of people who are entering the universities who would not have been admitted a century ago. In a chilling passage originally written in 1950, he says,

> In the past a rising class was aware of something valuable and enjoyed by others which it wished to share; but this is not so today. The leaders of the rising class are consumed with a contempt for everything which does not spring from their own desires, they are convinced in advance that they have nothing to learn and everything to teach, and consequently their aim is loot—to appropriate to themselves the organization, the shell of the institution, and convert it to their own purposes. The problem of the universities today is how to avoid destruction at the hands of men who have no use for their characteristic virtues, men who are convinced only that "knowledge is power."

Kimball or Bloom might have written something very like this passage today. The characterization was true of some members of the new class of students who were entering the British universities after 1945, but it was not true of most of them. In the United States of 1990, it accurately characterizes a small number of academics who are attacking the traditional standards of rationality, intelligence, truth, and excellence in order to advance a political ideology. But for the most part, the new groups of people coming into the universities, many of them from poor families, are sadly unformed. It is not their aim to "loot"; they are often too bewildered to have well-formed aspirations. On Oakeshott's own account of culture, they are waiting for people like himself to impart to them enough "learning" so that they can form aspirations.

Our lack of a satisfactory theory of what a general liberal education for undergraduates should consist of would not be reprehensible if in fact our practice was so good that no theory was required. To do a good job of teaching, you do not necessarily need a theory. However, I think we are not doing a good job in general education. Faced with the well-known cafeteria of courses, and obliged to fill very few requirements, a student is more likely to be well educated as the result of chance, or of his or her determination, than as a consequence of planning by the university authorities. Why do we lack the confidence to require that each undergraduate acquire the rudiments of a good general education? After all, we were not always so lacking in self-confidence. When my grandfather graduated from Oberlin after the Civil War, he set out on his horse for what was then Indian territory, carrying Milton's *Paradise Lost* and the Bible in his saddle-bags. After the Second World War, when I began my education, it was no longer a matter of educating "Christian gentlemen," but we were quite confident of our theory of a liberal education. One was supposed to acquire a solid grounding in the humanities, the social sciences, and the natural sciences, usually in the first two years; and this grounding in turn provided a base for the selection of a "major." Furthermore, one was expected to be fairly proficient in English and in a foreign language.

In our current educational practice, we often do well at educating graduate students in Ph.D. programs. In fact, our better Ph.D. programs are the envy of the world and many students come from the best European and British universities to do graduate work in America. Professors feel that they know what they are doing when they prepare someone for a doctorate in history, philosophy, or physics.

It is characteristic of American education that each stage is primarily designed to prepare the student for the next stage, so the best high schools prepare the student for graduate school. Since the professors think they know what they are doing in graduate education, it is not surprising that they also feel confident at designing undergraduate majors. The programs are designed to prepare the student for graduate work. In general education the failure of nerve derives from the fact that we do not know what we are preparing the student for.

Nonetheless, our lack of a well-defined objective is not a good enough reason to avoid stating some features of a general theory of education. In fact, it does not seem to me very difficult to describe some of the necessary conditions for being a well-educated person.

First, the student should have enough knowledge of his or her cultural tradition to know how it got to be the way it is. This involves both political and social history, on the one hand, as well as the mastery of some of the great philosophical and literary texts of the culture on the other. It involves reading not only texts that are of great value, like those of Plato, but many less valuable that have been influential, such as the works of Marx. For the United States, the dominant tradition is, and for the foreseeable future, will remain the European tradition. The United States is, after all, a product of the European Enlightenment. However, you do not understand your own tradition if you do not see it in relation to others. Works from other cultural traditions need to be studied as well.

If these two streams, both the political-social and the philosophical-literary, are well organized and well taught, the claims of the various minorities should have their place. Intelligently taught social and political histories of Europe and the United States, for example, should recognize the history of all of the major components of European and American society, including those that have been treated unjustly. It is important, however, to get rid of the ridiculous notion that there is something embarrassing or lamentable about the fact that most of the prominent political and intellectual leaders of our culture over the past two thousand years or so have been white males. This is just a historical fact whose causes should be explored and understood. To deny it or attempt to suppress the works of such thinkers is not simply racism, it is unintelligent.

Second, you need to know enough of the natural sciences so that you are not a stranger in the world. This means, at a minimum, that you need to know enough about physics and chemistry to understand how the physical world is constructed. This would also include at least a smattering of knowledge of the general and special theories of relativity, and an understanding of why quantum mechanics is so philosophically challenging. Furthermore, at a minimum, you must have enough biology to understand the Darwinian revolution, and to understand recent developments in genetics and microbiology.

Third, you need to know enough about how society works so that you understand what a trade cycle is, or how interest rates will affect the value of the currency, for example. In short, you need to have some knowledge of the subject matter that used to be called political economy.

Fourth, you need to know at least one foreign language well enough so that you can read the best literature that language has produced in the original, and so you carry on a reasonable conversation and have dreams in that language. There are several reasons why this is crucial, but the most important is perhaps this: You can never understand one language until you understand at least two.

Fifth, you need to know enough philosophy so that the methods of logical analysis are available to you to be used as a tool. One of the most depressing things about educated people today is that so few of them, even among professional intellectuals, are able to follow the steps of a simple logical argument.

Finally, and perhaps most importantly, you need to acquire the skills of writing and speaking that make for candor, rigor, and clarity. You cannot think clearly if you cannot speak and write clearly.

Just acquiring this amount of "education" will not, by itself, make you an educated person, even less will it give you what Oakeshott calls "judgment." But if the manner of instruction is adequate, the student should be able to acquire this much knowledge in a way that combines intellectual openness, critical scrutiny, and logical clarity. If so, learning will not stop when the student leaves the university. None of the books I have been reading about higher education makes even these elementary points.

PUBLIC IMAGE LIMITED: POLITICAL CORRECTNESS AND THE MEDIA'S BIG LIE

Michael Berubé

Michael Berubé is an assistant professor at the University of Illinois at Urbana-Champagne, where he holds appointments in the Department of English and the Unit for Criticism and Interpretive Theory. He published this article in *The Village Voice*, June 18, 1991.

Readers who've followed the tortuous course of political correctness (P.C.) in the national press now know that there is no American intellectual community so benighted and blinkered as that of young faculty members in the humanities. If deconstruction is nihilism, if multiculturalism is barbarism, and if feminism is the annihilation of all we hold dear, well, then, you can just imagine what happens when today's newly tenured and untenured professors put all these things in their big iron cauldrons, together with liberal doses of Foucault Helper. Let's just say that if we young whelps aren't quite the Great Satan, we're what one pundit calls "the new fundamentalists"—or worse yet, in Dinesh D'Souza's catchy phrase, "Visigoths in Tweed." But strange to say, though we're always mocked, derided, and reviled, we untenured radical Gothic fundamentalists are never quoted directly in any of the articles we "appear" in. It is as if, as Marx said (in another context, I think), the fundamentalist Visigoths cannot represent themselves; they must be represented.

Well, *ich bin ein* young faculty member. And what's more, I *know* a lot of young faculty members. We've been talking a great deal lately, trying to figure out what we think about this P.C. flap. If you've been hearing about us, though, you already know what we talk about: We "reduce" knowledge to power, we read "narrowly" for the ideological ramifications of literary texts. Yes, we plot no less than the destruction of the West. Just the other day a friend and I came up with the most pernicious academic scheme to date for toppling the West: He will kneel behind the West on all fours. I will push it backwards over him.

On January 7 of this year, a *Chicago Tribune* editorial convicted the professoriate of "crime against humanity." The *Tribune*'s editoralist had determined that our most heinous crime was our occasional scholarly engagement with the detritus of American mass culture (which presumably includes the *Chicago Tribune*), but you might easily have gotten the impression, if you scanned the editorial page quickly, that young American literary critics were occupying and despoiling Kuwait City.

The *Tribune*'s sole source for its editorial was the *Chicago Tribune*, whose Ron Grossman had just published an article on the annual meeting of the Modern Language Association. Grossman's theme was fatuous yet direct: The youngsters are abandoning the very idea of literary and scholarly "standards," devoting all their teaching and research to the production of revolutionary propaganda.

If I hear this nonsense one more time I'm going to deliberately step into the street and methodically knock people's hats off. After six years of graduate study, earning around $5,000 a year for teaching the history of English literature at a major university, reading as much as possible while working summers and part-time jobs, raising a child, paying tuition, and having the IRS declare my $5,000 per annum to be taxable income under the "tax reform" of 1986, I've finally gotten a real job at a real research university (and a real opportunity to begin paying off those real loans). No sooner have I begun to compose a syllabus or two than I am accused, along with every one of my colleagues within fifteen years of my age on either side, of "politicizing" literary study—by failing to treat literature as literature. Some of my friends and colleagues are incredulous that we are now rebuked for violating the autonomy of literature, when a few years ago we were rebuked for saying that literature is autonomous and self-referential; but as I've explained to my P.C. cadres, there are just some decades when you can't do anything right.

At first I thought this might not be a bad development: Since academic literary critics are normally considered to be roughly as necessary to contemporary American life as catapults and moats, undoubtedly there's a sense in which one is obligated to "politicize" a discipline with such vast potential for saying intelligent things to people who are curious about what they've read and haven't read, curious even to know why anyone should read anything, for what possible purposes, in what varieties of ways. But that's not what people think we do. Thanks to our limited public image, most folks now believe we brainwash our students by feeding them sixties radicalism alongside what one *New Republic* commentator calls "warmed-over Nietzscheanism," thus turning them into *agents of political correctness*. It's simple, really: Whenever my students hear me snap my fingers and quote Marx's eleventh thesis on Feuerbach, they spontaneously begin to decry sexism, racism, ageism, monologism, lookism, bagism, dragism, and journalism.

However, the last few years have been especially frustrating for your average beleaguered academic literary critic, because over the past decade, practically every intermediate, generalist critical forum in the United States has decided, slowly but surely, not to bother with the laborious process of *reading*, let alone discussing, recent literary criticism and theory. The reasons for this development vary from journal to journal; *The New York Times Book Review* seems solely interested in reviewing critical biographies of major literary figures, apparently having decided that its readers are more interested in whether Hemingway really slept with Mata Hari than if new historicism or "reception theory" constitutes a challenge to the dominant American models of literary theory and literary history. And *The New York Review of Books*, one gathers, will never forgive literary critics for using bizarre, jargon-laden neologisms like "discourse" and "sign," any more than the journal will forgive the women's movement for producing feminist scholarship the *Review* has neither the desire nor the competence to review. In this the *NYRB* resembles the *NYTBR*, for they share a profound intolerance for anything more "theoretical" than Samuel Johnson's *Lives of the Poets*—and, of course, lives of poets. The country still has some generalist criticism that's driving with its headlights on, but it's getting harder to find.

The result so far is that recent literary theory is so rarely accorded the privilege of representing itself in nonacademic forums that journalists, disgruntled professors, embittered ex-graduate students, and their families and friends now feel entitled to say anything at all about the academy without fear of contradiction by general readers. The field is wide open, and there's no penalty for charlatanism (quite the contrary), since few general readers are informed enough to spot even the grossest forms of misrepresentation and fraud. In fact, many journalist/critics, from Jonathan Yardley to Roger Kimball, profess outright disdain for a discipline in which you actually have to do research before you begin writing; in early 1988, for example, one of Yardley's columns attacking the "young fascists" of the academy derived every piece of its information from Joseph Berger's slight *New York Times* article of the previous week (thus confirming the suspicion that *The Washington Post* takes its cultural news from back issues of the *Times*).

However, most people don't have time to keep track of the myriad attacks on the academy, so let me fill you in on what's happened over the last ten years. Back in the late seventies and early eighties, people first got wind of critics like Harold Bloom, who'd been going around saying that poems could only be "about" other poems, and that authors are irrelevant to textual meaning. Well-pedigreed as this position is in the postwar American academy (versions of it date to the 1940s), it was for some reason taken to signal the death of Western culture. That relentless and perversely brilliant logician, the French poststructuralist philosopher Jacques Derrida, was called a traitor to Western reason, and suddenly the air was filled with denunciations of the "new New Criticism" at Yale: people went around saying that language *does* mean something, that literature *is* about "life," and that authors *do* matter. Many critics kicked stones for days in valiant efforts to reassert the existence of reality.

At about the same time, it became conventional wisdom among Norman Podhoretz et al. that American universities, especially Ivy League universities, were the most intolerant of American institutions, dominated by leftists left over from Stalin's purges. Back then, no one to the left of Genghis Khan believed this canard, especially since American universities seemed to be churning out little lawyers and investment bankers at an amazing clip, and American intellectuals like Irving Kristol were throwing around large sums of money to any campus organization that wanted to start a conservative campus magazine. For *Commentary* and the *National Review,* however, it was enough that American students were protesting and even heckling speakers like Jeane Kirkpartrick and Norman Podhoretz; this alone was prima facie evidence of intolerable intolerance.

Ten years and more, and these twin obsessions with deconstruction and intolerance have returned to the national press, this time as farce. They have not returned without friends. In 1987 we first met Allan Bloom, whose *The Closing of the American Mind* set the tone and pitch for the second wave of assaults, 1987–89. According to Bloom, today's American teachers and students are shallow "relativists," committed blandly to the principle that everyone is entitled to his or her or its opinion.

Bloom could not be more critical to the current debate, if only because, in John Searle's words, he has proven that "it is possible to write an alarmist book about the state of higher education with a long-winded title and make a great deal of money." However, Bloom himself has also proven to be something of an embarrassment, even to the Right. For every argument he's bestowed upon his sons, he's left them another that's nothing but a liability. For instance, thanks to Bloom, everyone now knows that you can't critique the West in good conscience, because the East is worse. As Bloom puts it, "only in the Western nations, i.e., those influenced by Greek philosophy, is there some willingness to doubt the identification of the good with one's own way."

This is almost a Cretan liar's paradox, from which it follows that the West is superior to other cultures because the West knows how to doubt its superiority to other cultures. Only the true Messiah denies his divinity. Very well. But a mere three pages prior to the one on which he intones that the West is the best, Bloom claims, rather less persuasively, that the "sexual adventurer" Margaret Mead, along with "all such teachers of openness," "either had no interest in or were actively hostile to the Declaration of Independence and the Constitution." I don't know what this means, and neither do you. Was it that Margaret Mead considered the United States to be a British colony?

Bloom's argument is full of unfathomable lapses like this, whether they take the form of rantings about rock and roll or of evocations of the days when truly erotic students ran "from prostitutes to Plato, and back." Besides, the American public doesn't thrill to the proposition that it has failed once again to read the *Symposium*, the *Republic*, *Ion*, and the *Phaedrus*, for never before in our history has the American public been so well-informed about the fact that it knows less than eight-year-olds in Sweden. But should you tell the American public that its children are being forcibly indoctrinated by communist fascist feminist deconstructionist multiculturalists, *then*, you've got a real best seller on your hands—and an argument even nonspecialists can follow.

In a way, Bloom's odd book was the jab that allowed the Right to set up the haymaker it's delivering now. Here's the strategy in a nutshell: First, accuse the academics of relativism. When the academics reply that they don't actually consider all opinions equally valid, that they take strong exception to student-goons, who demolish shanties, hold mock slave auctions, and scrawl swastikas on university structures, then follow the accusation of relativism with the accusation of political correctness.

Naturally, the next crucial text here is Roger Kimball's *Tenured Radicals*. Thanks to its handy soundbite title and its unswerving commitment to simplicity, Kimball's book has a bright future and an already illustrious past; until recently, Kimball was perhaps the most influential journalist working the academic beat and setting the terms for its public discussion. Kimball is a witty and capable writer, and Allan Bloom (apparently thinking that Kimball is working on a major motion picture) heads Kimball's front cover with the line, "All persons serious about education should see it." With uncanny symmetry, Bloom and Kimball now occupy the front covers of each other's books, but Kimball's salute to Bloom is more rigorous: "An unparalleled reflection on today's intellectual climate. . . . That rarest of documents, a genuinely profound book."

In Kimball's case, the book in question is a pastiche of *New Criterion* essays in which the author shows beyond all doubt that a bunch of academic conference papers and learned-society pamphlets are poppycock, blather, and rebarbative nonsense (I am not doing justice to Kimball's vast array of dismissive Edwardian interjections). But what makes Kimball's book so invaluable a resource is its comprehensiveness. If you've got a bone you'd like to pick with contemporary academic literary criticism, chances are Kimball's already picked that bone for you; thus, bonepickers of all competencies can today launch their accusations simply by citing *Tenured Radicals*.

For example: Some commentators, like William Bennett, have limited themselves to the complaint that academic critics have driven students away from careers in the humanities, because academic critics are trendy and incomprehensible. Others have charged that academic critics are corrupting and seducing an ever-growing number of students in the humanities, because academic critics are trendy and incomprehensible, and students find these qualities appealing. But Kimball, generously, accuses us of doing both: According to him, we drive students away *and* we lure them in. He opens his attack on the American Council of Learned Societies with the charge that "American education has suffered a wholesale flight from the humanities;" but he opens his book somewhat differently:

> *Second- and third-tier schools are rushing to embrace all manner of fashionable intellectual ideologies as so many formulas for gaining prestige, publicity, and "name" professors (and hoping thereby to attract more students and other sources of income).*

In other words, it's not that students have fled the humanities in search of more lucrative vocations; it's that greedy colleges are capitulating to intellectual fashion to attract students' tuition dollars. I don't see how it can be that we have such enormous drawing potential for all those students seeking to flee the humanities, but I trust this will be explained soon.

Page after page, Kimball's technique is too powerful and sweeping to be called "criticism"; devouring and dissolving its own self-contradictions as it fires round after round of verbal buckshot, Kimball's work does not argue so much as spray its points. And the moral of these excursions into the academy, as Kimball suggested in a January 1991 *New Criterion* postscript to his book, is that (to borrow a phrase from Colin Powell) we should cut off academic debate, and then kill it. For one thing, academic debate is confusing, and that's bad, because "it is in the nature of generalizations about life's difficult decisions to be perfectly obvious." Obvious then it is in our nature to be, even if we have to raze the syntax. And for another thing, academic debate is *dangerous,* like malaria or dengue fever:

> A *swamp yawns before us, ready to devour every-thing. The best response to all this—and finally the only serious and effective response—is not to enter these murky waters in the first place. As Nietzsche observed, we do not refute a disease. We resist it.*

This amazing passage follows Kimball's synopsis of questions about the contents of liberal-arts curricula; but it sums up his attitude toward modern academia quite well. Rarely has willful ignorance received so noble a defense, though I can't contemplate its intended audience without a shudder. Are there really readers out there who *fear* paging through their spring catalogues from the university presses? Do Kimball's readers have to be reminded to "just say no" if tempted by a book-length analysis of how our canonical texts have been read, misread, historically transmitted, celebrated, dismissed, and institutionalized?

It's hard to say, since the success of Kimball's thesis depends on the putative ignorance of its audience. Kimball claims that the academy is now run by the sixties radicals who are our most fashionable theorists; only a well-informed general reader would realize that most of Kimball's targets weren't student radicals in the 1960s. Indeed, the one critic Kimball treats in detail is Stanley Fish, who grew up in the fifties, and had nothing to do with the leftist political movements of the sixties, unless his 1967 book on *Paradise Lost* is really a cover for SDS propaganda.

Likewise, only a particularly attentive English major (or a sharp reader like Louis Menand, whose review of Kimball appeared in *The New Republic* of July 9–16, 1990) will know that Kimball's major premise is little short of mendacious. He castigates the academy for having abandoned the traditional mission of the humanities, yet he has overwhelming difficulty trying to say what this traditional mission was; and *New Criterion* readers, with their fervent libidinal attachment to the word "traditional," have not bothered to ask. Kimball's argument invoking "tradition" rests wholly on Matthew Arnold, whom Kimball construes as the father we have repudiated: Arnold, writes Kimball, "had looked to the preservation and transmission of the best that had been thought and written as a means of rescuing culture from anarchy in a democratic society." But although many culturally literate people know Arnold's *Culture and Anarchy* by title, very few will recall that Arnold had sought in 1869 to rescue culture from the anarchy *of* democratic society. Kimball's defense of "tradition" is thus cracked in its very foundation. It is no wonder he warns his fans away from the murk and disease of academic criticism; he may as well warn them away from the original texts by the original artists, too, since they are so capable of undermining his reliance on them.

And yet Kimball and Bloom, as our luck would have it, are the most intelligent of our attackers; from here it's all downhill, and in the pages of *New York* and *Newsweek,* one does well just to find the echoes of Kimball and Bloom that substitute for sustained argument. Frankly, this aspect of the debate startles me. Traditionalist that I am, I had long assumed that argumentation and investigative journalism were alike in their dependence on the adduction of evidence; then I came across John Taylor's piece in *New York*, "Are You Politically Correct?" (It has since then been reprinted in *Reader's Digest*.) In lieu of evidence for the proposition that academia's contemporary cultural left controls all campus thought and speech, Taylor's article deploys a number of subtle visual effects—typeface long associated with the Third Reich, pictures of book-burnings and the Parade of Dunces in Communist China's Cultural

Revolution. Taylor relies on Kimball not only for his thesis but for a few turns of phrase as well; the idea to link the academy to the religious Right, however, seems to be Taylor's.

> *In the past few years, a new sort of fundamentalism has arisen precisely among those people who were the most appalled by Christian fundamentalism. And it is just as demagogic and fanatical. The new fundamentalists are an eclectic group; they include multiculturalists, feminists, radical homosexuals, Marxists, New Historicists. What unites them—as firmly as the Christian fundamentalists are united in the belief that the Bible is the revealed word of God—is their conviction that Western culture and American society are thoroughly and hopelessly racist, sexist, oppressive.*

I want to remark on two striking phenomena mired in the innuendo and confusion of this Taylorized Kimballiana. First, Taylor implies here that only fanatical radical homosexual etceteras could possibly believe in the existence of racism and sexism in the United States. Second, Taylor bears out his claim, over the next five paragraphs, not by citing the work of Michel Foucault, or Toril Moi, or Paul Lauter, or Eve Sedgwick, or Henry Louis Gates—nor by citing *any* currently influential academic critic and theorist in the West—but by quoting a New York Board of Education task force, a Tulane draft report on race and gender, and a college administrator from the University of Pennsylvania. Whatever else they may be, these are not the texts we academic critics normally rely upon in writing scholarly articles, book reviews, tenure evaluations, or course descriptions; and one would have to be either unscrupulous or foolish to try to pass them off as examples of the "new conformity" of academic discourse.

In short, "Are You Politically Correct?," like *Tenured Radicals,* could not work as invective (far less as journalism) if it did not presume a high degree of ignorance among its readers. Nowhere is this principle clearer than in Taylor's discussion of feminism, which charges feminists with destroying the traditional family, hating men, and construing all women as victims. It's strange that Taylor should want to call feminism a "new fundamentalism," since the belief that feminism is bad for the family is prevalent chiefly among the religious Right. But aside from quoting Camille Paglia, who's become an instant celebrity in the past year for her absurdly dated attacks on feminisms that were prevalent around twenty years ago, *New York* doesn't seem interested in academic critics at all. Taylor's article instead provides us with a rogue's gallery of intolerant students, muddle-headed administrators, misguided activists, and the occasional "extremist" (i.e., "Afrocentrist"), but it really winds up with very little to say about the academic teachers and critics it purports to attack.

On the contrary, much of the piece is devoted to *defending* "traditional" professors from their students' verbal assaults. This emphasis should pose a problem for Taylor, but, curiously, it doesn't. Let me explain. He quotes with approval a passage from *Tenured Radicals* in which Kimball writes, "If the undergraduate population has moved quietly to the right in recent years, the men and women who are paid to introduce students to the great works and ideas of our civilization have by and large remained true to the emancipationist ideology of the sixties."

Of course, there's something disingenuous about Kimball's "if" clause, since he wrote it in the midst of a decade during which numerous American undergraduates moved to the right *noisily,* by flying Confederate flags and disrupting the classes of black professors, shouting slurs and spitting on minority students, quoting Hitler on Yom Kippur, and beating gays with baseball bats; but Taylor quotes the sentence all the same, even though he's writing an article whose most prominent villains turn out to be intolerant liberal students. The trouble, then, is this: Whereas Kimball's sweeping epic casts a right-wing student body against a passé and privileged "radical left" professoriate, Taylor's one-act drama, in which P.C. is everywhere, just can't make up its mind whether the P.C. students or their P.C. professors are the greater threat to contemporary learning.

Yet debate about P.C. is characterized by confusion; often, it's a specific confusion, with a specific source—*Newsweek.* Deciding to cover *P.C.* as the "new McCarthyism" in its December 24 issue on academic "thought police," *Newsweek* wisely chose to remain silent about *real* McCarthyism, during which American faculty—especially untenured faculty—who refused on Constitutional grounds to cooperate with investigating committees were fired, blacklisted, and jailed (for a chilling account of McCarthyism in American academia, see Ellen Schrecker's *No Ivory Tower*). Hence "McCarthyite," like "Orwellian," is now so fluid a term that it can be invoked by anyone about anything, and *Newsweek* has done its part to help this process along.

Linking literary theory and academic revision of core curricula to universities' administrative restrictions on virulent forms of "hate speech," *Newsweek* managed to suggest that *all* these recent developments are part of a radical "agenda." Our plan, it seems, is to displace Western culture by means of gay studies and minority literatures, so that we can punish offenders against P.C. The article's debt to Kimball should be obvious:

> *There is an experiment of sorts taking place in American colleges . . . directed at changing the consciousness of this entire generation of university students. The goal is to eliminate prejudice, not just of the petty sort that shows up on sophomore dorm walls, but the grand prejudice that has ruled American universities since their founding: that the intellectual tradition of Western Europe occupies the central place in the history of civilization. In this context it would not be enough for a student to refrain from insulting homosexuals or other minorities. He or she would be expected to "affirm" their presence on campus and to study their literature and culture alongside that of Plato, Shakespeare, and Locke. This agenda is broadly shared by most organizations of minority students, feminists, and gays. It is also the program of a generation of campus radicals who grew up in the sixties and are now achieving positions of academic influence.*

Just as the savants of earlier generations were able to find evidence of the global Jewish conspiracy both in the emergence of Jewish writers, lawyers, and entertainers *and* in the vicissitudes of international finance, so too can today's keener minds find in university classrooms as on university faculty as on university syllabi the growing presence of *feminists, gays, and minorities.* If you didn't think there was a common thread to literary theory, canon revision, and complaints about "lookism," *Newsweek* compels you to think again.

By the end of only the second paragraph, then, *Newsweek* had already framed the question in *The New Criterion*'s terms, as a choice between the West and all that opposes the West. As Kimball puts it, "The choice facing us today is not between a 'repressive' Western culture and

a multicultural paradise, but between culture and barbarism." The Right enjoys discussions that operate around
these terms, for they keep the arguments simple: Are you
for the West, or against it? And though many of us who
actually work in universities know very well that our deans,
provosts, and presidents are neither Marxists nor deconstructionists, *Newsweek* proves unable even to distinguish
between literary theory and campus administration: for as
Newsweek would have it, "political correctness" is politically
"Marxist in origin" and intellectually "informed by deconstructionism." To ask whether this claim is even remotely
true is to miss the point, for what *Newsweek*'s really saying
is that P.C. is bad stuff plus more bad stuff: In Orwell's
famous phrase, it's *doubleplusungood*.

The most alarming post-*Newsweek* phenomenon, however, must surely be *The Atlantic*'s publication of Dinesh
D'Souza's 12,000-word "Illiberal Education," a miniature
version of his recent book-length treatise of the same name.
D'Souza arrived in this country from India in 1978, and he
has spent the past thirteen years steadily moving up the
national conservative food chain. He has matured since his
early years in journalism, which he spent founding and
editing the infamous *Dartmouth Review*. What D'Souza
has, and John Taylor lacks, is the post-Reagan conservative's talent for sounding sensible: "It is not always possible
in such disputes," writes D'Souza, "for a reasonable person, in good conscience, to take any side; there is a good
deal of excess all around. The middle ground seems to
have disappeared on campus, and whether it can be restored is an open question."

Yes, well. It will not be restored by D'Souza, who ex-
pands the *Newsweek* program of reducing all current intellectual disputes to the question of whether or not the West
is a Good Thing. The debate, writes D'Souza, "has so far

been passionately superficial, posing false dichotomies . . . and missing the underlying principles that are shaping the dramatic changes in universities." The true dichotomies, as the far Right has always known, and as D'Souza will proceed to argue, are the dichotomies between the West and the Others, objectivity and special interests, good and evil.

D'Souza's work is uneven, ranging from provocative critiques of "affirmative action" campus politics, to passages of nothing less than moral and intellectual dishonesty. On the first page of "Illiberal Education" we are informed that:

> *There is little argument about the desirability of teaching the greatest works written by members of other cultures, by women, and by minority-group members. Many academic activists go beyond this to insist that texts be selected primarily or exclusively according to the author's race, gender, or sexual preference, and that the Western tradition be exposed in the classroom as hopelessly bigoted and oppressive in every way.*

If "many academic activists" insist such a thing, one would think that a writer as resourceful as D'Souza would be able to find one; but the quote that follows this passage comes not from any such "activist," but from Harvard sociologist David Riesman, who attacks "liberal closed-mindedness"; Riesman thus supports an argument for which no evidence has been adduced. Yet the first sentence of D'Souza's passage is worse still, for it is an outright falsehood: There have been—and there still are—tremendous arguments about revising reading lists even when such lists include the greatest works by women and non-whites. In fact, D'Souza himself goes on, only one paragraph later, to misrepresent once again Stanford's revision of its core course in "Western culture." Claiming that Stanford replaced this core "with a program called Cultures, Ideas, and Values, which stressed works on race and gender issues by Third World authors, minority-group members, and women," D'Souza neglects to mention that this notorious revision substantially affected only *one* of Stanford's eight core "tracks." D'Souza's own article, in other words, could afford us no better example of the Right's intolerance for the most minor kinds of tinkerings with core reading lists, and we're only on the second page of the piece.

In the end, D'Souza's attack on the academy, like Kimball's, relies on ignorance—his own, and ours. Deconstructionism, he writes toward the end of the essay, "appears uniformly hostile to all texts," but, as it turns out,

> *In fact deconstructionists treat some works with uncharacteristic respect, leaving their authority unchallenged. Marx, for instance, never seems to be deconstructed, nor does Foucault, or Lacan, or Derrida, or Barthes. Malcolm X and Martin Luther King, Jr., seem to enjoy immunity. There may be an entire gender exception for women. . . . Yet if, as we often read, Zora Neale Hurston is just as good as Milton, why not subject her to the same critical undoing?*

If someone were to publish an essay which claimed that *Paradise Lost* never really talks about theology, or that psychoanalysis fails to make use of the works of major Greek dramatists, certainly we would recognize such a person as a cultural illiterate. But because no one at *The Atlantic,* including even the journal's fact-checkers, is aware of the past twenty-five years' profusion of deconstruction work on Marx, or the extraordinary critical energy that's been expended on Foucault, Lacan, Derrida, and

Barthes by feminists, psychoanalytic critics, and deconstructionists (Jane Gallop and Teresa de Lauretis alone have
done much, throughout the eighties, to unseat the Four
French Horsemen), D'Souza is allowed to get away with
this series of inanities. Indeed, so inane is this passage that
by the time we've gotten to the Hurston sentence, we may
have forgotten that D'Souza began his minithesis with the
fuzzy idea that deconstruction is "hostile to all texts"—that
deconstructing a piece of writing is disrespectful, and not
something one does in front of ladies (from which it follows, conversely, that refusing to deconstruct a text is the
surest sign of love). And as for Zora Neale Milton: A mere
perusal of Barbara Johnson's "deconstructive" criticism on
Hurston will suffice to demonstrate that, when it comes to
academic criticism and theory, D'Souza has no idea what
he's talking about.

That *The Atlantic* would have published D'Souza, and
at such length, is an important sign of the extent to which
public discussion of American academia is now conducted
by the most callow and opportunistic elements of the
Right; it's also, sad to say, an important sign of how low are
our minimum standards for serious public exchange on
the status of American criticism. D'Souza's critique of
racial polarization in American academia is garden-variety
conservatism, although his account of the hiring dilemmas
consequent on the dearth of black Ph.D.'s is compelling;
but his attempt to link these to the hidden race-and-gender
biases of literary theory could not be more capricious or
unfounded..

And yet D'Souza's ignorance pales before his capacity
for feigning moral hysteria. To read D'Souza in *The Atlantic*
is to read D'Souza when he's on his best behavior; to read
D'Souza in *Forbes,* by contrast, is to visit him when he's
more at home. Speaking of the academy's "Visigoths in
Tweed," D'Souza claims that "the propaganda of the new

barbarians" threatens to "do us in." Toward the close of the piece, D'Souza turns up the rhetoric a notch: "Resistance on campus to the academic revolution is outgunned," he writes, "and sorely needs outside reinforcements." To our relief, D'Souza proceeds merely to call upon *Forbes* readers to defund the humanities, but his long-range plans should be clear from his choice of metaphor: To combat multiculturalism, especially at state institutions, he will eventually have to call out the National Guard.

D'Souza's program for "resistance" is the most extreme example of Right thinking to date, and it's worth asking how he can maintain any credibility at all even among conservative academics. The answer is simply this: According to D'Souza, deconstruction and affirmative action are two facets of the same thing, for they both involve attacks on "standards." Because deconstruction and affirmative action are both anathema to conservative thinkers of all ages, D'Souza's phantasmic version of academia has so far received an extraordinary level of financial and moral support on the Right. To wealthy conservative alumni of elite universities, D'Souza's message is refreshingly simple: If you return to your alma mater and find more women or blacks than you think belong there, on the faculty or in the student body, you can be sure that deconstruction is to blame. Keep your eyes open and your checkbook closed.

Really, to read the current assortment of conservative thugs, hitmen, and incompetents, you'd never know that deconstruction and canon revision have had practically nothing to do with each other. Of the four old Yale boys (J. Hills Miller, Paul de Man, Harold Bloom, and Geoffrey Hartmann) who originally put American deconstruction on the map in the seventies, not a single one ventured away from texts by "major" white Western men. For example, ex-Yalie Hillis Miller has come under ferocious attack in recent months, because he is a deconstructionist and admits it. Yet here's Hillis Miller talking about the canon: "I believe in the established canon of English and American literature and in the validity of the concept of privileged texts. I think it is more important to read Spenser, Shakespeare, or Milton than to read Borges in translation, or even, to say the truth, to read Virginia Woolf." Is this man too radical for the Right? Can it be true, as *Newsweek* and D'Souza have told us, that "it is impossible in deconstructionist terms to say that one text is superior to another?"

Allow me to offer a small dose of reality here. Neither I nor any of my known colleagues, past or present, have ever operated on the principle that all books are "equal." However, I confess that we *have* done a number of things no less corrosive: we have suggested that literary texts have many potential uses, and that some texts are better for some purposes than others; we have pointed out that "literary quality" has never been the sole criterion for canonical works, since many of them, like *Everyman,* are canonical today largely because they are of great historical interest; we have gone so far as to remark that the boundary between the "literary" and the "nonliterary" text does not rest on stable or self-evident distinctions, and that the boundary has shifted considerably over the history of the past few centuries (since the days when the English novel was considered a subliterary genre). And we have even written and argued to our undying chagrin, that the texts we value now have not always been valued (the poetry of John Donne), or have not always been valued for the same reasons *we* value them (*The Canterbury Tales*), or have occluded from our view the kinds of texts that different historical and social milieux considered central, vital, and—oh yes—timeless (Ariosto's *Orlando Furioso,* Elizabeth Barrett Browning's *Aurora Leigh*).

"Canon revision," in American media from *Newsweek* on down to *The New Criterion,* is made to appear the wholesale demolition of all the West has achieved and stood for, and the substitution of P.C. for literary merit. According to one of the recent ad campaigns undertaken by a conservative activist organization humorously calling itself the National Association of Scholars, canon revision involves replacing "generally applicable intellectual and aesthetic standards" with "the principle of proportional representation of authors, classified ethnically, biologically, or geographically." Within the academy, where it is actually taking place, canon revision is a good deal less glamorous (and less revolutionary), for it involves the dissemination of the principle that the university is a cultural institution, like the museum, that is entitled to take an active role in the creation and maintenance of its exhibits. No canon revision proceeds solely on the "principle of proportional representation."

And as it so happens, very little canon revision is launched at anything so large and ponderous as Western Civilization. Instead, canon revision is today most likely to involve redesigning and reshuffling the English department's standard "period" courses, teaching Mary Wollstonecraft alongside Samuel Coleridge, Aphra Behm next to Daniel Defoe; Wilkie Collins with George Eliot, Zora Neale Hurston after Ernest Hemingway. The most "radical" departments in the country have dismantled "periodicity" itself as an organizational tool, though at last report, even these departments were offering courses in Western culture.

For all the talk about "the West," the debate over canons gets most poisonous when it's conducted about American literature—partially because the canon of American literature has been redrawn substantially every thirty or forty years since it was solidified in the late nineteenth century (when it was conceived to be a moral representation of the Puritan national spirit), and partially because Americans have something of a history of debating what "American" means.

The "canon," of course, gets increasingly difficult to agree on the closer one gets to the present, and for this reason, some commentators believe that the university should have no business teaching or writing about anything that hasn't survived "the test of time"; in Kimball's words, we should transmit only those writers of "permanent interest" and "permanent value." It's a trickier proposition than it appears to be, if you recall that a great deal of work (like Hurston's) was originally dismissed by influential white men for no other reason than that its author was not a white man, or if you happen to know that the creation of what's now the "traditional canon" took place roughly from 1940–50, for American literature, and from 1920–30 for British literature. Herman Melville, John Donne, the Beowulf poet, and William Blake, for instance, get tossed out under the Kimball plan, since they have not been writers of "permanent interest"; Chaucer, Milton, and Shakespeare barely qualify; and as for Joyce, Eliot, Pound, and Lawrence, well, they've been of permanent interest for the past seventy years largely because F. R. Leavis and company accorded them canonization well before their deaths. For that matter, one cannot overestimate the importance of Eliot's criticism to his own canonization.

Still, if the university kept its hands off everything published after *The Waste Land* (the radical right "traditionalists" would not dream of losing Eliot, but they can do very well without Beckett), it is true that debate over the canon would be a lot more antiquarian, and a lot less acrimonious. It would also mean that academic critics would be prevented from practicing their trade on any test whose copyright had not expired.

Canon revision is neither more nor less than another form of textual reproduction, similar to and in competition with reviewing, marketing, and publishing. Preserving important texts and writers which our culture's various market forces have allowed to fall out of print, canon revision is both reformist and conservative. It is a project as deeply historical as it is deeply ethical; and this is a point so fundamental to the practices of contemporary professions in the humanities that it can only remain misunderstood today by critics with no sense of commitment to historical understanding. Some cultural conservatives will admit the university's right to dabble in work produced after 1922, just as some conservatives will admit that the content of "the canon" is and always has been subject to change. But what angers these people, much more than our canon tinkering and syllabus shuffling is that we tweedy Visigoths aren't teaching the great works the way they're supposed to be taught: Instead of reading the works of Shakespeare and Milton for timeless truths that speak to us all, instead of acknowledging that great literature conveys moral and spiritual lessons that ennoble all of humankind, we read the West's great works *ideologically*. But what are these spiritual lessons, these timeless truths? Lately we've noticed that our antagonists get uncharacteristically tongue-tied when we ask them what specific timeless truths they have in mind: Is *Paradise Lost* a 10,000-line version of "just say no"? Likewise, though conservative demagogues are fond of the claim that great works speak to us all, they begin to bluster when we ask them who they mean by us, and they get downright sullen when we ask whether these great works say the same thing every time they speak.

That's why nothing outrages the Right quite like the current academic interest in attempting to understand what literary works did and didn't say to their contemporary readers and audiences, and for what reasons. From the Right's perspective, inquiring into the historical production and reception of cultural artifacts is the most subversive enterprise of all, for it threatens to undo the very notion of artistic autonomy and timelessness; thus it is that as we expand our sense of literary meaning and value, the Right paradoxically charges us with *reducing* literature to "ideology," thereby depriving it of meaning and value.

Generally, when the Right complains that we're reading ideologically, it really means that we're reading historically. Insofar as we foreground literature's social meanings, and we argue that all meanings are social meanings (that is, human meanings), we do so because we take literature seriously; for if literary works were truly timeless, and truly "above" all ideology, they would be utterly meaningless. Let me not be misunderstood here: If meaning is produced by human agency then it is "ideological." What else could it be? To read a literary text as a work of art "about" social conflict, or power and its production, or gender relations, or imperialism, or even "about" its own possible interpretation, is merely to read literature as if it were produced and read by humans, and for humans. The only conservative alternatives to this position are to celebrate literature as pointless but very fine writing, or to believe that literary meaning has nothing to do with history or with readers. The latter is what the doctrine of the Right looks like at its best; but when this kind of authoriarian nihilism masquerades as a defense of literature's "integrity" and "autonomy," is it misguided, terrifying, or just plain stupid? I really don't know.

I myself am the product of more core curricula than most of you will ever want to see. Throughout my undergraduate years, I never once heard Zora Neale Hurston's name—or Mary Wollstonecraft's, or Aphra Behn's. Even as an English major specializing in American literature, I was assigned one book by a black writer—American literature's number one crossover hit, *Invisible Man*. That was nearly ten years ago, and it's safe to say it wouldn't happen quite that way today. But who knows? I was assigned a book by a writer of African descent only in my fourteenth of fourteen graduate courses at Virginia, when the English department managed to hire someone who could teach courses in which "American" was not automatically synonymous with "white."

In that fourteenth graduate course (on the modern American long poem), I came across Melvin Tolson, whose 170-page *Harlem Gallery*, published in 1965, is one of those neglected masterpieces that's fallen out of print and out of whatever passes for our cultural memory. It's Tolson who reminds me now that the canon revisions of the past fifteen years have not attacked Western culture; they have, above all, *enriched* our sense of Western culture. But precisely because we've done so much to recover some of the West's suppressed heterogeneities, we cannot stand mutely by while the West is defended by a phalanx of conservative journalists and political hacks who apparently read only each other. Under normal circumstances, it would be bad enough that the academy's attackers have so little understanding of what they're attacking; but what's truly scandalous about these people is that they so often have just as little understanding of what they're defending. If the legacy of Western culture is to be entrusted to the likes of Kimball, Taylor, D'Souza, and the scribes at *Newsweek*, then we can be sure that it will not truly be a legacy of "Western culture"—and it will not be a legacy worth preserving.

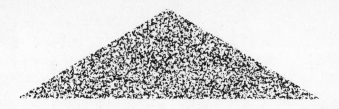

PART TWO

POLITICS AND THE CANON

THE VALUE OF THE CANON

Irving Howe

Irving Howe, the distinguished literary and social critic, is the author of, most recently, *Selected Writings: 1950–1990* and is the co-editor of the journal *Dissent*. He published this essay in *The New Republic*, February 18, 1991.

I.

Of all the disputes agitating the American campus, the one that seems to me especially significant is that over "the canon." What should be taught in the humanities and social sciences, especially in introductory courses? What is the place of the classics? How shall we respond to those professors who attack "Eurocentrism" and advocate "multiculturalism"? This is not the sort of tedious quarrel that now and then flutters through the academy; it involves matters of public urgency. I propose to see this dispute, at first, through a narrow, even sectarian lens, with the hope that you will come to accept my reasons for doing so.

Here, roughly, are the lines of division. On one side stand (too often, fall) the cultural "traditionalists," who may range politically across the entire spectrum. Opposing

them is a heterogeneous grouping of mostly younger teachers, many of them veterans of the 1960s, which includes
feminists, black activists, Marxists, deconstructionists, and
various mixtures of these.

At some colleges and universities traditional survey
courses of world and English literature, as also of social
thought, have been scrapped or diluted. At others they are
in peril. At still others they will be. What replaces them is
sometimes a mere option of electives, sometimes "multicultural" courses introducing material from Third World
cultures and thinning out an already thin sampling of
Western writings, and sometimes courses geared especially
to issues of class, race, and gender. Given the notorious
lethargy of academic decision-making, there has probably
been more clamor than change; but if there's enough
clamor, there will be change.

University administrators, timorous by inclination, are
seldom firm in behalf of principles regarding education.
Subjected to enough pressure, many of them will buckle
under. So will a good number of professors who vaguely
subscribe to "the humanist tradition" but are not famously
courageous in its defense. Academic liberalism has notable
virtues, but combativeness is not often one of them. In the
academy, whichever group goes on the offensive gains an
advantage. Some of those who are now attacking "traditionalist" humanities and social science courses do so out of
sincere persuasion; some, from a political agenda (what
was at first solemnly and now is half-ironically called P.C.—
politically correct); and some from an all-too-human readiness to follow the academic fashion that, for the moment,
is "in."

Can we find a neutral term to designate the antitradi-
tionalists? I can't think of a satisfactory one, so I propose
an unsatisfactory one: Let's agree to call them the insurgents, though in fact they have won quite a few victories.

In the academy these professors are often called "the left" or "the cultural left," and that is how many of them see themselves. But this is a comic misunderstanding, occasionally based on ignorance. In behalf of both their self-awareness and decent clarity of debate, I want to show that in fact the socialist and Marxist traditions have been close to traditionalist views of culture. Not that the left hasn't had its share of ranters (I exclude Stalinists and hooligans) who, in the name of "the revolution," were intent upon jettisoning the culture of the past; but generally such types have been a mere marginal affliction treated with disdain.

Let me cite three major figures. Here is Georg Lukacs, the most influential Marxist critic of the twentieth century:

> Those who do not know Marxism may be surprised at the respect for *the classical heritage of mankind* which one finds in the really great representatives of that doctrine. (Emphasis added.)

Here is Leon Trotsky, arguing in 1924 against a group of Soviet writers who felt that as the builders of "a new society" they could dismiss the "reactionary culture" of the past:

> If I say that the importance of *The Divine Comedy* lies in the fact that it gives me an understanding of the state of mind of certain classes in a certain epoch, this means that I transform it into *a mere historical document*. . . . How is it thinkable that there should be not a historical but *a directly aesthetic relationship* between us and a medieval Italian book? This is explained by the fact that in class society, in spite of its changeability, there are certain common features. Works of art developed in a medieval Italian city can affect us too. What does this

require? . . . That these feelings and moods shall have received such broad, intense, powerful expression as to have raised them above the limitations of the life of those days. (Emphasis added.)

Trotsky's remarks could serve as a reply to those American professors of literature who insist upon the omnipresence of ideology as it seeps into and perhaps saturates literary texts, and who scoff that only "formalists" believe that novels and poems have autonomous being and value. In arguing, as he did in his book *Literature and Revolution*, that art must be judged by "its own laws," Trotsky seems not at all P.C. Still less so is Antonio Gramsci, the Italian Marxist, whose austere opinions about education might make even our conservatives blanch:

Latin and Greek were learnt through their grammar, mechanically, but the accusation of formalism and aridity is very unjust. . . . In education one is dealing with children in whom one has to inculcate certain habits of diligence, precision, poise (even physical poise), ability to concentrate on specific subjects, which cannot be acquired without the mechanical repetition of disciplined and methodical acts.

These are not the isolated ruminations of a few intellectuals; Lukacs, Trotsky, and Gramsci speak with authority for a view of culture prevalent in the various branches of the Marxist (and also, by the way, the non-Marxist) left. And that view informed many movements of the left. There were the Labor night schools in England bringing to industrial workers elements of the English cultural past; there was the once-famous Rand School of New York City; there were the reading circles that Jewish workers, in both Eastern Europe and American cities, formed to acquaint themselves with Tolstoy, Heine, and Zola. And in Ignazio Silone's novel *Bread and Wine* we have a poignant account of an underground cell in Rome during the Mussolini years that reads literary works as a way of holding itself together.

My interest here is not to vindicate socialism or Marxism—that is another matter. Nor is there anything sacrosanct about the opinions I have quoted or their authors. But it is surely worth establishing that the claims of many academic insurgénts to be speaking from a left, let alone a Marxist, point of view are highly dubious. Very well, the more candid among them might reply, so we're not of the left, at least we're not of the "Eurocentric" left. To recognize that would at least help clear the atmosphere. More important, it might shrink the attractiveness of these people in what is perhaps the only area of American society where the lable of "the left" retains some prestige.

What we are witnessing on the campus today is a strange mixture of American populist sentiment and French critical theorizing as they come together in behalf of "changing the subject." The populism provides an underlying structure of feeling, and the theorizing provides a dash of intellectual panache. The populism releases anti-elitist rhetoric, the theorizing releases highly elitist language.

American populism, with its deep suspicion of the making of distinctions of value, has found expression not only in native sages (Henry Ford: "History is bunk") but also in the writings of a long line of intellectuals—indeed, it's only intellectuals who can give full expression to anti-intellectualism. Such sentiments have coursed through American literature, but only recently, since the counterculture of the 1960s, have they found a prominent place in the universities.

As for the French theorizing—metacritical, quasi-philosophical, and at times of a stupefying verbal opacity—it has provided a buttress for the academic insurgents. We are living at a time when all the once-regnant world systems that have sustained (also distorted) Western intellectual life, from theologies to ideologies, are taken to be in severe collapse. This leads to a mood of skepticism, an agnosticism of judgment, sometimes a world-weary nihilism in which even the most conventional minds begin to question both distinctions of value and the value of distinctions. If you can find projections of racial, class, and gender bias in both a Western by Louis L'Amour and a classical Greek play, and if you have decided to reject the "elitism" said to be at the core of literary distinctions, then you might as well teach the Western as the Greek play. You can make the same political points, and more easily, in "studying" the Western. And if you happen not to be well informed about Greek culture, it certainly makes things still easier.

I grew up with the conviction that what George Lukacs calls "the classical heritage of mankind" is a precious legacy. It came out of historical circumstances often appalling, filled with injustice and outrage. It was often, in consequence, alloyed with prejudice and flawed sympathies. Still, it was a heritage that had been salvaged from the nightmares, occasionally the glories, of history, and now we would make it "ours," we who came from poor and working-class families. This "heritage of mankind" (which also includes, of course, Romantic and modernist culture) had been denied to the masses of ordinary people, trained into the stupefaction of accepting, even celebrating, their cultural deprivations. One task of political consciousness was therefore to enable the masses to share in what had been salvaged from the past—the literature, art, music, thought—and thereby to reach an active relation with these. That is why many people, not just socialists but liberals, democrats, and those without political tags, kept struggling for universal education. It was not a given; it had to be won. Often, winning proved to be very hard.

Knowledge of the past, we felt, could humanize by promoting distance from ourselves and our narrow habits, and this could promote critical thought. Even partly to grasp a significant experience or literary work of the past would require historical imagination, a sense of other times, which entailed moral imagination, a sense of other ways. It would create a kinship with those who had come before us, hoping and suffering as we have, seeking through language, sound, and color to leave behind something of enduring value.

By now we can recognize that there was a certain naïveté in this outlook. The assumption of progress in education turned out to be as problematic as similar assumptions elsewhere in life. There was an underestimation of human recalcitrance and sloth. There was a failure to recognize what the twentieth century has taught us: that aesthetic sensibility by no means assures ethical value. There was little anticipation of the profitable industry of "mass culture," with its shallow kitsch and custom-made dreck. Nevertheless, insofar as we retain an attachment to the democratic idea, we must hold fast to an educational vision somewhat like the one I've sketched. Perhaps it is more an ideal to be approached than a goal to be achieved; no matter. I like the epigrammatic exaggeration, if it is an exaggeration, of John Dewey's remark that "the aim of education is to enable individuals to continue their education."

This vision of culture and education started, I suppose, at some point in the late eighteenth century or the early nineteenth century. It was part of a great sweep of human aspiration drawing upon Western traditions from the Renaissance to the Enlightenment. It spoke in behalf of such liberal values as the autonomy of the self, tolerance for a plurality of opinions, the rights of oppressed national and racial groups, and soon, the claims of the women's movements. To be sure, these vlaues were frequently violated— that has been true for every society in every phase of world history. But the criticism of such violations largely invoked the declared values themselves, and this remains true for all our contemporary insurgencies. Some may sneer at "Western hegemony," but knowingly or not, they do so in the vocabulary of Western values.

By invoking the "classical heritage of mankind" I don't propose anything fixed and unalterable. Not at all. There are, say, seven or eight writers and a similar number of social thinkers who are of such preeminence that they must be placed at the very center of this heritage; but beyond that, plenty of room remains for disagreement. All traditions change, simply through survival. Some classics die. Who now reads Ariosto? A loss, but losses form part of tradition too. And new arrivals keep being added to the roster of classics—it is not handed down from Mt. Sinai or the University of Chicago. It is composed and fought over by cultivated men and women. In a course providing students a mere sample of literature, there should be included some black and women writers who, because of inherited bias, have been omitted in the past. Yet I think we must give a central position to what Professor John Searle in a recent *New York Review of Books* article specifies as "a certain Western intellectual tradition that goes from, say, Socrates to Wittgenstein in philosophy, and from Homer to James Joyce in literature. . . . It is essential to the liberal education of young men and women in the United States that they should receive some exposure to at least some of the great works of this intellectual tradition."

Nor is it true that most of the great works of the past

are bleakly retrograde in outlook—to suppose that is a sign of cultural illiteracy. Bring together in a course on social thought selections from Plato and Aristotle, Machiavelli and Rousseau, Hobbes and Locke, Nietzsche and Freud, Marx and Mill, Jefferson and Dewey, and you have a wide variety of opinions, often clashing with one another, sometimes elusive and surprising, always richly complex. These are some of the thinkers with whom to begin, if only later to deviate from. At least as critical in outlook are many of the great poets and novelists. Is there a more penetrating historian of selfhood than Wordsworth? A more scathing critic of society than the late Dickens? A mind more devoted to ethical seriousness than George Eliot? A sharper critic of the corrupting effects of money than Balzac or Melville?

These writers don't necessarily endorse our current opinions and pieties—why should they? We read them for what Robert Frost calls "counterspeech," the power and brilliance of *other minds*, and if we can go "beyond" them, it is only because they are behind us.

What is being invoked here is not a stuffy obeisance before dead texts from a dead past, but rather a critical engagement with living texts from powerful minds still very much "active" in the present. And we should want our students to read Shakespeare and Tolstoy, Jane Austen and Kafka, Emily Dickinson and Leopold Senghor, not because they "support" one or another view of social revolution, feminism, and black self-esteem. They don't, in many instances; and we don't read them for the sake of enlisting them in a cause of our own. We should want students to read such writers so that they may learn to enjoy the activity of mind, the pleasure of forms, the beauty of language—in short, the arts in their own right.

By contrast, there is a recurrent clamor in the university for "relevance," a notion hard to resist (who wishes to be known as irrelevant?) but proceeding from an impoverished view of political life, and too often ephemeral in its excitements and transient in its impact. I recall seeing in the late 1960s large stacks of Eldridge Cleaver's *Soul on Ice* in the Stanford University bookstore. Hailed as supremely "relevant" and widely described as a work of genius, this book has fallen into disuse in a mere two decades. Cleaver himself drifted off into some sort of spiritualism, ceasing thereby to be "relevant." Where, then, is *Soul on Ice* today? What lasting value did it impart?

American culture is notorious for its indifference to the past. It suffers from the provincialism of the contemporary, veering wildly from fashion to fashion, each touted by the media and then quickly dismissed. But the past is the substance out of which the present has been formed, and to let it slip away from us is to acquiesce in the thinness that characterizes so much of our culture. Serious education must assume, in part, an adversarial stance toward the very society that sustains it—a democratic society makes the wager that it's worth supporting a culture of criticism. But if that criticism loses touch with the heritage of the past, it becomes weightless, a mere compendium of momentary complaints.

Several decades ago, when I began teaching, it could be assumed that entering freshmen had read in high school at least one play by Shakespeare and one novel by Dickens. That wasn't much, but it was something. These days, with the disintegration of the high schools, such an assumption can seldom be made. The really dedicated college teachers of literature feel that, given the bazaar of elective courses an entering student encounters and the propaganda in behalf of "relevance," there is likely to be only one opportunity to acquaint students with a smattering—indeed, the merest fragment—of the great works from the past. Such teachers take pleasure in watching the minds and sensibilities of young people opening up to a poem by Wordsworth, a story by Chekhov, a novel by Ellison. They feel they have planted a seed of responsiveness that, with time and luck, might continue to grow. And if this is said to be a missionary attitude, why should anyone quarrel with it?

II.

Let me now mention some of the objections one hears in academic circles to the views I have put down here, and then provide brief replies.

By requiring students to read what you call "classics" in introductory courses, you impose upon them a certain worldview—and that is an elitist act.

In some rudimentary but not very consequential sense, all education entails the "imposing" of values. There are people who say this is true even when children are taught to read and write, since it assumes that reading and writing are "good."

In its extreme version, this idea is not very interesting, since it is not clear how the human race could survive if there were not some "imposition" from one generation to the next. But in a more moderate version, it is an idea that touches upon genuine problems.

Much depends on the character of the individual teacher, the spirit in which he or she approaches a dialogue of Plato, an essay by Mill, a novel by D. H. Lawrence. These can be, and have been used to pummel an ideological line into the heads of students (who often show a notable capacity for emptying them out again). Such pummeling is possible for all points of view but seems most likely in behalf of totalitarian politics and authoritarian theologies, which dispose their adherents to fanaticism. On the other hand, the texts I've mentioned, as well as many others, can be taught in a spirit of openness, so that students are trained to read carefully, think independently, and ask questions. Nor does this imply that the teacher hides his or her opinions. Being a teacher means having a certain authority, but the student should be able to confront that authority freely and critically. This is what we mean by liberal education—not that a teacher plumps for certain political programs, but that the teaching is done in a "liberal" (open, undogmatic) style.

I do not doubt that there are conservative and radical teachers who teach in this "liberal" spirit. When I was a student at City College in the late 1930s, I studied philosophy with a man who was either a member of the Communist Party or was "cheating it out of dues." Far from being the propagandist of the Party line, which Sidney Hook kept insisting was the necessary role of Communist teachers, this man was decent, humane, and tolerant. Freedom of thought prevailed in his classroom. He had, you might say, a "liberal" character, and perhaps his commitment to teaching as a vocation was stronger than his loyalty to the Party. Were such things not to happen now and then, universities would be intolerable.

If, then, a university proposes a few required courses so that ill-read students may at least glance at what they do not know, that isn't (necessarily) "elitist." Different teachers will approach the agreed-upon texts in different ways, and that is as it should be. If a leftist student gets "stuck" with a conservative teacher, or a conservative student with a leftist teacher, that's part of what education should be. The university is saying to its incoming students: "Here are some sources of wisdom and beauty that have survived the centuries. In time you may choose to abandon them, but first learn something about them."

Your list of classics include only dead, white males, all

*tied in to notions and values of Western hegemony. Doesn't
this narrow excessively the horizons of education?*

All depends on how far forward you go to compose your
list of classics. If you do not come closer to the present
than the mid-eighteenth century, then of course there will
not be many, or even any, women in your roster. If you go
past the mid-eighteenth century to reach the present, it's
not at all true that only "dead, white males" are to be
included. For example—and this must hold for hundreds
of other teachers also—I have taught and written about
Jane Austen, Emily Brontë, Charlotte Brontë, Elizabeth
Gaskell, George Eliot, Emily Dickinson, Edith Wharton,
Katherine Anne Porter, Doris Lessing, and Flannery
O'Connor. I could easily add a comparable list of black
writers. Did this, in itself, make me a better teacher? I
doubt it. Did it make me a better person? We still lack
modes of evaluation subtle enough to say for sure.

The absence of women from the literature of earlier
centuries is a result of historical inequities that have only
partly been remedied in recent years. Virginia Woolf, in a
brilliant passage in *A Room of One's Own,* approaches this
problem by imagining Judith, Shakespeare's sister, perhaps
equally gifted but prevented by the circumstances of her
time from developing her gifts:

> Any woman born with a great gift in the sixteenth
> century would certainly have gone crazed, shot her-
> self, or ended her days in some lonely cottage outside
> the village, half witch, half wizard, feared and
> mocked at. . . . A highly gifted girl who had tried to
> use her gift of poetry would have been so thwarted
> and hindered by other people, so tortured and pulled
> asunder by her own contrary instincts, that she
> must have lost her health and sanity. . . .

The history that Virginia Woolf describes cannot be revoked. If we look at the great works of literature and thought through the centuries until about the mid-eighteenth century, we have to recognize that indeed they have been overwhelmingly the achievements of men. The circumstances in which these achievements occurred may be excoriated. The achievements remain precious.

To isolate a group of texts as the canon is to establish a hierarchy of bias, in behalf of which there can be no certainty of judgment.

There is mischief or confusion in the frequent use of the term "hierarchy" by the academic insurgents, a conflation of social and intellectual uses. A social hierarchy may entail a (mal)distribution of income and power, open to the usual criticisms; a literary "hierarchy" signifies a judgment, often based on historical experience, that some works are of supreme or abiding value, while others are of lesser value, and still others quite without value. To prefer Elizabeth Bishop to Judith Krantz is not of the same order as sanctioning the inequality of wealth in the United States. To prefer Shakespeare to Sidney Sheldon is not of the same order as approving the hierarchy of the nomenklatura in Communist dictatorships.

As for the claim that there is no certainty of judgment, all tastes being historically molded or individually subjective, I simply do not believe that the people who make it live by it. This is an "egalitarianism" of valuation that people of even moderate literacy know to be false and unworkable—the making of judgments, even if provisional and historically modulated, is inescapable in the life of culture. And if we cannot make judgments or demonstrate the grounds for our preferences, then we have no business teaching literature—we might just as well be teaching advertising—and there is no reason to have departments of literature.

The claim that there can be value-free teaching is a liberal deception or self-deception; so too the claim that there can be texts untouched by social and political bias. Politics or ideology is everywhere, and it's the better part of honesty to admit this.

If you look hard (or foolishly) enough, you can find political and social traces everywhere. But to see politics or ideology in all texts is to scrutinize the riches of literature through a single lens. If you choose, you can read all or almost all literary works through the single lens of religion. But what a sad impoverishment of the imagination, and what a violation of our sense of reality, this represents. Politics may be "in" everything, but not everything is politics. A good social critic will know which texts are inviting to a given approach and which it would be wise to leave to others.

To see politics everywhere is to diminish the weight of politics. A serious politics recognizes the limits of its reach; it deals with public affairs while leaving alone large spheres of existence; it seeks not to "totalize" its range of interest. Some serious thinkers believe that the ultimate aim of politics should be to render itself superfluous. That may seem an unrealizable goal; meanwhile, a good part of the struggle for freedom in recent decades has been to draw a line beyond which politics must not tread. The same holds, more or less, for literary study and the teaching of literature.

Wittingly or not, the traditional literary and intellectual canon was based on received elitist ideologies, the values of Western imperialism, racism, sexism, etc., and the teaching of the humanities was marked by corresponding biases. It is now necessary to enlarge the canon so that voices from Africa, Asia, and Latin America can be heard. This is especially important for minority students so that they may learn about their origins and thereby gain in self-esteem.

It is true that over the decades some university teaching has reflected inherited social biases—how, for better or worse, could it not? Most often this was due to the fact that many teachers shared the common beliefs of American society. But not all teachers! As long as those with critical views were allowed to speak freely, the situation, if not ideal, was one that people holding minority opinions and devoted to democratic norms had to accept.

Yet the picture drawn by some academic insurgents— that most teachers, until quite recently, were in the grip of the worst values of Western society—is overdrawn. I can testify that some of my school and college teachers a few decades ago, far from upholding Western imperialism or white supremacy, were sharply critical of American society, in some instances from a boldly reformist outlook. They taught us to care about literature both for its own sake and because, as they felt, it often helped confirm their world-views. (And to love it even if it didn't confirm their world-views.) One high school teacher introduced me to Hardy's *Jude the Obscure* as a novel showing how cruel society can be to rebels, and up to a point, she was right. At college, as a fervent anti-Stalinist Marxist, I wrote a thoughtless "class analysis" of Edmund Spenser's poetry for an English class, and the kindly instructor, whose politics were probably not very far from mine, suggested that there were more things in the world, especially as Spenser had seen it, than I could yet recognize. I mention these instances to suggest that there has always been a range of opinion among teachers, and if anything, the American academy has tilted more to the left than most other segments of our society. There were of course right-wing professors too; I remember an economics teacher we called "Steamboat" Fulton, the object of amiable ridicule among the students who nonetheless learned something from him.

Proposals to enlarge the curriculum to include non-Western writings—if made in good faith and not in behalf of an ideological campaign—are in principle to be respected. A course in ancient thought might well include a selection from Confucius; a course in the modern novel might well include a work by Tanizaki or García Márquez.

There are practical difficulties. Due to the erosion of requirements in many universities, those courses that survive are usually no more than a year or a semester in duration, so that there is danger of a diffusion to the point of incoherence. Such courses, if they are to have any value, must focus primarily on the intellectual and cultural traditions of Western society. That, like it or not, is where we come from and that is where we are. All of us who live in America are, to some extent, Western: it gets to us in our deepest and also our most trivial habits of thought and speech, in our sense of right and wrong, in our idealism and our cynicism.

As for the argument that minority students will gain in self-esteem through being exposed to writings by Africans and black Americans, it is hard to know. Might not entering minority students, some of them ill-prepared, gain a stronger sense of self-esteem by mastering the arts of writing and reading than by being told, as some are these days, that Plato and Aristotle plagiarized from an African source? Might not some black students feel as strong a sense of self-esteem by reading, say, Dostoyevsky and Malraux (which Ralph Ellison speaks of having done at a susceptible age) as by being confined to black writers? Is there not something grossly patronizing in the notion that while diverse literary studies are appropriate for middle-class white students, something else, racially determined, is required for the minorities? Richard Wright found sustenance in Dreiser, Ralph Ellison in Hemingway, Chinua Achebe in Eliot, Leopold Senghor in the whole of French poetry. Are there not unknown young Wrights and Ellisons, Achebes and Senghors in our universities who might also want to find their way to an individually achieved sense of culture?

In any case, is the main function of the humanities directly to inculcate self-esteem? Do we really know how this can be done? And if done by bounding the curriculum according to racial criteria, may that not perpetuate the very grounds for a lack of self-esteem? I do not know the answers to these questions, but do the advocates of multiculturalism?

One serious objection to "multicultural studies" remains; that it tends to segregate students into categories fixed by birth, upbringing, and obvious environment. Had my teachers tried to lead me toward certain writers because they were Jewish, I would have balked—I wanted to find my own way to Proust, Kafka, and Pirandello, writers who didn't need any racial credentials. Perhaps things are different with students today—we ought not to be dogmatic about these matters. But are there not shared norms of pride and independence among young people, whatever their race and color?

The jazz musician Wynton Marsalis testifies: "Everybody has two heritages, ethnic and human. The human aspects give art its real enduring power. . . . The racial aspect, that's a crutch so you don't have to go out into the world." David Bromwich raises an allied question: Should we wish "to legitimize the belief that the mind of a student deserves to survive in exactly the degree that it corresponds with one of the classes of socially constructed group minds? If I were a student today I would find this assumption frightening. It is, in truth, more than a license for conformity. It is a four-year sentence to conformity."

What you have been saying is pretty much the same as what conservatives say. Doesn't that make you feel uncomfortable?

No, it doesn't. There are conservatives—and conservatives. Some, like the editor of *The New Criterion*, are frantic ideologues with their own version of P.C., the classics as safeguard for the status quo. This is no more attractive than the current campus ideologizing. But there are also conservatives who make the necessary discriminations between using culture, as many have tried to use religion, as a kind of social therapy and seeing culture as a realm with its own values and rewards.

Similar differences hold with regard to the teaching of past thinkers. In a great figure like Edmund Burke you will find not only the persuasions of conservatism but also a critical spirit that does not readily lend itself to ideological coarseness. Even those of us who disagree with him fundamentally can learn from Burke the disciplines of argument and resources of language.

Let us suppose that in University X undergoing a curriculum debate there is rough agreement about which books to teach between professors of the democratic left and their conservative colleagues. Why should that trouble us—or them? We agree on a given matter, perhaps for different reasons. Or there may be a more or less shared belief in the idea of a liberal education. If there is, so much the better. If the agreement is momentary, the differences will emerge soon enough.

A Little Epilogue

A NEW REPUBLIC reader: "Good lord, you're becoming a virtuoso at pushing through open doors. All this carrying on just to convince us that students should read great books. It's so obvious . . ."

I reply: "Dear reader, you couldn't be more right. But that is where we are."

THE POLITICS OF KNOWLEDGE

Edward W. Said

Edward W. Said, the well-known author of *Orientalism* and other books, most recently including *Musical Explorations,* is Parr Professor of English and Comparative Literature at Columbia University. His essay originally appeared in the journal *Raritan,* Summer 1991.

Last fall I was invited to participate in a seminar at a historical studies center of a historically renowned American university. The subject of the seminar for this and the next academic year is imperialism, and the seminar discussions are chaired by the center's director. Outside participants are asked to send a paper before their arrival; it is then distributed to the members of the seminar, who are graduate students, fellows, and faculty. They will have read the paper in advance, precluding any reading of a lecture to them by the visitor, who is instead asked to summarize its main points for about ten minutes. Then for an hour and a half, there is an open discussion of the paper—a fairly rigorous but stimulating exercise. Since I have been working for some years on a sequel to *Orientalism*—it will be a long book that deals with the relationship between modern culture and imperialism—I sent a substantial extract from the introduction, in which I lay out the main lines of the book's argument. I there begin to describe the emergence of a global consciousness in Western knowledge at the end of the nineteenth century, particularly in such apparently unrelated fields as geography and comparative literature. I then go on to argue that the appearance of such cultural disciplines coincides with a fully global imperial perspective, although such a coincidence can only be made to seem significant from the point of view of later history, when nearly everywhere in the colonized world there emerged resistance to certain oppressive aspects of imperial rule like theories of subject races and peripheral regions, and the notions of backward, primitive, or undeveloped cultures. *Because* of that native resistance—for instance, the appearance of many nationalist and independence movements in India, the Caribbean, Africa, the Middle East—it is now evident that culture and imperialism in the West could be understood as offering support, each to the other. Here I referred to the extraordinary work of a whole range of non-Western writers and activists, including Tagore, Fanon, C. L. R. James, Yeats, and many others, figures who have given integrity to anti-imperialist cultural resistance.

The first question after my brief resumé was from a professor of history, a black woman of some eminence who had recently come to the university, but whose work was unfamiliar to me. She announced in advance that her question was to be hostile, "a very hostile one in fact." She then said something like the following: For the first thirteen pages of your paper you talked only about white European males. Thereafter, on page 14, you mention some names of non-Europeans. "How could you do such a thing?" I remonstrated somewhat, and tried to explain my argument in greater detail—after all, I said, I was discussing European imperialism, which would not have been likely to include in its discourse the work of African-American women. I pointed out that in the book I say quite a bit about the response to imperialism all over the world; that point was a place in my argument where it would be pertinent to focus on the work of such writers as—and here I again mentioned the name of a great Caribbean writer and intellectual whose work has a special importance for my own—C. L. R. James. To this my critic replied with a stupefying confidence that my answer was not satisfactory since C. L. R. James was dead! I must admit that I was nonplussed by the severity of this pronouncement. James indeed *was* dead, a fact that needn't, to a historian, have made further discussion impossible. I waited for her to resume, hoping that she might expatiate on what she meant by having suggested that even in discussions of what dead white European males said on a given topic it was inappropriate to confine oneself to what they said while leaving out the work of living African-American, Arab, and Indian writers.

But she did not proceed, and I was left to suppose that she considered her point sufficiently and conclusively made: I was guilty of not mentioning living non-European nonmales, even when it was not obvious to me or, I later gathered, to many members of the seminar what their pertinence might have been. I noted to myself that my antagonist did not think it necessary to enumerate what specifically in the work of living non-Europeans I should have used, or which books and ideas by them she found important and relevant. All I had been given to work with was the asserted necessity to mention some approved names—which names did not really matter—as if the very act of uttering them was enough. I was also left unmistakably with the impression that as a nonwhite—a category incidentally to which as an Arab I myself belong—she was saying that to affirm the existence of non-European "others" took the place of evidence, argument, discussion.

It would be pointless to deny that the exchange was unsettling. Among other things I was chagrined at the distortions of my position and for having responded to the distortions so clumsily. It did not seem to matter that a great deal of my own work has concerned itself with just the kind of omission with which I was being charged. What apparently mattered now was that having contributed to an early trend, in which Western and European intellectuals were arraigned for having their work constructed out of the suffering and deprivations of so many people of color, I was now allegedly doing what such complicit intellectuals had always done. For if in one place you criticize the exclusion of Orientals, as I did in *Orientalism,* the exclusion of "others" from your work in another place becomes on one level, difficult to justify or explain. I was disheartened not because I was being attacked, but because the general validity of the point made in *Orientalism* still obtained and yet was now being directed at me. It was *still* true that various Others—the word has acquired a sheen of modishness that has become extremely objectionable—were being represented unfairly, their reality distorted, their truth either denied or twisted with malice. Yet instead of joining in their behalf, I felt I was being asked to get involved in an inconsequential academic contest. I had wanted to say, but didn't, "Is all that matters about the issue of exclusion and misrepresentation the fact that *names* were left out? Why are you detaining us with such trivialities?"

To make matters worse, a few minutes later in the discussion I was attacked by a retired professor of Middle Eastern studies, himself an Orientalist. Like me, he was an Arab, but he had consistently identified himself with intellectual tendencies of which I had always been critical.

He now intervened to defend imperialism, saying in tones of almost comic reverence, that it had accomplished things that natives couldn't have done for themselves. It had taught them, among other things, he said, how to appreciate the cuneiform and hieroglyphics of their own traditions. As he droned on about the imperial schools, railroads, hospitals, and telegraphs in the Third World that stood for examples of British and French largesse, the irony of the whole thing seemed overpowering. It appeared to me that there had to be something to say that surrendered neither to the caricatural reductiveness of the two positions by then arrayed against me, and against each other, nor to that verbal quality in each that was determined to remain ideologically correct and little else.

I was being reminded by such negative flat-minded examples of thinking, that the one thing that intellectuals *cannot* do without is the full intellectual process itself. Into it goes historically informed research as well as the presentation of a coherent and carefully argued line that has taken account of alternatives. In addition, there must be, it seems to me, a theoretical presumption that in matters having to do with human history and society any rigid theoretical ideal, any simple additive or mechanical notion of what is or is not factual, must yield to the central factor of human work, the actual participation of peoples in the making of human life. If that is so then it must also be true that, given the very nature of human work in the construction of human society and history, it is impossible to say of it that its products are so rarified, so limited, so beyond comprehension as to exclude most other people, experiences, and histories. I mean further, that this kind of human work, which is intellectual work, is worldly, that it is situated in the world, and about that world. It is not about things that are so rigidly constricted and so forbiddingly arcane as to exclude all but an audience of like-minded, already fully convinced persons. While it would be stupid to deny the importance of constituencies and audiences in the construction of an intellectual argument, I think it has to be supposed that many arguments can be made to more than one audience and in different situations. Otherwise we would be dealing not with intellectual argument but either with dogma, or with a technological jargon designed specifically to repel all but a small handful of initiates or coteries.

Lest I fall into the danger myself of being too theoretical and specialized, I shall be more specific now and return to the episode I was discussing just a moment ago. At the heart of the imperial cultural enterprise I analyzed in *Orientalism* and also in my new book, was a politics of identity. That politics has needed to assume, indeed needed firmly to believe, that what was true about Orientals or Africans was *not* however true about or for Europeans. When a French or German scholar tried to identify the main characteristics of, for instance, the Chinese mind, the work was only partly intended to do that; it was also intended to show how different the Chinese mind was from the Western mind.

Such constructed things—they have only an elusive reality—as the Chinese mind or the Greek spirit have always been with us; they are at the source of a great deal that goes into the making of individual cultures, nations, traditions, and peoples. But in the modern world considerably greater attention has generally been given to such identities than was ever given in earlier historical periods, when the world was larger, more amorphous, less globalized. Today a fantastic emphasis is placed upon a politics of national identity, and to a very great degree, this emphasis is the result of the imperial experience. For when the great modern Western imperial expansion took place all across the world, beginning in the late eighteenth century, it accentuated the interaction between the identity of the French or the English and that of the colonized native peoples. And this mostly antagonistic interaction gave rise to a separation between people as members of homogenous races and exclusive nations that was and still is one of the characteristics of what can be called the epistemology of imperialism. At its core is the supremely stubborn thesis that everyone is principally and irreducibly a member of some race or category, and that race or category cannot ever be assimilated to or accepted by others—except as itself. Thus came into being such invented essences as the Oriental or Englishness, as Frenchness, Africanness, or American exceptionalism, as if each of those had a Platonic idea behind it that guaranteed it as pure and unchanging from the beginning to the end of time.

One product of this doctrine is nationalism, a subject so immense that I can treat it only very partially here. What interests me in the politics of identity that informed imperialism in its global phase is that just as natives were considered to belong to a different category—racial or geographical—from that of Western white man, it also became true that in the great anti-imperialist revolt represented by decolonization this same category was mobilized around, and formed the resisting identity of, the revolutionaries. This was the case everywhere in the Third World. Its most celebrated instance is the concept of *négritude,* as developed intellectually and poetically by Aimé Césaire, Leopold Senghor, and, in English, W. E. B. Du Bois. If blacks had once been stigmatized and given inferior status to whites, then it has since become necessary not to deny blackness, and not to aspire to whiteness, but to accept and celebrate blackness, to give it the dignity of poetic as well as metaphysical status. Thus *négritude* acquired positive Being where before it had been a mark of degradation and inferiority. Much the same revaluation of the native particularity occurred in India, in many parts of the Islamic world, China, Japan, Indonesia, and the Philippines, where the denied or repressed native essence emerged as the focus of, and even the basis for, nationalist recovery.

It is important to note that much of the early cultural resistance to imperialism on which nationalism and independence movements were built was salutary and necessary. I see it essentially as an attempt on the part of oppressed people who had suffered the bondage of slavery, colonialism, and—most important—spiritual disposession, to reclaim their identity. When that finally occurred in places such as Algeria, the grander nationalist efforts amounted to little short of a reconstructed communal political and cultural program of independence. Where the white man had once only seen lazy natives and exotic customs, the insurrection against imperialism produced, as in Ireland for example, a national revolt, along with political parties dedicated to independence, which, like the Congress party in India, was headed by nationalist figures, poets, and military heroes. There were remarkably impressive results from this vast effort at cultural reclamation, most of which are well known and celebrated.

But while the whole movement toward autonomy and independence produced in effect newly independent and separate states constituting the majority of new nations in the postcolonial world today, the nationalist politics of identity has nonetheless quickly proved itself to be insufficient for the ensuing period.

Inattentive or careless readers of Frantz Fanon, generally considered one of the two or three most eloquent apostles of anti-imperialist resistance, tend to forget his marked suspicions of unchecked nationalism. So while it is appropriate to draw attention to the early chapters on violence in *The Wretched of the Earth*, it should be noticed that in subsequent chapters he is sharply critical of what he called the pitfalls of national consciousness. He clearly meant this to be a paradox. And for the reason that while nationalism is a necessary spur to revolt against the colonizer, national consciousness must be immediately transformed into what he calls "social consciousness," just as soon as the withdrawal of the colonizer has been accomplished.

Fanon is scathing on the abuses of the postindependence nationalist party, on, for instance, the cult of the Grand Panjandrum (or maximum leader), or the centralization of the capital city, which Fanon said flatly needed to be deconsecrated, and most importantly, on the hijacking of common sense and popular participation by bureaucrats, technical experts, and jargon-wielding obfuscators. Well before V. S. Naipaul, Fanon was arguing against the politics of mimicry and separatism which produced the Mobutus, Idi Amins, and Saddams, as well as the grotesqueries and pathologies of power that gave rise to tyrannical states and praetorian guards while obstructing democratic freedoms in so many countries of the Third World. Fanon also prophesied the continuing dependency of numerous postcolonial governments and philosophies, all of which preached the sovereignty of the newly independent people of one or another new Third World State, and, having failed to make the transition from nationalism to true liberation, were in fact condemned to practice the politics, and the economics, of a new oppression as pernicious as the old one.

At bottom, what Fanon offers most compellingly is a critique of the separatism and mock autonomy achieved by a pure politics of identity that has lasted too long and been made to serve in situations where it has become simply inadequate. What invariably happens at the level of knowledge is that signs and symbols of freedom and status are taken for the reality: You want to be named and considered. In effect this really means that just to be an independent postcolonial Arab, or black, or Indonesian is not a program, nor a process, nor a vision. It is no more than a convenient starting point from which the real work, the hard work, might begin.

As for that work, it is nothing less than the reintegration of all those people and cultures, once confined and reduced to peripheral status, with the rest of the human race. After working through *négritude* in the early sections of *Cahier d'un retour*, Aimé Césaire states this vision of integration in his poem's climatic moment: "No race possesses the monopoly of beauty, of intelligence, of force, and there is a place for all at the rendez-vous of victory."

Without this concept of "place for all at the rendez-vous of victory," one is condemned to an impoverishing politics of knowledge based only upon the assertion and reassertion of identity, an ultimately uninteresting alternation of presence and absence. If you are weak, your affirmation of identity for its own sake amounts to little more than saying that you want a kind of attention easily and superficially granted, like the attention given an individual in a crowded room at roll call. Once having such recognition, the subject has only to sit there silently as the proceedings unfold as if in his or her absence. And, on the other hand, though the powerful get acknowledged by the sheer force of presence, this commits them to a logic of displacement, as soon as someone else emerges who is as, or more, powerful.

This has proved a disastrous process, whether for postcolonials, forced to exist in a marginal and dependent place totally outside the circuits of world power, or for powerful societies, whose triumphalism and imperious wilfullness have done so much to devastate and destabilize the world. What has been at issue between Iraq and the United States is precisely such a logic of exterminism and displacement, as unedifying as it is unproductive. It is risky, I know, to move from the realm of interpretation to the realm of world politics, but it seems to me true that the relationship between them is a real one, and the light that one realm can shed on the other is quite illuminating. In any case the politics of knowledge that is based principally on the affirmation of identity is very similar, is indeed directly related to, the unreconstructed nationalism that has guided so many postcolonial states today. It asserts a sort of separatism that wishes only to draw attention to itself; consequently it neglects the integration of that earned and achieved consciousness of self within "the rendez-vous of victory." On the national and on the intellecutal level the problems are very similar.

Let me return therefore to one of the intellectual debates that has been central to the humanities in the past decade, and which underlies the episode with which I began. The ferment in minority, subaltern, feminist, and postcolonial consciousness has resulted in so many salutary achievements in the curricular and theoretical approach to the study of the humanities as quite literally to have produced a Copernican revolution in all traditional fields of inquiry. Eurocentrism has been challenged definitively; most scholars and students in the contemporary American academy are now aware, as they were never aware before, that society and culture have been the heterogenous product of heterogenous people in an enormous variety of cultures, traditions, and situations. No longer does T. S. Eliot's idea of the great Western masterpieces enduring together in a constantly redefining pattern of monuments have its old authority; nor do the sort of patterns elucidated with such memorable brilliance in formative works like *Mimesis* or *The Anatomy of Criticism* have the same cogency for today's student or theorist as they did even quite recently.

And yet the great contest about the canon continues. The success of Allan Bloom's *The Closing of the American* one center for another. It was always a matter of opening and participating in a central strand of intellectual and cultural effort and of showing what had always been, though indiscernibly, a part of it, like the work of women, or of blacks and servants—but which had been either denied or derogated. The power and interest of—to give two examples particularly dear to me—Tayib Salih's *Season of Migration to the North* is not only how it memorably describes the quandary of a gifted young Sudanese who has lived in London but then returns home to his ancestral village alongside the Nile; the novel is also a rewriting of Conrad's *Heart of Darkness*, seen now as the tale of someone who voyages into the heart of light, which is modern Europe, and discovers there what has been hidden deep within him. To read the Sudanese writer is of course to interpret an Arabic novel written during the late 60s at a time of nationalism and a rejection of the West. The novel is therefore affiliated with other Arabic novels of the postwar period including the works of Mahfouz and Idriss; but given the historical and political meaning of a narrative that quite deliberately recalls and reverses Conrad—something impossible for a black man at the time *Heart of Darkness* was written—Tayib Salih's masterpiece is necessarily to be viewed as, along with other African, Indian, and Caribbean works, enlarging, widening, refining the scope of a narrative form at the center of which had heretofore always been an exclusively European observer or center of consciousness.

There is an equally complex resonance to Ghassan Kanafani's *Men in the Sun*, a compelling novella about the travails of three Palestinian refugees who are trying to get from Basra in Iraq to Kuwait. Their past in Palestine is evoked in order to contrast it with the poverty and dispossession of which they are victims immediately after 1948. When they find a man in Basra whose occupation is in part

Mind, the subsequent publication of such works as Alv
Kernan's *The Death of Literature* and Roger Kimbal
Tenured Radicals, as well as the rather posthumous ene
gies displayed in journals like *The American Scholar* (no
a neoconservative magazine), *The New Criterion,* and *Con
mentary*—all this suggests that the work done by those
us who have tried to widen the area of awareness in th
study of culture is scarcely finished or secure. But ou
point, in my opinion, cannot be simply and obdurately
reaffirm the paramount importance of formerly suppresse
or silenced forms of knowledge and leave it at that, nor ca
it be to surround ourselves with the sanctimonious piety
historical or cultural victimhood as a way of making ou
intellectual presence felt. Such strategies are woefully in
sufficient. The whole effort to deconsecrate Eurocentrism
cannot be interpreted, least of all by those who participat
in the enterprise, as an effort to supplant Eurocentrism
with, for instance, Afrocentric or Islamocentric ap
proaches. On its own, ethnic particularity does not provide
for intellectual process—quite the contrary. At first, you
will recall, it was a question, for some, of adding Jane
Austen to the canon of male Western writers in humanitie
courses; then it became a matter of displacing the entire
canon of American writers like Hawthorne and Emersor
with best-selling writers of the same period like Harrie
Beecher Stowe and Susan Warner. But after that the logi
of displacement became even more attenuated, and th
mere names of politically validated living writers becam
more important than anything about them or their works.

I sumit that these clamorous dismissals and swoopin
assertions are in fact caricatural reductions of what th
great revisionary gestures of feminism, subaltern or blac
studies, and anti-imperialist resistance originally intende
For such gestures it was never a matter of replacing one se
of authorities and dogmas with another, nor of substitutir

to smuggle refugees across the border in the belly of his empty watertruck, they strike a deal with him, and he takes them as far as the border post where he is detained in conversation in the hot sun. They die of asphyxiation, unheard and forgotten. Kanafani's novella belongs to the genre of immigrant literature contributed to by an estimable number of postwar writers—Rushdie, Naipaul, Berger, Kundera, and others. But it is also a poignant meditation on the Palestinian fate, and of course eerily prescient about Palestinians in the current Gulf crisis. And yet it would do the subject of the work and its literary merit an extraordinary disservice were we to confine it to the category of national allegory, to see in it only a mirroring of the actual plight of Palestinians in exile. Kanafani's work is literature connected both to its specific historical and cultural situations as well as to a whole world of other literatures and formal articulations, which the attentive reader summons to mind as the interpretation proceeds.

The point I am trying to make can be summed up in the useful notion of worldliness. By linking works to each other we bring them out of the neglect and secondariness to which for all kinds of political and ideological reasons they had previously been condemned. What I am talking about therefore is the opposite of separatism, and also the reverse of exclusivism. It is only through the scrutiny of these works *as* literature, as style, as pleasure and illumination, that they can be brought in, so to speak, and kept in. Otherwise they will be regarded only as informative ethnographic specimens, suitable for the limited attention of experts and area specialists. *Worldliness* is therefore the restoration to such works and interpretations of their place in the global setting, a restoration that can only be accomplished by an appreciation not of some tiny, defensively constituted corner of the world, but of the large many-windowed house of human culture as a whole.

It seems to me absolutely essential that we engage with cultural works in this unprovincial, interested manner while maintaining a strong sense of the contest for forms and values which any decent cultural work embodies, realizes, and contains. A great deal of recent theoretical speculation has proposed that works of literature are completely determined as such by their situation, and that readers themselves are totally determined in their responses by their respective cultural situations, to a point where no value, no reading, no interpretation can be anything other than the merest reflection of some immediate interest. All readings and all writing are reduced to an assumed historical emanation. Here the indeterminacy of deconstructive reading, the airy insouciance of postaxiological criticism, the casual reductiveness of some (but by not means all) ideological schools are principally at fault. While it is true to say that because a text is the product of an unrecapturable past, and that contemporary criticism can to some extent afford a neutral disengagement or opposed perspective impossible for the text in its own time, there is no reason to take the further step and exempt the interpreter from *any* moral, political, cultural, or psychological commitments. All of these remain at play. The attempt to read a text in its fullest and most integrative context commits the reader to positions that are educative, humane, and engaged, positions that depend on training and taste and not simply on a technologized professionalism, or on the tiresome playfulness of "postmodern" criticism, and its repeated disclaimers of anything but local games and pastiches. Despite Lyotard and his acolytes, we are still in the era of large narratives, of horrendous cultural clashes, and of appallingly destructive war—as witness the recent conflagration in the Gulf—and to say that we are against theory, or beyond literature, is to be blind and trivial.

I am not arguing that every interpretive act is equivalent to a gesture either for or against life. How could anyone defend or attack so crudely general a position? I am saying that once we grant intellectual work the right to exist in a relatively disengaged atmosphere, and allow it a status that isn't disqualified by partisanship, we ought then to reconsider the ties between the text and the world in a serious and uncoercive way. Far from repudiating the great advances made when Eurocentrism and patriarchy began to be demystified, we should consolidate these advances, using them so as to reach a better understanding of the degree to which literature and artistic genius belong to and are some part of the world where all of us also do other kinds of work.

This wider application of the ideas I've been discussing cannot even be attempted if we simply repeat a few names or refer to a handful of approved texts ritualistically or sanctimoniously. Victimhood, alas, does not guarantee or necessarily enable an enhanced sense of humanity. To testify to a history of oppression is necessary, but it is not sufficient unless that history is redirected into intellectual process and universalized to include all sufferers. Yet too often testimony to oppression becomes only a justification for further cruelty and inhumanity, or for high sounding cant and merely "correct" attitudes. I have in mind, for instance, not only the antagonists mentioned at the beginning of this essay but also the extraordinary behavior of an Elie Wiesel who has refused to translate the lessons of his own past into consistent criticisms of Israel for doing what it has done and is doing right now to Palestinians.

So while it is not necessary to regard every reading or interpretation of a text as the moral equivalent of a war or a political crisis, it does seem to me to be important to underline the fact that whatever else they are, works of literature are not merely texts. They are in fact differently constituted and have different values, they aim to do different things, exist in different genres, and so on. One of the great pleasures for those who read and study literature is the discovery of longstanding norms in which all cultures known to me concur: such things as style and performance, the existence of good as well as lesser writers, and the exercise of preference. What has been most unacceptable during the many harangues on both sides of the so-called Western canon debate is that so many of the combatants have ears of tin, and are unable to distinguish between good writing and politically correct attitudes, as if a fifth-rate pamphlet and a great novel have more or less the same significance. Who benefits from leveling attacks on the canon? Certainly not the disadvantaged person or class whose history, if you bother to read it at all, is full of evidence that popular resistance to injustice has always derived immense benefits from literature and culture in general, and very few from invidious distinctions made between ruling-class and sub-servient cultures. After all, the crucial lesson of C. L. R. James's *Black Jacobins*, or of E. P. Thompson's *Making of the English Working Class* (with its reminder of how important Shakespeare was to nineteenth-century radical culture), is that great antiauthoritarian uprisings made their earliest advances, not by denying the humanitarian and universalist claims of the general dominant culture, but by attacking the adherents of that culture for failing to uphold their own declared standards, for failing to extend them to all, as opposed to a small fraction, of humanity. Toussaint L'Ouverture is the perfect example of a downtrodden slave whose struggle to free himself and his people was informed by the ideas of Rousseau and Mirabeau.

Although I risk over-simplifiction, it is probably correct to say that it does not finally matter *who* wrote what, but rather *how* a work is written and *how* it is read. The idea that because Plato and Aristotle are male and the products of a slave society they should be disqualified from receiving contemporary attention is as limited an idea as suggesting that *only* their work, because it was addressed to and about elites, should be read today. Marginality and homelessness are not, in my opinion, to be gloried in; they are to be brought to an end, so that more, and not fewer, people can enjoy the benefits of what has for centuries been denied the victims of race, class, or gender.

WHOSE CANON IS IT, ANYWAY?

Henry Louis Gates, Jr.

Henry Louis Gates, Jr., the author of *The Signifying Monkey* and other books, is the W. E. B. Du Bois professor of the humanities at Harvard and co-editor of the journal *Transition*. He first published this essay in *The New York Times Book Review*, February 26, 1989.

William Bennett and Allan Bloom, the dynamic duo of the new cultural right, have become the easy targets of the cultural left, which I am defining here loosely and generously as that uneasy, shifting set of alliances formed by feminist critics, critics of so-called minority culture and Marxist and poststructuralist critics generally—in short, the rainbow coalition of contemporary critical theory. These two men (one a former United States Secretary of Education and now President Bush's "drug czar," the other a professor at the University of Chicago and author of *The Closing of the American Mind*) symbolize the nostalgic return to what I think of as the "antebellum esthetic position," when men were men and men were white, when

scholar-critics were white men and when women and
people of color were voiceless, faceless servants and laborers, pouring tea and filling brandy snifters in the board-
rooms of old boys' clubs. Inevitably, these two men have
come to play the roles that George Wallace and Orville
Faubus played for the civil rights movement, or that Richard Nixon and Henry Kissinger played during Vietnam—
the "feel good" targets who, despite internal differences
and contradictions, the cultural left loves to hate.

And how tempting it is to juxtapose their "civilizing
mission" to the racial violence that has swept through our
campuses since 1986—at traditionally liberal Northern institutions such as the University of Massachusetts at Am-
herst, Mount Holyoke College, Smith College, the University of Chicago, Columbia, the University of Pennsylvania,
and at Southern institutions such as the University of
Alabama, the University of Texas and the Citadel. Add to
this the fact that affirmative action programs on campus
have become window dressing operations, necessary "ev-
ils" maintained to preserve the fiction of racial fairness and
openness but deprived of the power to enforce their stated
principles. When unemployment among black youth is 40
percent, when 44 percent of black Americans can't read
the front page of a newspaper, when less than 2 percent of
the faculty on campuses is black, and when only 40 percent of black students in higher education are men, well,
you look for targets close at hand.

And yet there's a real danger of localizing our grievances;
of the easy personification, assigning celebrated faces to
the forces of reaction and so giving too much credit to a
few men who are really symptomatic of a larger political
current. (In a similar vein, our rhetoric sometimes depicts
the high canonical as the reading matter of the power elite.
You have to imagine James Baker curling up with the *Pisan*

Cantos, Dan Quayle leafing through *The Princess Casa-massima.*) Maybe our eagerness to do so reflects a certain vanity that academic cultural critics are prone to. We make dire predictions, and when they come true, we think we've changed the world.

It's a tendency that puts me in mind of my father's favorite story about Father Divine, that historic con man of the cloth. In the 1930s, he was put on trial and convicted for using the mails to defraud. At sentencing, Father Divine stood up and told the judge: I'm warning you, you send me to jail, something terrible is going to happen to you. Father Divine, of course, was sent to prison, and a week later, by sheer coincidence, the judge had a heart attack and died. When the warden and the guards found out about it in the middle of the night, they raced to Father Divine's cell and woke him up. Father Divine, they said, your judge just dropped dead of a heart attack. Without missing a beat, Father Divine lifted his head and told them: "I *hated* to do it."

As writers, teachers or intellectuals, most of us would like to claim greater efficacy for our labors than we're entitled to. These days, literary criticism likes to think of itself as "war by other means." But it should start to wonder: have its victories come too easily? The recent turn toward politics and history in literary studies has turned the analysis of texts into a marionette theater of the political, to which we bring all the passions of our real-world commitments. And that's why it is sometimes necessary to remind ourselves of the distance from the classroom to the streets. Academic critics write essays, "readings" of litera-ture, where the bad guys (you know, racism or patriarchy) lose, where the forces of oppression are subverted by the boundless powers of irony and allegory that no prison can contain, and we glow with hard-won triumph. We pay homage to the marginalized and demonized, and it feels almost as if we've righted an actual injustice. (Academic battles are so fierce—the received wisdom has it—because so little is truly at stake.) I always think of the folk tale about the fellow who killed seven with one blow: flies, not giants.

Ours was the generation that took over buildings in the late 1960s and demanded the creation of black and women's studies programs and now, like the return of the repressed, has come back to challenge the traditional curriculum. And some of us are even attempting to redefine the canon by editing anthologies. Yet it sometimes seems that blacks are doing better in the college curriculum than they are in the streets or even on the campuses.

This is not a defeatist moan, just an acknowledgment that the relation between our critical postures and the social struggles they reflect is far from transparent. That doesn't mean there's no relation, of course, only that it's a highly mediated one. In all events, I do think we should be clear about when we've swatted a fly and when we've toppled a giant. Still, you can't expect people who spend their lives teaching literature to be dispassionate about the texts they teach; no one went into literature out of an interest in literature-in-general.

I suppose the literary canon is, in no very grand sense, the commonplace book of our shared culture, the archive of those texts and titles we wish to remember. And how else did those of us who teach literature fall in love with our subject than through our very own commonplace books, in which we inscribed secretly, as we might in a private diary, those passages of books that named for us what we had deeply felt, but could not say?

I kept mine from the age of 12, turning to it to repeat those marvelous words that named me in some private way. From H. H. Munro to Dickens and Austen, to Hugo and de Maupassant, each resonant sentence would find its way into my book. (There's no point in avoiding the narcissism here: We are always transfixed by those passages that seem to read us.) Finding James Baldwin and writing him down at an Episcopal church camp in 1965—I was fifteen, and the Watts riots were raging—probably determined the direction of my intellectual life more than anything else I could name. I wrote and rewrote verbatim his elegantly framed paragraphs, full of sentences that were somehow both Henry Jamesian and King Jamesian, garbed as they were in the figures and cadences of the spirituals. Of course, we forget the private pleasures that brought us to the subject in the first place once we adopt the alienating strategies of formal analysis; our professional vanity is to insist that the study of literature be both beauty and truth, style and politics and everything in between.

In the swaddling clothes of our academic complacencies, then, few of us are prepared when we bump against something hard, and sooner or later, we do. One of the first talks I ever gave was to a packed audience at a college honors seminar, and it was one of those mistakes you don't make twice. Fresh out of graduate school, immersed in the arcane technicalities of contemporary literary theory, I was going to deliver a crunchy structuralist analysis of a slave narrative by Frederick Douglass, tracing the intricate play of its "binary oppositions." Everything was neatly schematized, formalized, analyzed; this was my Sunday-best structuralism: crisp white shirt and shiny black shoes. And it wasn't playing. If you've seen an audience glaze over, this was double glazing. Bravely, I finished my talk and, of course, asked for questions. "Yeah, brother," said a young man in the very back of the room, breaking the silence that ensued, "all we want to know is, was Booker T. Washington an Uncle Tom or not?"

The funny thing is, this happens to be an interesting question, a lot more interesting than my talk was. It raised all the big issues about the politics of style, about what it means to speak for another, about how you were to distinguish between canny subversion and simple co-optation—who was manipulating whom? And while I didn't exactly appreciate it at the time, the exchange did draw my attention, a little rudely perhaps, to the yawning chasm between our critical discourse and the traditions they discourse upon.

Obviously, some of what I'm saying is by way of *mea culpa,* because I'm speaking here as a participant in a moment of canon formation in a so-called marginal tradition. As it happens, W. W. Norton, the "canonical" anthology publisher, will be publishing *The Norton Anthology of Afro-American Literature.* The editing of this anthology has been a great dream of mine for a long time, and it represents, in the most concrete way, the project of black canon formation. But my pursuit of this project has required me to negotiate a position between those on the cultural right who claim that black literature can have no canon, no masterpieces, and those on the cultural left who wonder why anyone wants to establish the existence of a canon, any canon, in the first place.

We face the outraged reactions of those custodians of Western culture who protest that the canon, that transparent decanter of Western values, may become—breathe the word—*politicized.* That people can maintain a straight face while they protest the irruption of politics into something that has always been political—well, it says something about how remarkably successful official literary histories have been in presenting themselves as natural objects, untainted by worldly interests.

I agree with those conservatives who have raised the alarm about our students' ignorance of history. But part of the history we need to teach has to be the history of the very idea of the "canon," which involves the history both of literary pedagogy and the very institution of the school. One function of literary history is then to conceal all connections between institutionalized interests and the literature we remember. Pay no attention to the men behind the curtain, booms the Great Oz of literary history.

Cynthia Ozick once chastised feminists by warning that strategies become institutions. But isn't that really another way of warning that their strategies, Heaven forfend, may *succeed*?

Here we approach the scruples of those on the cultural left who worry about, well, the price of success. "Who's co-opting whom?" might be their slogan. To them, the very idea of the canon is hierarchical, patriarchal and otherwise politically suspect. They'd like us to disavow it altogether.

But history and its institutions are not just something we study, they're also something we live, and live through. And how effective and how durable our inventions in contemporary cultural politics will be depends upon our ability to mobilize the institutions that buttress and reproduce that culture. We could seclude ourselves from the real world and keep our hands clean, free from the taint of history. But that is to pay obeisance to the status quo, to the entrenched arsenal of sexual and racial authority, to say that things shouldn't change, become something other and, let's hope, better.

Indeed, this is one case where we've got to borrow a leaf from the right, which is exemplarily aware of the role of education in the reproduction of values. We must engage in this sort of canon reformation precisely because Mr. Bennett is correct: the teaching of literature *is* the teaching of values, not inherently, no, but contingently, yes; it is—it has become—the teaching of an esthetic and political order, in which no person of color, no woman, was ever able to discover the reflection or representation of his or her cultural image or voice. The return of "the" canon, the high canon of Western masterpieces, represents the return of an order in which my people were the subjugated, the voiceless, the invisible, the unpresented and the unrepresentable.

Let me be specific. Those of us working in my own tradition confront the hegemony of the Western tradition, generally, and of the larger American tradition, more locally, as we theorize about our tradition and engage in canon formation. Long after white American literature has been anthologized and canonized, and recanonized, our efforts to define a black American canon are often decried as racist, separatist, nationalist, or "essentialist." Attempts to derive theories about our literary tradition from the black tradition—a tradition, I might add, that must include black vernacular forms as well as written literary forms—are often greeted by our colleagues in traditional literature departments as a misguided desire to secede from a union that only recently, and with considerable kicking and screaming, has been forged. What is wrong with you people? our friends ask us in genuine passion and concern; after all, aren't we all just citizens of literature here?

Well, yes and no. Every black American text must confess to a complex ancestry, one high and low (that is, literary and vernacular) but also one white and black. There can be no doubt that white texts inform and influence black texts (and vice versa), so that a thoroughly integrated canon of American literature is not only politically sound, it is intellectually sound as well. But the attempts of black scholars to define a black American canon, and to derive indigenous theories of interpretation from within this canon, are not meant to refute the soundness of these gestures of integration. Rather, it is a question of perspective, a question of emphasis. Just as we can and must cite a black text within the larger American tradition, we can and must cite it within its own tradition, a tradition not defined by a pseudoscience of racial biology, or a mystically shared essence called blackness, but by the repetition and revision of shared themes, topoi and tropes, the call and response of voices, their music and cacophony.

And this is our special legacy: what in 1849 Frederick Douglass called the "live, calm, grave, clear, pointed, warm, sweet, melodious and powerful human voice." The presence of the past in the African-American tradition comes to us most powerfully as *voice*, a voice that is never quite our own—or *only* our own—however much we want it to be. One of my earliest childhood memories tells this story clearly.

I remember my first public performance, which I gave at the age of four in the all-black Methodist church that my mother attended, and that her mother had attended for fifty years. It was a religious program, at which each of the children of the Sunday school was to deliver a "piece"—as the people in our church referred to a religious recitation. Mine was the couplet "Jesus was a boy like me, / And like Him I want to be." Not much of a recitation, but then I *was* only four. So, after weeks of practice in elocution, hair pressed and greased down, shirt starched and pants pressed, I was ready to give my piece. I remember skipping along to the church with all of the other kids, driving everyone crazy, repeating that couplet over and over. "Jesus was a boy like me, / And like Him I want to be."

Finally we made it to the church, and it was packed—bulging and glistening with black people, eager to hear pieces, despite the fact that they had heard all of the pieces already, year after year, like bits and fragments of a repeated master text. Because I was the youngest child on the program, I was the first to go. Miss Sarah Russell (whom we called Sister Holy Ghost—behind her back, of course) started the program with a prayer, then asked if little Skippy Gates would step forward. I did so.

And then the worst happened: I completely forgot the words of my piece. Standing there, pressed and starched, just as clean as I could be, in front of just about everybody in our part of town, I could not for the life of me remember one word of that piece.

After standing there I don't know how long, struck dumb and captivated by all of those staring eyes, I heard a voice from near the back of the church proclaim, "Jesus was a boy like me, / And like Him I want to be."

And my mother, having arisen to find my voice, smoothed her dress and sat down again. The congregation's applause lasted as long as its laughter as I crawled back to my seat.

What this moment crystallizes for me is how much of my scholarly and critical work has been an attempt to learn how to speak in the strong, compelling cadences of my mother's voice. As the black feminist scholar Hortense Spillers has recently insisted, in moving words that first occasioned this very recollection, it is "the heritage of the *mother* that the African-American male must regain as an aspect of his own personhood—the power of 'yes' to the 'female' within.

To reform core curriculums, to account for the comparable eloquence of the African, the Asian and the Middle Eastern traditions, is to begin to prepare our students for their roles as citizens of a world culture, educated through a truly human notion of "the humanities," rather than—as Mr. Bennett and Mr. Bloom would have it—as guardians at the last frontier outpost of white male Western culture, the keepers of the masterpieces. And for us as scholar-critics, learning to speak in the voice of the black mother is perhaps the ultimate challenge of producing a discourse of the Other.

WHY DO WE READ?

Katha Pollitt

Katha Pollitt won the National Book Critics' Circle Award
for Poetry for her collection, *Antarctic Traveler*. She is a
well-known essayist on literary and political themes and a
contributing editor of *The Nation*, where this commentary
on the canon debate first appeared in the issue of September 23, 1991.

For the past couple of years, we've all been witness to a
furious debate about the literary canon. What books should
be assigned to students? What books should critics discuss? What books should the rest of us read—and who are
we, anyway? Like everyone else, I've given these questions
some thought and, when an invitation came my way,
leaped to produce my own manifesto. But to my surprise,
when I sat down to write—in order to discover, as E. M.
Forster once said, what I really think—I found that I agreed
with all sides in the debate at once.

Take the conservatives. Now, this rather dour collection
of scholars and diatribists—Allan Bloom, Hilton Kramer,
John Silber, and so on—are not, to my mind, a particularly
appealing group of people. They are arrogant, they are

rude, they are gloomy, they do not suffer fools gladly—and everywhere they look, fools are what they see. All good reasons not to elect them to public office, as the voters of Massachusetts recently decided. But what is so terrible, really, about what they are saying? I too believe that some books are profounder, more complex, more essential to an understanding of our culture than others; I too am appalled to think of students graduating from college not having read Homer, Plato, Virgil, Milton, Tolstoy—all writers, dead white Western men though they be, whose works have meant a great deal to me. As a teacher of literature and of writing, I too have seen at first hand how ill-educated many students are and how little aware they are of this important fact about themselves. Last year, for instance, I taught a graduate seminar in the writing of poetry. None of my students had read more than a smattering of poems by anyone, male or female, published more than ten years ago. Robert Lowell was as far outside their frame of reference as Alexander Pope. When I gently suggested to one student that it might benefit her to read some poetry if she planned to spend her life writing it, she told me that yes, she knew she should read more, but when she encountered a really good poem it only made her depressed. That contemporary writing has a history which it profits us to know in some depth, that we ourselves were not born yesterday, seems too obvious even to argue.

But ah, say the liberals, the canon exalted by the conservatives is itself an artifact of history. Sure, some books are more rewarding than others, but why can't we revise the list of which books those are? The canon itself was not always the list we know today: Until the 1920s, *Moby-Dick* was shelved with the boys' adventure stories. If T. S. Eliot could singlehandedly dethrone the Romantic poets in favor of the neglected Metaphysicals and place John Webster alongside Shakespeare, why can't we dip into the sea of stories and pluck out Edith Wharton or Virginia Woolf? And this position too makes a great deal of sense to me. After all, alongside the many good reasons why a book might end up on the required reading shelf are some rather suspect reasons why it might be excluded—because it was written by a woman and therefore presumed to be too slight; because it was written by a black person and therefore presumed to be too unsophisticated or, in any case, to reflect too special an instance. By all means, say the liberals, let's have great books and a shared culture. But let's make sure that all the different kinds of greatness are represented and that the culture we share reflects the true range of human experience.

If we leave the broadening of the canon up to the conservatives, it will never happen because, to them, change only means defeat. Look at the recent fuss over the latest edition of the Great Books series published by the Encyclopedia Britannica, headed by that old snake-oil salesman Mortimer Adler. Four women have now been added to the series: Virginia Woolf, Willa Cather, Jane Austen, and George Eliot. That's nice, I suppose, but really! Jane Austen has been a certified great writer for a hundred years! Lionel Trilling said so! There's something truly absurd about the conservatives, earnestly sitting in judgment on the illustrious dead as though up in Writers' Heaven Jane and George and Willa and Virginia were breathlessly waiting to hear if they'd finally made it into the club, while Henry Fielding, newly dropped from the list, howls in outer darkness and the Brontës, presumably, stamp their feet in frustration and hope for better luck in twenty years, when *Jane Eyre* and *Wuthering Heights* will suddenly turn out to have qualities of greatness never before detected in their pages. It's like Poets' Corner over at Manhattan's Cathedral of St. John the Divine, where mortal men—and a woman or two—of letters actually vote on which immortals to put up a plaque to—complete, no doubt, with electoral campaigns, compromise candidates, and all the rest of the underside of the literary life. "No, I'm sorry, I just can't vote for Whitman. I'm a Washington Irving man myself."

Well, being a liberal is not a very exciting thing to be, and so we have the radicals, who attack the concepts of "greatness," "shared," "culture," and "lists." (I'm overlooking here the ultra-radicals, who attack the "privileging," horrible word, of "texts," as they insist on calling books, and think one might as well spend one's college years "deconstructing," i.e., watching reruns of *Leave It to Beaver*.) Who is to say, ask the radicals, what is a great book? What's so terrific about complexity, ambiguity, historical centrality, and high seriousness? If *The Color Purple*, say, gets students thinking about their own experience, maybe they ought to read it and forget about—and here you can fill in the name of whatever classic work you yourself found dry and tedious and never got around to finishing. For the radicals, the notion of a shared culture is a lie, because it means presenting as universally meaningful and politically neutral books that reflect the interests and experiences and values of privileged white men at the expense of those of others—women, blacks, Hispanics, Asians, the working class, whatever. Why not scrap the one-list-for-everyone idea and let people connect with books that are written by people like themselves about people like themselves? It will be a more accurate reflection of a multifaceted and conflict-ridden society and do wonders for everyone's self-esteem, except, of course, for living white men—but they have too much self-esteem already.

Now, I have to say that I dislike the radicals' vision intensely. How foolish to argue that Chekhov has nothing to say to a black woman—or, for that matter, myself— merely because he is Russian, long dead, a man. The notion that one reads to increase one's self-esteem sounds to me like more snake oil: literature is not a session at the therapist's. But then I think of myself as a child, leafing through anthologies of poetry for the names of women. I never would have admitted that I needed a role model, even if that awful term had existed back in the prehistory of which I speak, but why was I so excited to find a female name, even when, as was often the case, it was attached to a poem of no interest to me whatsoever? Anna Laetitia Barbauld, author of "Life! I know not what thou art/ But know that thou and I must part!," Lady Anne Lindsay, writer of languid ballads in incomprehensible Scots dialect, and the other minor female poets included by chivalrous Sir Arthur Quiller-Couch in the old *Oxford Anthology of English Verse*—I have to admit it, just by their presence in that august volume they did something for me. And although it had nothing to do with reading or writing, it was an important thing they did.

Now, what are we to make of this spluttering debate, in which charges of imperialism are met by equally passionate accusations of vandalism, in which each side hates the others, and yet each seems to have its share of reason? It occurs to me that perhaps what we have here is one of those debates in which the opposing sides, unbeknownst to themselves, share a myopia that will turn out to be the most interesting and important feature of the whole discussion, a debate, for instance, like that of our Founding Fathers over the nature of the franchise. Think of all the energy and passion spent debating the question of property qualifications, or direct versus legislative elections, while all along, unmentioned and unimagined, was the fact—to us so central—that women and slaves were never considered for any kind of vote.

While everyone is busy fighting over the canon, something is being overlooked. That is the state of reading, and books, and literature in our country, at this time. Why, ask yourself, is everyone so hot under the collar about what to put on the required-reading shelf? It is because, while we have been arguing so fiercely about which books make the best medicine, the patient has been slipping deeper and deeper into a coma.

Let us imagine a country in which reading was a popular voluntary activity. There, parents read books for their own edification and pleasure and are seen by their children at this silent and mysterious pastime. These parents also read to their children, give them books for presents, talk to them about books, and underwrite, with their taxes, a public library system that is open all day, every day. In school—where an attractive library is invariably to be found—the children study certain books together but also have an active reading life of their own. Years later, it may even be hard for them to remember if they read *Jane Eyre* at home and Judy Blume in class or the other way around. In college, young people continue to be assigned certain books, but far more important are the books they discover for themselves browsing in the library, in bookstores, on the shelves of friends, one book leading to another, back and forth in history and across languages and cultures. After graduation, they continue to read and in the fullness of time produce a new generation of readers. Oh happy land! I wish we all lived there.

In that other country of real readers, voluntary, active, self-determined readers, a debate like the current one over the canon would not be taking place. Or if it did, it would be as a kind of parlor game: What books would *you* take to a desert island? Everyone would know that the top-ten list was merely a tiny fraction of the books one would read in a lifetime. It would not seem racist or sexist or hopelessly hidebound to put Hawthorne on the list and not Toni

Morrison. It would be more like putting oatmeal and not noodles on the breakfast menu—a choice part arbitrary, part a nod to the national past, part, dare one say it, a kind of reverse affirmative action: School might frankly *be* the place where one read the books that are a little off-putting, that have gone a little cold, that you might overlook because they do not address, in reader-friendly contemporary fashion, the issues most immediately at stake in modern life but that, with a little study, turn out to have a great deal to say. Being on the list wouldn't mean so much. It might even add to a writer's cachet *not* to be on the list, to be in one way or another too heady, too daring, too exciting to be ground up into institutional fodder for teenagers. Generations of high-school kids have been turned off to George Eliot by being forced to read *Silas Marner* at a tender age. One can imagine a whole new readership for her if grown-ups were left to approach *Middlemarch* and *Daniel Deronda* with open minds, at their leisure.

But, of course, they rarely do. In America today, the underlying assumption behind the canon debate is that the books on the list are the only books that are going to be read and if the list is dropped, *no* books are going to be read. Becoming a textbook is a book's only chance—all sides take that for granted. And so all sides agree not to mention certain things that they themselves, as highly educated people and, one assumes, devoted readers, know perfectly well. For example, that if you read only twenty-five, or fifty, or a hundred books, you can't understand them, however well-chosen they are. And that if you don't have an independent reading life—and very few students do—you won't *like* reading the books on the list and will forget them the minute you finish them. And that books have, or should have, other lives than as items in a syllabus—which is why there is now a totally misguided attempt to put current literature in the classroom. How strange to think that people need professorial help to read John Updike or Alice Walker, writers people actually *do* read for fun. But all sides agree, if it isn't taught, it doesn't count. What a peculiar notion!

Let's look at the canon question from another angle. Instead of asking what books do we want others to read, let's ask, why do we read books ourselves? I think it will become clear very quickly that the canon debaters are being a little disingenuous here, are suppressing, in the interest of their own positions, their own experience of reading. Sure, we read to understand our own American culture and history, and we also read to recover neglected masterpieces, and to learn more about the accomplishments of our subgroup and thereby, as I've admitted about myself, increase our self-esteem. But what about reading for the aesthetic pleasures of language, form, image? What about reading to learn something new, to have a vicarious adventure, to follow the workings of an interesting, if possibly skewed, narrow and ill-tempered, mind? What about reading for the story? For an expanded sense of sheer human variety? There are a thousand reasons why a book might have a claim on our time and attention, other than its canonization. I once infuriated an acquaintance by asserting that Trollope, although in many ways a lesser writer than Dickens, possessed some wonderful qualities Dickens lacked: a more realistic view of women, a more skeptical view of good intentions, a subtler sense of humor—a drier vision of life that I myself found congenial. You'd think I'd advocated throwing Dickens out and replacing him with a toaster. Because Dickens is a certified Great Writer, and Trollope is not.

Am I saying anything different than what Randall Jarrell said in his great 1953 essay, "The Age of Criticism"? Not really, so I'll quote him. Speaking of the literary social gatherings of the era, Jarrell wrote: "If, at such parties, you wanted to talk about *Ulysses* or *The Castle* or *The Brothers Karamazov* or *The Great Gatsby* or Graham Greene's last novel—Important books—you were at the right place. (Though you weren't so well off if you wanted to talk about *Remembrance of Things Past.* Important, but too long.) But if you wanted to talk about Turgenev's novelettes, or *The House of the Dead,* or *Lavengro,* or *Life on the Mississippi,* or *The Old Wives' Tale,* or *The Golovlyov Family,* or Cunningham-Grahame's stories, or Saint-Simon's memoirs, or *Lost Illusions,* or *The Beggar's Opera,* or *Eugen Onegin,* or *Little Dorrit,* or the *Burnt Njal Saga,* or *Persuasion,* or *The Inspector-General,* or *Oblomov,* or *Peer Gynt,* or *Far From the Madding Crowd,* or *Out of Africa,* or the *Parallel Lives,* or *A Dreary Story,* or *Debits and Credits,* or *Arabia Deserta,* or *Elective Affinities,* or *Schweik,* or—any of a thousand good or interesting but Unimportant books, you couldn't expect a very ready knowledge or sympathy from most of the readers there. They had looked at the big sights, the current sights, hard, with guides and glasses; and those walks in the country, over unfrequented or thrice-familiar territory, all alone—those walks from which most of the joy and good of reading come—were walks that they hadn't gone on very often."

I suspect that most canon debaters have, in fact, taken those solitary rambles, if only out of boredom—how many times, after all, can you reread the *Aeneid,* or *Mrs. Dalloway,* or *Cotton Comes to Harlem* (to pick one book from each column)? But those walks don't count, because of another assumption all sides hold in common. And that is that the purpose of reading is not the many varied and delicious satisfactions I've mentioned; it's medicinal. The chief end of reading is to produce a desirable kind of person and a desirable kind of society—a respectful high-minded citizen of a unified society for the conservatives, an up-to-date and flexible sort for the liberals, a subgroup-identified, robustly confident one for the radicals. How pragmatic, how moralistic, how American! The culture debaters turn out to share a secret suspicion of culture itself, as well as the anti-pornographer's belief that there is a simple, one-to-one correlation between books and behavior. Read the conservatives' list and produce a nation of sexists and racists—or a nation of philosopher kings. Read the liberals' list and produce a nation of spineless relativists—or a nation of open-minded world citizens. Read the radicals' list, and produce a nation of psychobabblers and ancestor-worshippers—or a nation of stalwart proud-to-be-me pluralists.

But is there any list of a few dozen books that can have such a magical effect, for good or for ill? Of course not. It's like arguing that the perfectly nutritional breakfast cereal is enough food for the whole day. And so the canon debate is really an argument about what books to cram down the resistant throats of a resentful captive populace of students—and the trick is never to mention the fact that, under such circumstances, one book is as good, or as bad, as another. Because, as the debaters know from their own experience as readers but never acknowledge because it would count against all sides equally, books are not pills that produce health when ingested in measured doses. Books do not shape character in any simple way, if indeed they do so at all, or the most literate would be the most virtuous instead of just the ordinary run of humanity with larger vocabularies. Books cannot mold a common national purpose when, in fact, people are honestly divided about what kind of country they want—and are divided, moreover, for very good and practical reasons, as they always have been.

For these burly purposes, books are all but useless. The way books affect us is an altogether more subtle, delicate, wayward, and individual, not to say private, affair. And that reading, at the present moment, is being made to bear such an inappropriate and simplistic burden speaks to the poverty both of culture and of frank political discussion in our time.

On his deathbed, Dr. Johnson—once canonical, now more admired than read—is supposed to have said to a friend who was energetically rearranging his bedclothes, "Thank you, this will do all that a pillow can do." One might say that the canon debaters are all asking of their handful of chosen books that they do a great deal more than any handful of books can do.

PART THREE

FREE
SPEECH
AND
SPEECH
CODES

"Speech Codes" on the Campus and Problems of Free Speech

Nat Hentoff

Nat Hentoff, the veteran battler for free speech and other causes, is a columnist at *The Village Voice* and *The Washington Post* and a staff writer at *The New Yorker*. He published this article in *Dissent*, Fall 1991.

During three years of reporting on anti–free-speech tendencies in higher education, I've been at more than twenty colleges and universities—from Washington and Lee and Columbia to Mesa State in Colorado and Stanford.

On this voyage of initially reverse expectations—with liberals fiercely advocating censorship of "offensive" speech and conservatives merrily taking the moral high ground as champions of free expression—the most dismaying moment of revelation took place at Stanford.

In the course of a two-year debate on whether Stanford, like many other universities, should have a speech code punishing language that might wound minorities, women, and gays, a letter appeared in the *Stanford Daily*. Signed by the African-American Law Students Association, the Asian-American Law Student Association, and the Jewish Law Students Association, the letter called for a harsh code. It reflected the letter and the spirit of an earlier declaration by Canetta Ivy, a black leader of student government at Stanford during the period of the grand debate. "We don't put as many restrictions on freedom of speech," she said, "as we should."

Reading the letter by this rare ecumenical body of law students (so pressing was the situation that even Jews were allowed in), I thought of twenty, thirty years from now. From so bright a cadre of graduates, from so prestigious a law school would come some of the law professors, civic leaders, college presidents, and even maybe a Supreme Court Justice of the future. And many of them would have learned—like so many other university students in the land—that censorship is okay provided your motives are okay.

The debate at Stanford ended when the president, Donald Kennedy, following the prevailing winds, surrendered his previous position that once you start telling people what they can't say, you will end up telling them what they can't think. Stanford now has a speech code.

This is not to say that these gags on speech—every one of them so overboard and vague that a student can violate a code without knowing he or she has done so—are invariably imposed by student demand. At most colleges, it is the administration that sets up the code. Because there have been racist or sexist or homophobic taunts, anonymous notes or graffiti, the administration feels it must *do something*. The cheapest, quickest way to demonstrate that it cares is to appear to suppress racist, sexist, homophobic speech.

Usually, the leading opposition among the faculty consists of conservatives—when there is opposition. An exception at Stanford was law professor Gerald Gunther, arguably the nation's leading authority on constitutional law. But Gunther did not have much support among other faculty members, conservative or liberal.

At the University of Buffalo Law School, which has a code restricting speech, I could find just one faculty member who was against it. A liberal, he spoke only on condition that I not use his name. He did not want to be categorized as a racist.

On another campus, a political science professor for whom I had great respect after meeting and talking with him years ago, has been silent—students told me—on what Justice William Brennan once called "the pall of orthodoxy" that has fallen on his campus.

When I talked to him, the professor said, "It doesn't happen in my class. There's no 'politically correct' orthodoxy here. It may happen in other places at this university, but I don't know about that." He said no more.

One of the myths about the rise of P.C. (politically correct) is that, coming from the left, it is primarily intimidating conservatives on campus. Quite the contrary. At almost every college I've been, conservative students have their own newspaper, usually quite lively and fired by a muckraking glee at exposing "politically correct" follies on campus.

By and large, those most intimidated—not so much by the speech codes themselves but by the Madame Defarge-like spirit behind them—are liberal students and those who can be called politically moderate.

I've talked to many of them, and they no longer get involved in class discussions where their views would go against the grain of P.C. righteousness. Many, for instance, have questions about certain kinds of affirmative action. They are not partisans of Jesse Helms or David Duke, but they wonder whether progeny of middle-class black families should get scholarship preference. Others have a question about abortion. Most are not pro-life, but they believe that fathers should have a say in whether the fetus should be sent off into eternity.

Jeff Shesol, a recent graduate of Brown and now a Rhodes scholar at Oxford, became nationally known while at Brown because of his comic strip, "Thatch," which, not too kindly, parodied P.C. students. At a forum on free speech at Brown before he left, Shesol said he wished he could tell the new students at Brown to have no fear of speaking freely. But he couldn't tell them that, he said, advising the new students to stay clear of talking critically about affirmative action or abortion, among other things, in public.

At that forum, Shesol told me, he said that those members of the left who regard dissent from their views as racist and sexist should realize that they are discrediting their goals. "They're honorable goals," said Shesol, "and I agree with them. I'm against racism and sexism. But these people's tactics are obscuring the goals. And they've resulted in Brown no longer being an open-minded place." There were hisses from the audience.

Students at New York University Law School have also told me that they censor themselves in class. The kind of chilling atmosphere they describe was exemplified last year as a case assigned for a moot court competition became subject to denunciation when a sizable number of law students said it was too "offensive" and would hurt the feelings of gay and lesbian students. The case concerned a divorced father's attempt to gain custody of his children on the grounds that their mother had become a lesbian. It was against P.C. to represent the father.

Although some of the faculty responded by insisting that you learn to be a lawyer by dealing with all kinds of cases, including those you personally find offensive, other faculty members supported the rebellious students, praising them for their sensitivity. There was little public opposition from the other students to the attempt to suppress the case. A leading dissenter was a member of the conservative Federalist Society.

What is P.C. to white students is not necessarily P.C. to black students. Most of the latter did not get involved in the N.Y.U. protest, but throughout the country many black students do support speech codes. A vigorous exception was a black Harvard law school student during a debate on whether the law school should start punishing speech. A white student got up and said that the codes are necessary because without them, black students would be driven away from colleges and thereby deprived of the equal opportunity to get an education.

A black student rose and said that the white student had a hell of a nerve to assume that he—in the face of racist speech—would pack up his books and go home. He's been familiar with that kind of speech all his life, and he had never felt the need to run away from it. He'd handled it before and he could again.

The black student then looked at his white colleague and said that it was condescending to say that blacks have to be "protected" from racist speech. "It is more racist and insulting," he emphasized, "to say that to me than to call me a nigger."

But that would appear to be a minority view among black students. Most are convinced they do need to be protected from wounding language. On the other hand, a good many black student organizations on campus do not feel that Jews have to be protected from wounding language.

Though it's not much written about in reports of the language wars on campuses, there is a strong strain of anti-Semitism among some—not all, by any means—black students. They invite such speakers as Louis Farrakhan, the former Stokely Carmichael (now Kwame Touré), and such lesser but still burning bushes as Steve Cokely, the Chicago commentator who has declared that Jewish doctors inject the AIDS virus into black babies. That distinguished leader was invited to speak at the University of Michigan.

The black student organization at Columbia University brought to the campus Dr. Khallid Abdul Muhammad. He began his address by saying: "My leader, my teacher, my guide is the honorable Louis Farrakhan. I thought that should be said at Columbia Jewniversity."

Many Jewish students have not censored themselves in reacting to this form of political correctness among some blacks. A Columbia student, Rachel Stoll, wrote a letter to the *Columbia Spectator*: "I have an idea. As a white Jewish American, I'll just stand in the middle of a circle comprising. . . . Khallid Abdul Muhammad and assorted members of the Black Students Organization and let them all hurl large stones at me. From recent events and statements made on this campus, I gather this will be a good cheap method of making these people feel good."

At UCLA, a black student magazine printed an article indicating there is considerable truth to the *Protocols of the Elders of Zion*. For months, the black faculty, when asked their reactions, preferred not to comment. One of them did say that the black students already considered the black faculty to be insufficiently militant, and the professors didn't want to make the gap any wider. Like white liberal faculty members on other campuses, they want to be liked—or at least not too disliked.

Along with quiet white liberal faculty members, most

black professors have not opposed the speech codes. But unlike the white liberals, many honestly do believe that minority students have to be insulated from barbed language. They do not believe—as I have found out in a number of conversations—that an essential part of an education is to learn to demystify language, to strip it of its ability to demonize and stigmatize you. They do not believe that the way to deal with bigoted language is to answer it with more and better language of your own. This seems very elementary to me, but not to the defenders, black and white, of the speech codes.

Consider University of California president David Gardner. He has imposed a speech code on all the campuses in his university system. Students are to be punished—and this is characteristic of the other codes around the country—if they use "fighting words"—derogatory references to "race, sex, sexual orientation, or disability."

The term "fighting words" comes from a 1942 Supreme Court decision, *Chaplinsky* v. *New Hampshire,* which ruled that "fighting words" are not protected by the First Amendment. That decision, however, has been in disuse at the High Court for many years. But it is thriving on college campuses.

In the California code, a word becomes "fighting" if it is directly addressed to "any ordinary person" (presumably, extraordinary people are above all this). These are the kinds of words that are "inherently likely to provoke a violent reaction, *whether or not they actually do.*" (Emphasis added).

Moreover, he or she who fires a fighting word at any ordinary person can be reprimanded or dismissed from the university because the perpetrator should "reasonably know" that what he or she has said will interfere with the "victim's ability to pursue effectively his or her education or otherwise participate fully in university programs and activities."

Asked Gary Murikami, chairman of the Gay and Lesbian Association at the University of California, Berkeley: "What does it mean?"

Among those—faculty, law professors, college administrators—who insist such codes are essential to the university's purpose of making *all* students feel at home and thereby able to concentrate on their work, there has been a celebratory resort to the Fourteenth Amendment.

That amendment guarantees "equal protection of the laws" to all, and that means to all students on campus. Accordingly, when the First Amendment rights of those engaging in offensive speech clash with the equality rights of their targets under the Fourteenth Amendment, the First Amendment must give way.

This is the thesis, by the way, of John Powell, legal director of the American Civil Liberties Union, even though that organization has now formally opposed all college speech codes—after a considerable civil war among and within its affiliates.

The battle of the amendments continues, and when harsher codes are called for at some campuses, you can expect the Fourteenth Amendment—which was not intended to censor *speech*—will rise again.

A precedent has been set at, of all places, colleges and universities, that the principle of free speech is merely situational. As college administrators change, so will the extent of free speech on campus. And invariably, permissible speech will become more and more narrowly defined. Once speech can be limited in such subjective ways, more and more expression will be included in what is forbidden.

One of the exceedingly few college presidents who speaks out on the consequences of the anti–free-speech movement is Yale University's Benno Schmidt:

Freedom of thought must be Yale's central commitment. It is not easy to embrace. It is, indeed, the effort of a lifetime. . . . Much expression that is free may deserve our contempt. We may well be moved to exercise our own freedom to counter it or to ignore it. But universities cannot censor or suppress speech, no matter how obnoxious in content, without violating their justification for existence. . . .

On some other campuses in this country, values of civility and community have been offered by some as paramount values of the university, even to the extent of superseding freedom of expression.

Such a view is wrong in principle and, if extended, is disastrous to freedom of thought. . . . The chilling effects on speech of the vagueness and open-ended nature of many universities' prohibitions . . . are compounded by the fact that these codes are typically enforced by faculty and students who commonly assert that vague notions of community are more important to the academy than freedom of thought and expression. . . .

This is a flabby and uncertain time for freedom in the United States.

On the Public Broadcasting System in June, I was part of a Fred Friendly panel at Stanford University in a debate on speech codes versus freedom of expression. The three black panelists strongly supported the codes. So did the one Asian-American on the panel. But then so did Stanford law professor, Thomas Grey, who wrote the Stanford code, and Stanford president Donald Kennedy, who first opposed and then embraced the code. We have a new ecumenicism of those who would control speech for the greater good. It is hardly a new idea, but the mix of advocates is rather new.

But there are other voices. In the national board debate at the ACLU on college speech codes, the first speaker— and I think she had a lot to do with making the final vote against codes unanimous—was Gwen Thomas.

A black community college administrator from Colorado, she is a fiercely persistent exposer of racial discrimination.

She started by saying, "I have always felt as a minority person that we have to protect the rights of all because if we infringe on the rights of any persons, we'll be next."

"As for providing a nonintimidating educational environment, our young people have to learn to grow up on college campuses. We have to teach them how to deal with adversarial situations. They have to learn how to survive offensive speech they find wounding and hurtful."

Gwen Thomas is an educator—an endangered species in higher education.

FREEDOM OF HATE SPEECH

Richard Perry and Patricia Williams

Richard Perry is a researcher in linguistics at the University of Louvain, Belgium, and Patricia Williams is an associate professor of law and women's studies at the University of Wisconsin at Madison. Her recent book is *The Alchemy of Race and Rights*. The two authors published this essay as part of a symposium on political correctness in the journal *Tikkun*, July/August 1991.

Until well after the Second World War, American institutions of higher education were bastions of a sort of cheery and thoughtlessly jingoistic nativism (isn't this some part of what we've always meant when we spoke of "that old college spirit"?). Except for the historically black and women's colleges and a couple of schools serving immigrant populations (such as the City College of New York), the vast majority of the student bodies of America's hundreds of colleges were overwhelmingly U.S.-born, male, Christian, and of Northern European descent, and their faculties were even more so. The structure of the core liberal arts curriculum suggested that the university understood itself as an umpire of timeless values, high above the rough and tumble of mere politics, standing at the summit of Western civilization, which from this vantage point could be seen to have risen in an unbroken crescendo from Plato to NATO.

However, the assumptions that made the university an arbiter of "universal values" have been questioned, as multinational business and research institutions have evolved into ever more global and ethnically diverse enterprises. On the home front, meanwhile, the hard-won material gains of women and ethnic minorities have produced halting progress toward the goal of making American universities truly representative of the country's population as a whole. Responding to these historical developments, many have sought to make the core curriculum a more effective preparation for the diverse, multicultural environments of both the contemporary United States and the world. There have also been efforts to make the campus itself a more hospitable place for its newly heterogeneous population, most notably amendments to the campus conduct rules intended to discourage harassment on the basis of race, religion, ethnicity, gender, and sexual orientation.

These reform efforts have been met with a virulent backlash. This backlash has recently been fueled by a series of often scurrilous stories in the most visible national magazines and by fervent denunciations from the Left, Right, and center of political debate.

This confusion stems largely from the dishonest manner in which the debates have been reported. Most accounts of this campus dispute have been characterized by repeated distortions of fact and a profound bad faith with history. First, it is preposterous to claim, as many opponents of multiculturalism have, that these debates are about some supposed new infringement of the First Amendment rights of American citizens. No position seriously advocated by multiculturalists would have the slightest effect upon our right as Americans to be nativist, racist, anti-Semitic, sexist, homophobic, or just as narrowly monocultural-as-we-wanna-be in our personal lives. So too it remains entirely possible to stand in the public arena and call one another any of the whole litany of terms with which we as Americans have learned throughout our history to abuse one another. One might instructively compare this situation with the new Canadian constitution, which specifically limits the protection of certain kinds of hate speech, without much evidence that this provision has started Canada down that slippery slope toward being a Stalinist police state.

Nor do the multiculturalist reforms pose any institutional threat to the many securely tenured professors on the most prestigious faculties who teach doctrines (such as sociobiology and kindred theories on the margins of intellectual respectability) that are patently demeaning to members of the most long-abused groups. And the debate over multiculturalism scarcely disturbs the work of eminent scholars who regularly contrive to put a revisionist happy face upon the history of slavery, the Czarist pogroms, the Nazi genocides, the colonial subjugation of indigenous peoples, or the oppression of women.

What has *never* been true is that one member of an institution has an unrestrained legal right to harass another member and remain in the good graces of the institution.

Yet the recent barrage of media coverage would have us believe that some *novel* restriction is being imposed in multiculturalist speech and behavior codes. This misinformation has been conveyed by those who are apparently unable to distinguish between a liberty interest on the one hand and, on the other, a quite specific interest in being able to spout racist, sexist, and homophobic epithets completely unchallenged—without, in other words, the terrible inconvenience of feeling bad about it.

There is a sharp paradox at the heart of all this, a contradiction whose effective message is: "I have the right to express as much hatred as I want, so you shut up about it." It may be appropriate to defend the First Amendment rights of students who, for example, openly advocate Nazi policies. However, there has been a good deal of unacknowledged power-brokering that has informed the refusal even to think about the effect of relentless racist propagandizing on educational institutions in particular. Now those who even criticize this selective invocation of the First Amendment on the behalf of one social group over another are themselves called Nazis.

This fundamental paradox has bred a host of others. Conservatives such as George Will hurriedly discard their hallowed distinction between the public and private spheres when expediency beckons. Not long ago right-wingers were asserting that the evangelical Bob Jones University should be allowed to practice segregation and still be given a tax exemption—because it was a *private* institution. Where were these free-speech patriots in 1986 when Captain Goldman, a U.S. Air Force officer and an Orthodox Jew, was denied by the Reagan Supreme Court the right to wear a yarmulke at his desk job? And where are they now, when the new Supreme Court of our new world order has just asserted that the government *can* control speech between doctor and patient—heretofore one of the most sacred of privacy privileges—when the clinic receives federal funds and the topic of conversation is reproductive choice?

These ironies of free-speech opportunism have been accompanied by a breathtaking effort to rewrite our history. The multiculturalist reforms on campus have been characterized as being at odds with the two moral touchstones of recent political memory: the World War II-era fight against Nazi theory of Aryan supremacy and the American anti-slavery and civil rights movements. Both of these struggles were in fact fought over—among other things—the sort of contested social meanings that can be traced directly to the present university discussions. The new interpretation of these two contests, however, rewrites them as triumphs of the inevitable, forward-marching progress of modern liberal individualism. Commentators from George Will to Shelby Steele have consistently depicted Martin Luther King, Jr., for example, as having pursued the higher moral ground of individual achievement rather than the validation of African-American collective social identity—as though these notions were inherently in opposition to one another. We are to imagine, for example, that the brave people who faced fire hoses and police dogs and who sat-in at lunch counters in the 1950s and 1960s were after nothing more than, say, the market freedom of an individual black American to eat a grilled cheese sandwich in the company of raving bigots. Conservative opponents of multiculturalism would have us forget about the other part of that struggle: the fight to expand the social space of all blacks and to re-articulate the political semantics of the collective identity of the descendants of slaves.

Another striking paradox is the way that much of this backlash proceeds in the name of democratic values, while mounting a sustained assault precisely on the democratic process of academic self-governance. The academic Right devotes itself to attacks on changes in curricula and conduct codes that have been adopted only after lengthy deliberation and votes by the faculty senates (such as in the Stanford Western civilization reforms or the Berkeley ethnic studies requirement), administrative committees, or student bodies. More curiously still, these assaults are typically said to be conducted in defense of something like "a free marketplace of ideas." Yet the recent multiculturalist changes might accurately be viewed as shifts in an intellectual marketplace where several positions have been rising in value, while another, older position, adamantly refusing to innovate, has been steadily losing its market share. There is a certain irony, therefore, in the spectacle of William Bennett and company engaged in a kind of status brokerage, trading on their appointed positions of authority for advantage they cannot gain via democratic votes in faculty senates or in the governing bodies of professional organizations.

Such distortions of the debate have worked to obscure what could be a genuine opportunity. The market idea, considered not simply as the nineteenth-century social-Darwinist mechanism whereby big fish eat little fish for the greater good, might serve as a multidimensional matrix for the representation of certain types of social information. If, for example, we could ever get to the point where we can honestly speak of having achieved a level playing-field in the marketplace of ideas (for this is precisely what is at stake in the present debates), then we might begin to understand the market as one means of representing multicentered networks of social interaction. Just as the American monetary system went off the gold standard in 1934, it is now time to get off the traditional *rational man* standard (the straight, white, male, Christian, English-speaking, middle-class individualist) as the universal measure of humanity. It is time to initiate a *perestroika* of personhood—to make a world in which all of us, in our multiple, overlapping, individual and collective identities can come to terms.

THERE'S NO SUCH THING AS FREE SPEECH AND IT'S A GOOD THING, TOO

Stanley Fish

Stanley Fish, who is a professor of English and law at Duke University, is a well-known literary theorist and Milton scholar. He is the author of *Doing What Comes Naturally: Change, Rhetoric, and the Practise of Theory in Literary and Legal Studies*. His article is an excerpt from an essay-in-progress that will, in its fuller version, consider Supreme Court cases and opposing arguments in detail.

"Nowadays the First Amendment is the first refuge of scoundrels."

—Samuel Johnson and Stanley Fish

Not far from the end of his *Aereopagitica*, and after having celebrated the virtues of toleration and unregulated publication in passages that find their way into every discussion of free speech and the First Amendment, John Milton catches himself up short and says, of course I didn't mean Catholics, them we exterminate:

> I mean not tolerated popery, and open superstition, which as it extirpates all religious and civil suprem-acies, so itself should be extirpated . . . that also which is impious or evil absolutely against faith or manners no law can possibly permit that intends not to unlaw itself.

Notice that Milton is not simply stipulating a single excep-tion to a rule generally in place; the kinds of utterance that might be regulated and even prohibited on pain of trail and punishment comprise an open set; popery is named only as a particularly perspicuous instance of the advocacy that cannot be tolerated. No doubt there are other forms of speech and action that might be categorized as "open superstitions" or as subversive of piety, faith, and manners, and presumably these too would be candidates for "extir-pation." Nor would Milton think himself culpable for hav-ing failed to provide a list of unprotected utterances. The list will fill itself out as utterances are put to the test implied by his formulation: Would this form of speech or advocacy, if permitted to flourish, tend to undermine the very pur-poses for which our society is constituted? One cannot answer this question with respect to a particular utterance in advance of its emergence on the world's stage; rather, one must wait and ask the question in the full context of its production and (possible) dissemination. It might ap-pear that the result would be ad hoc and unprincipled, but for Milton the principle inheres in the core values in whose name men of like mind come together in the first place. Those values, which include the search for truth and the promotion of virtue, are capacious enough to accommodate a diversity of views. But at some point—again impossible of in-advance specification—capaciousness will threaten to become shapelessness, and at that point fidelity to the original values will demand acts of extirpation.

I want to say that all affirmations of freedom of expression are like Milton's, dependent for their force on an
exception that literally carves out the space in which
expression can then emerge. I do not mean that expression
(saying something) is a realm whose integrity is sometimes
compromised by certain restrictions but that restriction, in
the form of an underlying articulation of the world that
necessarily (if silently) negates alternatively possible articulations, is constitutive of expression. Without restriction,
without an in-built sense of what it would be meaningless
to say or wrong to say, there could be no assertion and no
reason for asserting it. The restriction or the exception
comes first, and the expression, *shaped* by the exception,
then follows. It is in relation to the underlying and constituting exception that speech is recognized as intolerable.
Speech, in short, is never and could not be an independent
value, but is always asserted against a background of some
assumed conception of the good to which it must yield in
the event of conflict. When the pinch comes (and sooner
or later it will always come) and the institution (be it
church, state, or university) is confronted by behavior
subversive of its core rationale, it will respond by declaring
"of course we mean not tolerated ⸺, that we extir-
pate"; not because an exception to a general freedom has
suddenly and contradictorily been announced but because
the freedom has never been general and has always been
understood against the background of an originary exclusion that gives it meaning.

This is a large thesis, but before tackling it directly I
want to buttress my case with another example, taken not
from the seventeenth century but from the charter and
case law of Canada. Canadian thinking about freedom of
expression departs from the line usually taken in the
United States in ways that bring that country very close to
the *Areopagitica* as I have expounded it. The differences

are fully on display in a recent landmark case, *R. V. Keegs-tra*. James Keegstra was a high school teacher in Alberta who, it was established by evidence, "systematically denigrated Jews and Judaism in his classes." He described Jews as treacherous, subversive, sadistic, money-loving, power-hungry, and child-killers. He declared them "responsible for depressions, anarchy, chaos, wars, and revolution" and required his students "to regurgitate these notions in essays and examinations." Keegstra was indicted under section 319(2) of the Criminal Code and convicted. The Court of Appeal reversed, and the Crown appealed to the Supreme Court, which reinstated the lower court's verdict.

Section 319(2) reads in part, "Every one who, by communicating statements other than in private conversation, willfully promotes hatred against any identifiable group is guilty of . . . an indictable offense and is liable to imprisonment for a term not exceeding two years." In the United States, this provision of the code would almost certainly be struck down because, under the First Amendment, restrictions on speech are apparently prohibited without qualification. To be sure, the Canadian charter has its own version of the First Amendment, in section 2(b): "Everyone has the following fundamental freedoms . . . (b) freedom of thought, belief, opinion, and expression, including freedom of the press and other media of communication." But section 2(b), like every other section of the charter, is qualified by section 1: "The Canadian Charter of Rights and Freedoms guarantees the rights and freedoms set out in it subject only to such reasonable limits prescribed by law as can be demonstrably justified in a free and democratic society." Or in other words, every right and freedom herein granted can be trumped if its exercise is found to be in conflict with the principles that underwrite the society.

This is what happens in *Keegstra,* as the majority finds

that section 319(2) of the Criminal Code does in fact violate the right of freedom of expression guaranteed by the charter but is nevertheless a *permissible* restriction because it accords with the principles proclaimed in section 1. There is, of course, a dissent which reaches the conclusion that would have been reached by most, if not all, U.S. courts; but even in dissent the minority is faithful to Canadian ways of reasoning, accepting the contextualism that contrasts so markedly with the categorical absolutism of American First Amendment law. Like the majority, the minority assumes that "freedom of expression must in certain circumstances give way to countervailing considerations"; it just doesn't believe that the present case is one of those circumstances. "The question," it declares, "is always one of balance," and thus even when a particular infringement of Charter section 2(b) has been declared unconstitutional, as it would have been by the minority, the question remains open with respect to the next case. In the United States the question is presumed closed and can be pried open only by special tools. In our legal culture as it is presently constituted, if one yells "free speech" in a crowded courtroom and makes it stick, the case is over.

Of course, it is not that simple. Despite the apparent absoluteness of the First Amendment, there are any number of ways to getting around it, ways that are known to every student of the law. In general, the strategy is to manipulate the distinction between speech and action which is at bottom a distinction between inconsequential and consequential behavior. In Archibald Cox's formulation, the First Amendment protects "expressions separable from conduct harmful to other individuals and the community." The difficulty of managing this segregation is well known: Speech always seems to be crossing the line into action where it becomes, at least potentially, consequential. In the face of this categorical instability, First

Amendment theorists and jurists fashion a distinction within the distinction: Some forms of speech are not really speech because they have a tendency to incite violence; they are, as the court declares in *Chaplinsky* v. *New Hampshire* (1941), "fighting words," words "likely to provoke the average person to retaliation, and thereby cause a breach of the peace."

The trouble with this definition is the following: It distinguishes not between fighting words and words that remain safely and merely expressive but between words that are provocative to one group (the group that falls under the rubric "average person") and words that might be provocative to other groups, groups of persons not now considered average. And if you ask what words are likely to be provocative to those non-average groups, what are likely to be *their* fighting words, the answer is anything and everything, for as Justice Holmes said long ago (in *Gitlow* v. *New York*), every idea is an incitement to somebody, and since ideas come packaged in sentences, in words, every sentence is potentially, in some situation that might occur tomorrow, a fighting word and therefore a candidate for regulation. That is why the doctrine of "fighting words" has always been a problematic tool since its appearance in 1941; for there is nothing to prevent the category from being extended to everything which would lead us to the conclusion (in fact, my conclusion) that there is nothing for the First Amendment to protect, no such thing as "speech alone" or speech separable from harmful conduct, no such thing as "mere speech" or the simple nonconsequential expression of ideas. It would follow that when a court rules in the name of these nonexistent things, it is really doing something else; it is deciding to permit certain harms done by words because it believes that by permitting them it upholds a value greater than the value of preventing them. This will not be the value of speech but of whatever set of concerns is judged by the court to outweigh the concerns of those who find a form of speech assaultive.

At this point a First Amendment purist might ask, "Why couldn't that overriding concern be the protection of speech?" "Why couldn't freedom of speech be the greater value to which other values must yield in the event of a clash?" The answer is that freedom of expression would be a primary value only if it didn't matter what was said, didn't matter in the sense that no one gave a damn, but just liked to hear talk. There are contexts like that, a Hyde Park corner or a radio talk show where people get to sound off for the sheer fun of it. These, however, are special contexts, artificially bounded spaces designed to ensure that talking is not taken seriously. In ordinary contexts, talk is produced with the goal of trying to move the world in one direction rather than another. In these contexts—the contexts of everyday life—you go to the trouble of asserting that x is y only because you suspect that some people are asserting that x is z or that x doesn't exist. You assert, in short, because you give a damn, not about assertion—as if it were a value in and of itself—but about what your assertion is about. It may seem paradoxical, but free expression could only be a primary value if what you are valuing is the right to make noise; but if you are engaged in some purposive activity in the course of which speech happens to be produced, sooner or later you will come to a point when you decide that some forms of speech do not further but endanger that purpose.

Take the case of universities and colleges. Could it be the purpose of such places to encourage free expression? If the answer were "yes," it would be hard to say why there would be any need for classes, or examinations, or departments, or disciplines or libraries, since freedom of expression requires nothing but a soapbox or an open telephone line. The very fact of the university's machinery—of the events, rituals and procedures that fill its calendar—argues for some other, more substantive, purpose. There can be, of course, disputes as to just what that purpose is, but let me offer what I hope will be a noncontroversial (because minimal) stipulation of it as "the investigation and study of matters of fact and interpretation." In relation to that purpose (which will be realized differently in different kinds of institutions), the flourishing of free expression will in almost all circumstances be an obvious good; but in some circumstances, freedom of expression may pose a threat to that purpose, and at that point, it may be necessary to discipline or regulate speech, lest, to paraphrase Milton, the institution were to sacrifice itself to one of its accidental features.

Interestingly enough, the same conclusion is reached (inadvertently) by Congressman Henry Hyde, who is addressing these very issues in a recently offered amendment to Title VI of the Civil Rights Act. The first section of the amendment states its purpose, to protect "the free speech rights of college students" by prohibiting private as well as public educational institutions from "subjecting any student to disciplinary sanctions solely on the basis of conduct that is speech." The second section enumerates the remedies available to students whose speech rights may have been abridged; and the third, which is to my mind the nub of the matter, declares as an exception to the amendment's jurisdiction any "educational institution that is controlled by a religious organization," on the reasoning that the application of the amendment to such institutions "would not be consistent with the religious tenets of such organizations." In effect, what Congressman Hyde is saying is that at the heart of these colleges and universities is a set of beliefs, and it would be wrong to require them to tolerate behavior, including speech behavior, inimical to those beliefs. But insofar as this logic is persuasive, it applies across the board; for all educational institutions rest on some set of beliefs—no institution is "just there" independent of any purpose—and it is hard to see why the rights of an institution to protect and preserve its basic "tenets" should be restricted only to those that are religiously controlled. Read strongly, the third section of the amendment undoes sections one and two—the exception becomes, as it always was, the rule—and points us to a balancing test very much like that employed in Canadian law: Given that any college or university is informed by a core rationale, an administrator faced with complaints about offensive speech should ask whether damage to the core would be greater if the speech were tolerated or regulated, or, in other words (words Milton might have used), is the spirit of the enterprise strengthened or threatened by the protection of this kind of expression? Since an educational setting is one in which expression is privileged by definition (as opposed, for example, to the settings of military or medical activities), the presumption will normally be in favor of its protection, but the presumption is not absolute and can be overriden, as in Canadian law, by a judgment (difficult and imprecise) that is is outweighed by a danger.

The objection to this line of reasoning is well known and has recently been reformulated by Benno Schmidt, president of Yale University. According to Schmidt, speech codes on campuses constitute "well-intentioned but misguided efforts to give values of community and harmony a higher place than freedom" (*Wall Street Journal*, May 6, 1991). "When the goals of harmony collide with freedom of expression," he continues, "freedom must be the paramount obligation of an academic community." The flaw in this logic is on display in the phrase "academic community"; for the phrase recognizes what Schmidt would deny, that expression occurs only in communities, if not in an academic community, then in a shopping mall community or a dinner-party community or an airplane-ride community or an office community. Arguments like Schmidt's get their purchase only by imagining expression occurring in *no* community, in an environment without the pervasive pressures and pressurings that come along with any socially organizing activity. The same (impossibly) quarantined and pristine space is the location of his preferred value, freedom, which in his conception is not freedom *for* anything but just "freedom," an urge without direction, as expression is for him an emission without assertive content. Of course the speech to which campus codes are a response is full of content and productive of injury but Schmidt is able to skirt this difficulty by reducing the content to a matter of style and the injury to an offense against sensibility. This is the work done by the word "obnoxious" when Schmidt urges us to protect speech "no matter how obnoxious in content." In this formulation, obnoxiousness becomes the content of the speech and the deeper affront that might provoke efforts to curtail it is pushed into the background. "Obnoxious" suggests that the injury or offense is a surface one that a large-minded ("liberated and humane") person should be able to tolerate if not embrace. The idea that the effects of speech can penetrate to the core—either for good or for ill—is never entertained; everything is kept on the level of weightless verbal exchange; there is no sense of the lacerating harms that speech of certain kinds can inflict.

To this Schmidt would no doubt reply, as he does in his essay, that harmful speech should be answered not by regulation but by more speech; but that would make sense only if the effects of speech could be canceled out by additional speech, only if the pain and humiliation caused by racial or religious epithets could be ameliorated by saying something like, "So's your old man." What Schmidt fails to realize at every level of his argument is that expression is more than a matter or proffering and receiving propositions, that words do work in the world of a kind that cannot be confined to a purely cognitive realm of "mere" ideas.

There could, however, be still another turn to the argument. A holder of a Schmidt-like position could acknowledge the extent of the damage done by speech and even acknowledge that the remedy provided by the opportunity to talk back will be inadequate to the injury but complain that I have too instrumental a view of the work words do. That is, I am too focused on short-run outcomes and fail to understand that the work assigned by the First Amendment to speech has its fruition not in the present but in a future whose emergence regulation could only inhibit. This line of reasoning would also have the advantage of blunting one of my key points, that speech in and of itself cannot be a value and is only worth worrying about if it is in the service of something with which it cannot be identical. My mistake, it could be said, is to equate the something in whose service speech is with some locally espoused value (e.g., the end of racism, the empowerment of disadvantaged minorities), whereas in fact we should think of that something as a now inchoate shape that will be given firm lines only by time's pencil. That is why the shape now receives such indeterminate characterizations (e.g., true self-fulfillment, a more perfect polity, a more capable citizenry, a less partial truth); we cannot now know it, and therefore we must not prematurely fix it in ways that will bind successive generations to error.

This forward-looking view of what the First Amendment protects has a great appeal, in part because it continues in a secular form the Puritan celebration of millenarian hopes, but it imposes a requirement so severe that one would expect more justification than is usually provided. The requirement is that we endure whatever pain racist and hate speech inflicts for the sake of a future whose emergence we can only take on faith. In a specifically religious vision like Milton's, this makes perfect sense (it is indeed the whole of Christianity), but in the context of a politics that puts its trust in the world and not in the Holy Spirit, it raises more questions than it answers and could be seen as the other prong of a strategy designed to delegitimize the complaints of victimized groups. The first strategy, as I have noted, is to define speech in such a way as to render it inconsequential (on the model of "sticks and stones will break my bones, but . . ."); the second strategy is to acknowledge the (often grievous) consequences but declare that we must suffer them in the name of something that cannot be named.

I find both strategies unpersuasive, but my own skepticism concerning them is less important than the fact that in general they seem to have worked; in the parlance of the marketplace (a parlance First Amendment commentators love), many in the society seemed to have bought them. Why? The answer, I think, is that people cling to First Amendment pieties because they do not wish to face what they take to be the alternative. That alternative is politics, the realization (at which I have already hinted) that decisions about what is and is not protected in the realm of expression will rest not on principle or firm doctrine but on the ability of persons and groups to so operate (some would say manipulate) the political process that the speech they support is labelled "protected" while the speech inimical to their interests is declared to be fair game. It is from this realization that First Amendment commentators recoil, saying things like "this could render the First Amendment a dead letter," or "this would leave us with no normative guidance in determining when and what speech to protect," or "this effaces the distinction between speech and action," or "this is incompatible with any viable notion of freedom of expression." To these statements (culled more or less at random from recent law review pieces) I would reply that the First Amendment has always been a dead letter if one understood its "liveness" to depend on the identification and protection of a realm of "mere" expression or discussion distinct from the realm of regulatable conduct; that the distinction between speech and action has always been effaced in principle, although in practice it can take whatever form the prevailing political conditions mandate; that we have never had any normative guidance for marking off protected from unprotected speech; rather, that the guidance we have has been fashioned (and refashioned) in the very political struggles over which it then (for a time) presides. In short, the name of the game has always been politics, even when (indeed, especially when) it is played by stigmatizing politics as the area to be avoided.

It is important to be clear as to what this means. It does *not* mean that in the absence of normative guidelines we should throw up our hands and either regulate everything or allow everything. Rather it means that the question of whether or not to regulate will always be a local one and that we can not rely on abstractions that are either empty of content or filled with the content of some partisan agenda to generate a "principled" answer. Instead we must be frankly ad hoc in our consideration of what is at stake and what are the risks and gains of alternative courses of action. In the course of this consideration many things will be of help, but among them will not be phrases like "freedom of speech" or "the right of individual expression," which, at least as they are used now, tend to obscure rather than clarify our dilemmas. Once they are removed or (more possibly) deprived of their talismanic force, once it is no longer strategically effective simply to invoke them in the act of walking away from a problem, the conversation could continue in directions that are now blocked by conceptual will-o-the-wisps. To the student reporter who complains that in the wake of the promulgation of a speech code at the University of Wisconsin there is now something in the back of his mind as he writes, one could reply, "There was always something in the back of your mind and perhaps it might be better to have this code in the back of your mind than whatever was in there before." And when someone warns about the slippery slope and predicts mournfully that if you restrict one form of speech, you never know what will be restricted next, one could reply, "Some form of speech is always being restricted; else there could be no meaningful assertion; we have always and already slid down the slippery slope; someone is always going to be restricted next, and it is your job to make sure that the someone is not you." And when someone observes, as someone surely will, that anti-harassment codes chill speech, one could reply that since speech becomes intelligible only against the background of what isn't being said, the background of what has already been silenced, the only question is the political one of which speech is going to be chilled, and, all things considered, it seems a good thing to chill speech like "nigger," "cunt," "kike," and "faggot." And if someone then says, "But what happened to free-speech principles?," one could say what I have now said a dozen times—free speech principles don't exist except as a component in a bad argument in the context of which their invocation will often be a mask for motives that would not withstand close scrutiny.

This sounds sweeping and even corrosive, but it is time to acknowledge that the content of this essay has been less startling than its title may have suggested. When I say that there is no such thing as free speech, I mean that there is no class of utterances separable from the world of conduct, no "merely" cognitive expressions whose effects can be confined to some prophylactically sealed area of public discourse. And since it is just such expressions that are privileged by the First Amendment (it is expressions free of certain consequences that are to be freely allowed), there is nothing for the amendment to protect, no items in the category "free expression." That is the bad news. The good news is that precisely *because* there is nothing in the category of "free expression," speech always matters; because everything we say impinges on the world in ways indistinguishable from the effects of physical action, we must take responsibility for our verbal performances and not assume that they are being taken care of by a clause in the Constitution. Of course with responsibility come risks, but they have always been our risks, and no doctrine of free speech has ever insulated us from them. They are the risks of either allowing or policing the flow of discourse. They are the risks, respectively, of permitting speech that does obvious harm and of shutting off speech in ways that might deny us the benefit of Joyce's *Ulysses* or Lawrence's *Lady Chatterly's Lover* or Titian's paintings. Nothing, I repeat, can insulate us from those risks. And, moreover, nothing can provide us with a principle for deciding which risk in the long run is the best to take. I am persuaded that at the present moment, right now, the risk of not attending to hate speech is greater than the risk that by regulating it we will deprive ourselves of valuable voices and insights or slide down the slippery slope toward tyranny. This is a judgment for which I can offer reasons but no guarantees. All I am saying is that the judgments of those who would come down on the other side carry no guarantees either and cannot claim the support of the abstractions that usually accompany them. It is not that there are no choices to make or means of making them; it is just that the choices as well as the means are inextricable from the din and confusion of partisan struggle. There is no safe place.

PART FOUR

TEXAS SHOOT-OUT

Nowhere has political correctness been debated more fiercely than at the University of Texas, Austin. Here are three documents pertaining to that debate. The three documents do not pretend to represent every one of the positions that emerged, but they do suggest the range of opinion and something of the atmosphere.

THE STATEMENT OF THE BLACK FACULTY CAUCUS

Ted Gordon and Wahneema Lubiano

This essay on multiculturalism at the University of Texas appeared in a slightly different form in the *Daily Texan*, May 3, 1990. It was written by Ted Gordon, who is an assistant professor of anthropology, and Wahneema Lubiano, who has subsequently moved from the University of Texas to Princeton, where she is assistant professor of English.

Multiculturalism is not a tourist's eye view of "ethnicity," nor is it a paean to the American mythology defining this nation as a collection of diverse and plural groups living happily together and united by their knowledge of, and proper respect for, something called "Western culture." Multiculturalism, as an organizing principle to which universities are increasingly paying at least lip service, is understood at its most simplistic to mean exposure to different cultures. Simple exposure, however, is absolutely meaningless without a reconsideration and restructuring of the ways in which knowledge is organized, disseminated, and used to support inequitable power differentials.

Within the parameters of the present University hierarchical power structure, multiculturalism—an idea whose time has apparently come—can be thoroughly appropriated, diluted, and neutralized so that the domination of Eurocentric areas of knowledge remains completely unchallenged. The concept can be as useless as the idea of the melting pot where multiple cultures are thrown together in such a way that the end result isn't recognizable as anything in particular and the issues raised by the presence of diverse cultures, racial groups, gender groups, and power relations among these groups get ignored.

In the name of multiculturalism, for example, any university can simply continue business as usual by making available a smorgasbord of "ethnic" or "racially specific" courses without ever addressing the ways in which the focus of what we understand as "Western" culture has a political relationship to the way in which our world is constructed.

Nonetheless, to some limited extent, this University *is* multicultural—the racial constituencies that represent the multiplicity of American culture are present here in some numbers, but their presence is not empowered within the institution, and the specific knowledges that inhere within the terms of those cultures have no consistent curricular presence or force. Therefore, in order for multiculturalism to be something other than an empty abstraction used by administrators to take political heat off the institution, those of us interested in a transformative multiculturalism must insist that it cannot be held to exist within dominance.

In other words, if there are present at the University

people from various minority groups, and some minority or "ethnic" courses are made available within the terms of degree requirements, are we practicing multiculturalism if minority groups are not represented adequately within the various levels of *authority*—from the Board of Regents through the faculty? No. Research universities such as this one are in the business of investments, of initiating and cooperating in corporate business projects, of producing research that contributes to the way in which the United States shapes and contributes to the world economy. Therefore, it is important that minority people be part of *all* levels of the University chain of command, that they be an empowered presence at the levels of policy-making in order to insert different perspectives into the kinds of the decisions that the University as a corporate entity makes— decisions as whether or not to invest in South Africa, whether or not to focus on high-tech military research instead of contributing to research on meeting U.S. housing needs, and other such vexed issues. Further, as a corporate entity, the University is an employer of many kinds of laborers. A transformative multiculturalism project ought to address its relations to staff workers and their racial, gender, and class makeup.

Multiculturalism requires more than the perspective of non-dominant groups, more than the representations of specific histories and cultural expressions, more than additional numbers of minority faculty, staff and students. It requires that the curricula of the "West," as it is currently understood, be placed under scrutiny and transformed in order to fairly represent the variegated nature of American culture; it requires that materials and knowledge from marginalized groups be a part of degree and area requirements; it requires that "minority" people be empowered here. Dictatorial lines of power not only maintain the politics of the status quo, but they ensure that those with power stay safely distant from and unchanged by the ongoing complexities and challenges of multiculturalism.

Multiculturalism forces us to ask hard questions. How do we ensure that traditional courses do not remain strong-holds of dominance? If areas that are considered part of "Western" culture are to be transformed in order to more fully represent the real diversity of the "West," how do we ensure that faculty, within the boundaries of such courses, who might be presenting materials outside of their own area of knowledge, do so with attention to the ways in which those materials exist within their originating cultures?

If American literature, for example, is to be enlarged so as to include representative texts from "minority" groups, how do those groups' perspectives get into the course if the person teaching American literature is a "non-minority" person? A critical mass of "minority" people *empowered at all levels* could contest unfair and inadequate representations.

Additional questions raise their heads. How do we make specific minority courses available when the numbers of minority faculty nationally remain insufficient? How, for example, does the University address problems of the relatively small number of specialists in African-American literature available and the even smaller numbers currently in the academic pipeline? And if minority professors can function in "traditional" fields by virtue of their exposure to Eurocentric educational systems, are non-minority professors, educated within that same system, able to work in minority fields? Our thinking is that such cross-cultural work is possible, but difficult, and, as we argue above, such work depends upon the presence of a critical mass of people of color (at all levels of the University) who could *contest* what we felt to be unfair or inadequate use of the materials.

Nonetheless, we need to keep in mind an understanding that under the best circumstances, given the present political realities, Euro-Americans teaching the materials of people of color cannot make the University multicultural because multiculturalism demands empowered *people* of color as well as empowered *areas* of knowledge. What we're describing is a continuing process that includes elements of self and mutual critiques, a process that builds multicultural perspectives into all aspects of the curriculum, especially those courses generally considered "traditional."

This work, by definition, must be undertaken in part by Euro-American scholars, also; unfortunately, however, that participation is problematized by virtue of the fact that Euro-American scholars are products of the same educational system as the students they would be asked to "enlighten" in the name of a multiculturalist agenda. How can they teach students what some of them have not yet learned themselves? In other words, how do we deal with the relation of faculty members to their own undergraduate and graduate histories? What has to be created is an atmosphere of critique and exchange that evolves into the education of Euro-American faculty as part of a multicultural agenda.

Following this argument, the Black Faculty Caucus has a specific multicultural agenda. . . . We set out below detailed recommendations for multiculturalism here at the university. It must be understood from the outset that we are arguing here, finally, for a transformative, not reformist project. Making multiculturalism work requires radical changes because the present system can neither accommodate the magnitude of systemic alterations necessary, nor can it act as a catalyst for creative construction.

Since multiculturalism as a concrete reality requires bodies, an increase in the minority representation at all levels of the University in proportion to their presence in the general population of Texas is necessary. In order for this representation to be a reality, the University and other universities have to be willing to actively address the problems. Because the elite research universities are not producing enough "minority" scholars, the present trend among them is to go "raiding" each others' faculties. We suggest instead that this University turn its attention both to places that fall outside of the top "tier" or the two top tiers of elite research centers and to the historically black colleges and universities, places which graduate the majority of black Ph.Ds.

Further, departments can commit themselves to aggressive on-site training. Minority graduate students from other places and from within this institution can be brought into departments to establish themselves while they finish their graduate work. These suggestions are radical departures from current practices, but adhering to current practices will ensure that the problem of minority faculty representation will go unredressed throughout the twenty-first century. The process could also be the model for the recruitment of administrators. Multiculturalism demands increased numbers of and retained minority faculty and administrators; however, and most importantly, it demands their empowerment. That empowerment is needed because their work will be threefold:

1) They will produce and teach specific knowledges.

2) They will contest dominant knowledges.

3) They will participate in decision-making processes in the corporate university.

The problem of increasing the number of and retaining a higher percentage of minority undergraduate and graduate students will require the same kind of innovation, aggressive focus, and material support. The University could intervene at the high school level, or even below it, in order to help students prepare themselves for undergraduate education; it could also establish links with historically Black colleges and universities like Prairie View and Huston-Tillotson as a way of facilitating the entrance of African-American students, for example, into graduate and professional schools. These kinds of programs have been undertaken already at other universities in the United States.

Multiculturalism at the level of curriculum does not just make available information about the cultures of specific groups, but places such information within a world context; it ensures that students see themselves against a panorama of world and social formations. No one can be educated within the terms of their own limited reality, without looking at the ways in which groups have interacted with each other. Marginalized cultures and groups are objects of domination; multiculturalism, therefore, requires examination of issues of race, gender, class, and sexuality. That is to say, multiculturalism is not just about what constitutes culture, but how power is wielded between cultures and the ways in which cultures reflect racial diversity, the ways in which culture is organized by contemporary and historical politics.

Specifically in regard to curriculum restructuring we have four areas of concern.

1) All aspects of the University curriculum have to be subjected to critique and reformation in order to ensure that the curriculum reflects not only the presence of multiple cultures in specific bodies of knowledge, but also the ways in which those presences have to be inserted *now* because of the *historical* reasons for their absences.

2) A multiculturalist project requires a critique and reformation—not elimination—of generally required "traditional" courses such as American history and Texas government in order to reflect the complexities of minority

cultures' participation in those discourses and their relation to the ways in which those subject areas have themselves historically marginalized minority knowledge and
engagements.

3) Degree and area requirements should be transformed so that undergraduate students are required to take
two minority studies courses.

One course would be based on an examination of a
particular group within the American context—a focus on
a significant American minority group but with attention
to the ways in which the relations between groups are
customarily masked. Such a course would not just present
and consider alternative aesthetic appreciation or cultural
enrichment, but would deal with the ways in which that
group comes to be constructed against the dominant
group.

The second course would be based on a particular
group within the *world* context. It would not be a broad
survey of a number of cultures, but would focus on one
culture in order to teach students about the diversity of
human experience in a world context that examines a
specific cultural situation with attention to the ways in
which issues of social formations (race, gender, class, and
sexuality) are played out in contexts that are outside of the
students' immediate reality.

4) Graduate students should be required to take a
course that critiques the formation of disciplinary canons,
methodologies, and discourses. Given the fact that graduate programs produce the faculty of the future, who will in
turn be required to participate in multicultural programs
at other colleges and universities, UT graduate students
need to become aware of the manner in which their own
disciplines have historically reproduced the power differentials that result in minority cultures' marginal status

within the academy and within the terms of our social formation.

What we are talking about here is no less than transforming the University into a center of multicultural learning: anything less continues a system of education that ultimately reproduces racism and racists.

RADICAL ENGLISH

George F. Will

In the spring of 1990, a policy committee of the University of Texas proposed a new syllabus for the freshman writing requirement, English 306, to be called "Writing About Difference." The course aroused so much opposition on the part of members of the National Association of Scholars and other critics that the entire policy committee felt obliged to resign.

Part of the argument revolved around a textbook edited by Paula Rothenberg called *Racism and Sexism: An Integrated Study*, which at first was going to be assigned to students but later was dropped. Here is a nationally syndicated commentary from September 16, 1990, by George F. Will, the columnist, discussing the course and the textbook.

At the University of Texas in Austin, as on campuses across the country, freshmen are hooking up their stereos and buckling down to the business of learning what they should have learned in high school—particularly English composition. Thousands of young Texans will take English 306, the only required course on composition. The simmering controversy about that course illustrates the political tensions that complicate, dilute, and sometimes defeat higher education today.

Last summer an attempt was made to give a uniform political topic and text to all sections of E306. It was decided that all sections would read *Racism and Sexism,* an anthology of writings with a pronounced left-wing slant.

The text explains that a nonwhite "may discriminate against white people or even hate them" but cannot be called "racist." The book's editor, a New Jersey sociologist, sends her students to make "class analysis of shopping malls." "They go to a boutiquey mall and a mall for the masses. I have them count how many public toilets are in each and bring back samples of the toilet paper. It makes class distinctions visible."

After some faculty members protested the subordination of instruction to political indoctrination, that text was dropped and the decision about recasting E306 was postponed until next year. But the pressure is on for political content, thinly disguised under some antiseptic course title such as "Writing about Difference—Race and Gender."

Such skirmishes in the curricula wars occur because campuses have become refuges for radicals who want universities to be as thoroughly politicized as they are. Like broken records stashed in the nation's attic in 1968, these politicized professors say:

America is oppressive, imposing subservience on various victim groups. The culture is permeated with racism, sexism, heterosexism, classism (oppression of the working class), so the first task of universities is "consciousness-raising." This is done with "diversity education," which often is an attempt to produce intellectual uniformity by promulgating political orthodoxy.

Such "value clarification" aims at the moral reformation of young people who are presumed to be burdened with "false consciousness" as a result of being raised within the "hegemony" of America's "self-perpetuating power structure."

The universities' imprimatur is implicitly bestowed on a particular view of American history, a political agenda, and specific groups deemed authoritative regarding race, sex, class, etc.

This orthodoxy is reinforced—and enforced—by codes of conduct called "anti-harassment" codes, under which designated groups of victims are protected from whatever they decide offends them. To cure the offensiveness of others, therapists and thought police are proliferating on campuses, conducting "racial awareness seminars" and other "sensitivity training."

These moral tutors have a professional interest in the exacerbation of group tensions, to which university administrations contribute by allowing, even encouraging, the Balkanization of campus life. This is done by encouraging group identities—black dorms, women's centers, gay studies, etc.

The status of victim is coveted as a source of moral dignity and political power, so nerves are rubbed raw by the competitive cultivation of grievances. The more brittle campus relations become, the more aggressive moral therapy becomes, making matters worse.

The attempt to pump E306 full of politics is a manifestation of a notion common on campuses: Every academic activity must have an ameliorative dimension, reforming society and assuaging this or that group's grievance. From that idea, it is but a short step down the slippery slope to this idea: All education, all culture, is political, so it should be explicitly so.

And any academic purpose is secondary to political consciousness-raising. The classroom is an "arena of struggle" and teaching should be grounded in the understanding that even teaching English composition is a political activity.

Recently at the University of Michigan, a teacher's description of a freshman composition course said that writing skills should be learned "in connection to social and political contexts" so "all of the readings I have selected focus on Latin America, with the emphasis on the U.S. government's usually detrimental role in Latin American politics . . . damning commentary on the real meaning of U.S. ideology . . . responsibility for 'our' government's often brutal treatment of. . . ." And so on.

This, remember, for a course on composition. But, then, the teacher is candid about sacrificing writing skills to indoctrination: "Lots of reading . . . Consequently, I will assign considerable (sic) less writing than one would normally expect . . ."

On other campuses, writing requirements are reduced to the mere writing of a journal, a virtually standardless exercise in "self-expression" that "empowers" students. This is regarded as political liberation because rules of grammar and elements of style are "political" stratagems reinforcing the class structure to the disadvantage of the underclass, which has its own rich and authentic modes of expression from the streets.

So it goes on many campuses. The troubles at Texas are, as yet, mild. But the trajectory is visible: down. So is the destination: political indoctrination supplanting education.

CRITICS OF ATTEMPTS TO DEMOCRATIZE THE CURRICULUM ARE WAGING A CAMPAIGN TO MISREPRESENT THE WORK OF RESPONSIBLE PROFESSORS

Paula Rothenberg

Here is a reply to George F. Will's column by Paula Rothenberg, the editor of the textbook that was singled out for criticism. The reply ran in *The Chronicle of Higher Education*, April 10, 1991.

Paula Rothenberg is director of the New Jersey Project, a statewide curriculum-transformation project financed by the New Jersey Department of Higher Education. She is also professor of philosophy and women's studies at the William Paterson College of New Jersey.

I remember watching hearings of the House Un-American Activities Committee on television as a very young girl, sharing my mother's horror at the way in which Wisconsin Senator Joseph McCarthy trampled on the Bill of Rights. I knew kids whose parents were public-school teachers who had hidden books away in the cellar or destroyed them for fear of being accused wrongly of some amorphous crime and losing their jobs.

Later, I was moved to tears by Eric Bentley's dramatization of the hearings, which I heard on the radio. I have read endless accounts of that terrible time of redbaiting and blacklisting, ranging from the much-publicized stories of Lillian Hellman and Dashiell Hammett to the recent article in *The New York Times Magazine* by television producer Mark Goodson, father of a childhood friend and classmate. Each one chills my soul.

Imagine my feeling then, when I picked up the December 24 issue of *Newsweek* and found the cover story on integrating issues of race and gender into college curricula asking the question, "Is This the New Enlightenment—or the New McCarthyism?" and referring to my own book, *Racism and Sexism: An Integrated Study* (St. Martin's Press, 1988) as the "primer of politically correct thought." In fact, rather than trying to direct thought into approved channels, the book is an interdisciplinary text designed to allow students and teachers to examine the comprehensive and interconnected nature of racism, sexism, and class privilege within the United States. It employs scholarly writings from the humanities and social sciences, Supreme Court decisions and other historical documents, newspaper and magazine articles, poetry, and fiction.

But I suppose I should not have been surprised by the headline. Three months earlier George Will, in a nationally syndicated column, had announced "Political Indoctrination Supplants Education in Nation's Universities," referring to me (mistakenly) as a "New Jersey sociologist" (my graduate training was in philosophy) and describing some of my work in terms so ludicrous they would have been funny were the man not so widely read or his conclusions so dangerous.

Earlier, *The New York Times,* as well as *The Chronicle,* had reported on the decision at the University of Texas at Austin to use my book as the primary text in its required composition course—and the subsequent retraction of that decision in response to political pressure from inside and outside the university. Since that time, a steady stream of articles on "politically correct" thought have appeared in countless national, regional, and local publications. None of them, whether news stories or opinion pieces, makes even a pretense of presenting a fair and balanced account of the issues; each of them seems content to repeat the same set of half-truths and distortions being circulated by the National Association of Scholars, a Princeton-based organization of academics seemingly committed to curricula based on the Orwellian slogans: *War Is Peace, Freedom Is Slavery,* and *Ignorance Is Strength.*

For example, the writer of an article in *The New Republic* reduced the comments I had made during a lengthy telephone interview to a single sentence that misrepresented what I had said. The article reported that I couldn't name a single book that was so racist and sexist that it should be dropped from the canon. In fact, when asked to specify such works during the interview, I had refused on the grounds that transforming the college curriculum was not about banning books. I had added that other teachers might use very effectively books that I might find objectionable. Needless to say, this comment did not appear in the article.

In response to a curriculum-reform movement that seeks to expand the horizons of students' learning to include all peoples and all places, the N.A.S. and other opponents of a multicultural, gender-balanced curriculum propose the continued silencing of all but a tiny fraction of the world's population. They have so little faith in this nation's potential to realize the democratic values we have so long espoused that they mistakenly believe that identifying the racism and sexism in our past and present will weaken this nation rather than strengthen it. They have even managed to persuade some people that those who seek to decrease the violence of our language and our behavior somehow seek to limit the Bill of Rights rather than to extend its protections to all.

Recoiling in horror from those who advocate a critical reading of Shakespeare or Milton (I thought scholarship was about critical readings), they show no equivalent concern for the peoples and cultures rendered invisible by the traditional curriculum. At another time in history opponents' attempts to misrepresent so completely the goals of curriculum reform might well have attracted little serious attention; at this moment they have gained a hearing because they express the collective fears of a small but still dominant group within the academy that sees its continued power and privilege in jeopardy. What exactly is the critique of the traditional curriculum they have tried so hard to silence—and failing that—to misrepresent? How does the traditional curriculum serve their interests and perpetuate their power?

The traditional curriculum teaches all of us to see the world through the eyes of privileged, white, European males and to adopt their interests and perspectives as our own. It calls books by middle-class, white, male writers "literature" and honors them as timeless and universal, while treating the literature produced by everyone else as idiosyncratic and transitory. The traditional curriculum introduces the (mythical) white, middle-class, patriarchal, heterosexual family and its values and calls it "Introduction to Psychology." It teaches the values of white men of property and position and calls it "Introduction to Ethics." It reduces the true *majority* of people in this society to "women and minorities" and calls it "political science." It teaches the art produced by privileged white men in the West and calls it "art history."

The curriculum effectively defines this point of view as "reality" rather than as a point of view itself, and then assures us that it and it alone is "neutral" and "objective." It teaches all of us to use white male values and culture as the standard by which everyone and everything else is to be measured and found wanting. It defines "difference" as "deficiency" (deviance, pathology). By building racism, sexism, heterosexism, and class privilege into its very definition of "reality," it implies that the current distribution of wealth and power in the society, as well as the current distribution of time and space in the traditional curriculum, reflects the natural order of things.

In this curriculum, women of all colors, men of color, and working people are rarely if ever subjects or agents. They appear throughout history at worst as objects, at best as victims. According to this curriculum, only people of color have a race and only women have a gender, only lesbians and gays have a sexual orientation—everyone else is a human being. This curriculum values the work of killing and conquest over the production and reproduction of life. It offers abstract, oppositional thinking as the paradigm for intellectual rigor.

The traditional curriculum is too narrow. It leaves out too much. Its narrow approach to defining knowledge implies that people who look different, talk differently, and embrace different cultural practices are not studied because they have nothing to teach "us."

Not content to debate curriculum reform in a straight-forward and intellectually honest fashion, the opponents of such reform are mounting a nationwide campaign to smear and misrepresent the work of responsible teachers and scholars all across the country who are committed to democratizing the curriculum. After serving as "thought police" for generations, effectively silencing the voices and issues of all but a few, they now attempt to foist that label on the very forces in the university seeking to expand, rather than to contract, the discourse. The opponents of curriculum reform seek to effectively ban books like my own that, among other things, survey U.S. history by asking students to read our Constitution, Supreme Court decisions, and other public documents so that the "founding fathers" and their descendants can speak for themselves. Perhaps their fear is justified. I read the *Dred Scott* decision in ninth grade and have never been the same since.

And what of white males' scholarship and perspectives in this new and evolving curriculum? Will there be a place for them? The question is absurd, and the need to answer it reflects how far the misrepresentations have gone. The perspectives and contributions of that group are valid and valuable: there is much to be learned from them. The difficulty is not with their inclusion but with the exclusion of everyone else. The difficulty is with universalizing that experience and those interests.

Yes, *Newsweek,* there may well be a new McCarthyism. If so, it is coming directly from the irresponsible right and its fellow travelers. How ironic that those who actively attempt to dictate what books students will and will not read portray themselves as defenders of academic freedom. How ironic that those of us seeking to make the curriculum and campus climate *less* racist, *less* sexist, and *less* heterosexist are portrayed as threats to democratic freedoms rather than their champions. But in the end, war is *not* peace, slavery is *not* freedom, and no matter what the N.A.S. may believe, ignorance is *not* strength.

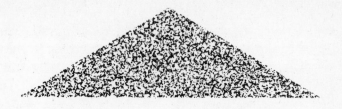

PART FIVE

THE
PUBLIC
SCHOOLS

MULTICULTURALISM:
E PLURIBUS PLURES

Diane Ravitch

Diane Ravitch, the Assistant United States Secretary of Education, published this essay in *The American Scholar* in the Summer 1990 issue. She is the author of, among other books, *The Troubled Crusade: American Education, 1945–1980*.

Questions of race, ethnicity, and religion have been a perennial source of conflict in American education. The schools have often attracted the zealous attention of those who wish to influence the future, as well as those who wish to change the way we view the past. In our history, the schools have been not only an institution in which to teach young people skills and knowledge but an arena where interest groups fight to preserve their values, or to revise the judgments of history, or to bring about fundamental social change. In the nineteenth century, Protestants and Catholics battled over which version of the Bible should be used in school, or whether the Bible should be used at all. In recent decades, bitter racial disputes—

provoked by policies of racial segregation and discrimination—have generated turmoil in the streets and in the schools. The secularization of the schools during the past century has prompted attacks on the curricula and textbooks and library books by fundamentalist Christians, who object to whatever challenges their faith-based views of history, literature, and science.

Given the diversity of American society, it has been impossible to insulate the schools from pressures that result from differences and tensions among groups. When people differ about basic values, sooner or later those disagreements turn up in battles about how schools are organized or what the schools should teach. Sometimes these battles remove a terrible injustice, like racial segregation. Sometimes, however, interest groups politicize the curriculum and attempt to impose their views on teachers, school officials, and textbook publishers. Across the country, even now, interest groups are pressuring local school boards to remove myths and fables and other imaginative literature from children's readers and to inject the teaching of creationism in biology. When groups cross the line into extremism, advancing their own agenda without regard to reason or to others, they threaten public education itself, making it difficult to teach any issues honestly and making the entire curriculum vulnerable to political campaigns.

For many years, the public schools attempted to neutralize controversies over race, religion, and ethnicity by ignoring them. Educators believed, or hoped, that the schools could remain outside politics; this was, of course, a vain hope since the schools were pursuing policies based on race, religion, and ethnicity. Nonetheless, such divisive questions were usually excluded from the curriculum. The textbooks minimized problems among groups and taught a sanitized version of history. Race, religion, and ethnicity were presented as minor elements in the American saga;

slavery was treated as an episode, immigration as a sidebar, and women were largely absent. The textbooks concentrated on presidents, wars, national politics, and issues of state. An occasional "great black" or "great woman" received mention, but the main narrative paid little attention to minority groups and women.

With the ethnic revival of the 1960s, this approach to the teaching of history came under fire, because the history of national leaders—virtually all of whom were white, Anglo-Saxon, and male—ignored the place in American history of those who were none of the above. The traditional history of elites had been complemented by an assimilationist view of American society, which presumed that everyone in the American melting pot would eventually lose or abandon those ethnic characteristics that distinguished them from mainstream Americans. The ethnic revival demonstrated that many groups did not want to be assimilated or melted. Ethnic studies programs popped up on campuses to teach not only that "black is beautiful" but also that every other variety of ethnicity is "beautiful" as well; everyone who had "roots" began to look for them so that they too could recover that ancestral part of themselves that had not been homogenized.

As ethnicity became an accepted subject for study in the late 1960s, textbooks were assailed for their failure to portray blacks accurately; within a few years, the textbooks in wide use were carefully screened to eliminate bias against minority groups and women. At the same time, new scholarship about the history of women, blacks, and various ethnic minorities found its way into the textbooks. At first, the multicultural content was awkwardly incorporated as little boxes on the side of the main narrative. Then some of the new social historians (like Stephan Thernstrom, Mary Beth Norton, Gary Nash, Winthrop Jordan, and Leon Litwack) themselves wrote textbooks, and the main narrative itself began to reflect a broadened historical understanding of race, ethnicity, and class in the American past. Consequently, today's history textbooks routinely incorporate the experiences of women, blacks, American Indians, and various immigrant groups.

Although most high school textbooks are deeply unsatisfactory (they still largely neglect religion, they are too long, too encyclopedic, too superficial, and lacking in narrative flow), they are far more sensitive to pluralism than their predecessors. For example, the latest edition of Todd and Curti's *Triumph of the American Nation,* the most popular high school history text, has significantly increased its coverage of blacks in America, including profiles of Phillis Wheatley, the poet; James Armistead, a revolutionary war spy for Lafayette; Benjamin Banneker, a self-taught scientist and mathematician; Hiram Revels, the first black to serve in the Congress; and Ida B. Wells-Barnett, a tireless crusader against lynching and racism. Even better as a textbook treatment is Jordan and Litwack's *The United States,* which skillfully synthesizes the historical experiences of blacks, Indians, immigrants, women, and other groups into the mainstream of American social and political history. The latest generation of textbooks bluntly acknowledges the racism of the past, describing the struggle for equality by racial minorities while identifying individuals who achieved success as political leaders, doctors, lawyers, scholars, entrepreneurs, teachers, and scientists.

As a result of the political and social changes of recent decades, cultural pluralism is now generally recognized as an organizing principle of this society. In contrast to the idea of the melting pot, which promised to erase ethnic and group differences, children now learn that variety is the spice of life. They learn that America has provided a haven for many different groups and has allowed them to maintain their cultural heritage or to assimilate, or—as is often the case—to do both; the choice is theirs, not the state's. They learn that cultural pluralism is one of the norms of a free society; that differences among groups are a national resource rather than a problem to be solved. Indeed, the unique feature of the United States is that its common culture has been formed by the interaction of its subsidiary cultures. It is a culture that has been influenced over time by immigrants, American Indians, Africans (slave and free) and by their descendants. American music, art, literature, language, food, clothing, sports, holidays, and customs all show the effects of the commingling of diverse cultures in one nation. Paradoxical though it may seem, the United States has a common culture that is multicultural.

Our schools and our institutions of higher learning have in recent years begun to embrace what Catharine R. Stimpson of Rutgers University has called "cultural democracy," a recognition that we must listen to a "diversity of voices" in order to understand our culture, past and present. This understanding of the pluralistic nature of American culture has taken a long time to forge. It is based on sound scholarship and has led to major revisions in what children are taught and what they read in school. The new history is—indeed, must be—a warts-and-all history; it demands an unflinching examination of racism and discrimination in our history. Making these changes is difficult, raises tempers, and ignites controversies, but gives a more interesting and accurate account of American history. Accomplishing these changes is valuable, because there is also a useful lesson for the rest of the world in America's relatively successful experience as a pluralistic society. Throughout human history, the clash of different cultures, races, ethnic groups, and religions has often been the cause of bitter hatred, civil conflict, and international war. The ethnic tensions that now are tearing apart Lebanon, Sri Lanka, Kashmir, and various republics of the Soviet Union remind us of the costs of unfettered group rivalry. Thus, it is a matter of more than domestic importance that we closely examine and try to understand that part of our national history in which different groups competed, fought, suffered, but ultimately learned to live together in relative peace and even achieved a sense of common nationhood.

Alas, these painstaking efforts to expand the understanding of American culture into a richer and more varied tapestry have taken a new turn, and not for the better. Almost any idea, carried to its extreme, can be made pernicious, and this is what is happening now to multiculturalism. Today, pluralistic multiculturalism must contend with a new, particularistic multiculturalism. The pluralists seek a richer common culture; the particularists insist that no common culture is possible or desirable. The new particularism is entering the curriculum in a number of school systems across the country. Advocates of particularism propose an ethnocentric curriculum to raise the self-esteem and academic achievement of children from racial and ethnic minority backgrounds. Without any evidence, they claim that children from minority backgrounds will do well in school *only* if they are immersed in a positive, prideful version of their ancestral culture. If children are of, for example, Fredonian ancestry, they must hear that Fredonians were important in mathematics, science, history, and literature. If they learn about great Fredonians and if their studies use Fredonian examples and Fredonian concepts, they will do well in school. If they do not, they will have low self-esteem and will do badly.

At first glance, this appears akin to the celebratory activities associated with Black History Month or Women's History Month, when schoolchildren learn about the achievements of blacks and women. But the point of those celebrations is to demonstrate that neither race nor gender is an obstacle to high achievement. They teach all children that everyone, regardless of their race, religion, gender, ethnicity, or family origin, can achieve self-fulfillment, honor, and dignity in society if they aim high and work hard.

By contrast, the particularistic version of multicultural-ism is unabashedly filiopietistic and deterministic. It teaches children that their identity is determined by their "cultural genes." That something in their blood or their race memory or their cultural DNA defines who they are and what they may achieve. That the culture in which they live is not their own culture, even though they were born here. That American culture is "Eurocentric," and there-fore hostile to anyone whose ancestors are not European. Perhaps the most invidious implication of particularism is that racial and ethnic minorities are not and should not try to be part of American culture; it implies that American culture belongs only to those who are white and European; it implies that those who are neither white nor European are alienated from American culture by virtue of their race or ethnicity; it implies that the only culture they do belong to or can ever belong to is the culture of their ancestors, even if their families have lived in this country for genera-tions.

The war on so-called Eurocentrism is intended to foster self-esteem among those who are not of European descent. But how, in fact, is self-esteem developed? How is the sense of one's own possibilities, one's potential choices, devel-oped? Certainly, the school curriculum plays a relatively small role as compared to the influence of family, commu-nity, mass media, and society. But to the extent that curriculum influences what children think of themselves, it should encourage children of all racial and ethnic groups to believe that they are part of this society and that they should develop their talents and minds to the fullest. It is enormously inspiring, for example, to learn about men and women from diverse backgrounds who overcame poverty, discrimination, physical handicaps, and other obstacles to achieve success in a variety of fields. Behind every such biography of accomplishment is a story of heroism, perseverance, and self-discipline. Learning these stories will encourage a healthy spirit of pluralism, of mutual respect, and of self-respect among children of different backgrounds. The children of American society today will live their lives in a racially and culturally diverse nation, and their education should prepare them to do so.

The pluralist approach to multiculturalism promotes a broader interpretation of the common American culture and seeks due recognition for the ways that the nation's many racial, ethnic, and cultural groups have transformed the national culture. The pluralists say, in effect, "American culture belongs to us, all of us; the U.S. is us, and we remake it in every generation." But particularists have no interest in extending or revising American culture; indeed, they deny that a common culture exists. Particularists reject any accommodation among groups, any interactions that blur the distinct lines between them. The brand of history that they espouse is one in which everyone is either a descendant of victims or oppressors. By doing so, ancient hatreds are fanned and recreated in each new generation. Particularism has its intellectual roots in the ideology of ethnic separatism and in the black nationalist movement. In the particularist analysis, the nation has five cultures: African-American, Asian-American, European-American, Latino/Hispanic, and Native American. The huge cultural, historical, religious, and linguistic differences within these categories are ignored, as is the considerable inter-marriage among these groups, as are the linkages (like gender, class, sexual orientation, and religion) that cut across these five groups. No serious scholar would claim that all Europeans and white Americans are part of the same culture, or that all Asians are part of the same culture, or that all people of Latin American descent are of the same culture, or that all people of African descent are of the same culture. Any categorization this broad is essentially meaningless and useless.

Several districts—including Detroit, Atlanta, and Washington, D.C.—are developing an Afrocentric curriculum. *Afrocentricity* has been described in a book of the same name by Molefi Kete Asante of Temple University. The Afrocentric curriculum puts Africa at the center of the student's universe. African-Americans must "move away from an [*sic*] Eurocentric framework" because "it is difficult to create freely when you use someone else's motifs, styles, images, and perspectives." Because they are not Africans, "white teachers cannot inspire in our children the visions necessary for them to overcome limitations." Asante recommends that African-Americans choose an African name (as he did), reject European dress, embrace African religion (not Islam or Christianity), and love "their own" culture. He scorns the idea of universality as a form of Eurocentric arrogance. The Eurocentrist, he says, thinks of Beethoven or Bach as classical, but the Afrocentrist thinks of Ellington or Coltrane as classical; the Eurocentrist lauds Shakespeare or Twain, while the Afrocentrist prefers Baraka, Shange, or Abiola. Asante is critical of black artists like Arthur Mitchell and Alvin Ailey who ignore Afrocentricity. Likewise, he speaks contemptuously of a group of black university students who spurned the Afrocentrism of the local Black Student Union and formed an organization called Inter-race: "Such madness is the direct consequence of self-hatred, obligatory attitudes, false assumptions about society, and stupidity."

The conflict between pluralism and particularism turns on the issue of universalism. Professor Asante warns his readers against the lure of universalism: "Do not be captured by a sense of universality given to you by the Eurocentric viewpoint; such a viewpoint is contradictory to your own ultimate reality." He insists that there is no alternative to Eurocentrism, Afrocentrism, and other ethnocentrisms. In contrast, the pluralist says, with the Roman playwright Terence, "I am a man: nothing human is alien to me." A contemporary Terence would say "I am a person" or might be a woman, but the point remains the same: You don't have to be black to love Zora Neale Hurston's fiction or Langston Hughes's poetry or Duke Ellington's music. In a pluralist curriculum, we expect children to learn a broad and humane culture, to learn about the ideas and art and animating spirit of many cultures. We expect that children, whatever their color, will be inspired by the courage of people like Helen Keller, Vaclav Havel, Harriet Tubman, and Feng Lizhe. We expect that their response to literature will be determined by the ideas and images it evokes, not by the skin color of the writer. But particularists insist that children can learn only from the experiences of people from the same race.

Particularism is a bad idea whose time has come. It is also a fashion spreading like wildfire through the education system, actively promoted by organizations and individuals with a political and professional interest in strengthening ethnic power bases in the university, in the education profession, and in society itself. One can scarcely pick up an educational journal without learning about a school district that is converting to an ethnocentric curriculum in an attempt to give "self-esteem" to children from racial minorities. A state-funded project in a Sacramento high school is teaching young black males to think like Africans and to develop the "African Mind Model Technique," in order to free themselves of the racism of American culture. A popular black rap singer, KRS-One, complained in an op-ed article in the *New York Times* that the schools should be teaching blacks about their cultural heritage, instead of trying to make everyone Americans. "It's like trying to teach a dog to be a cat," he wrote. KRS-One railed about having to learn about Thomas Jefferson and the Civil War, which had nothing to do (he said) with black history.

Pluralism can easily be transformed into particularism, as may be seen in the potential uses in the classroom of the Mayan contribution to mathematics. The Mayan example was popularized in a movie called *Stand and Deliver*, about a charismatic Bolivian-born mathematics teacher in Los Angeles who inspired his students (who are Hispanic) to learn calculus. He told them that their ancestors invented the concept of zero; but that wasn't all he did. He used imagination to put across mathematical concepts. He required them to do homework and to go to school on Saturdays and during the Christmas holidays, so that they might pass the Advanced Placement mathematics examination for college entry. The teacher's reference to the Mayans' mathematical genius was a valid instructional device: It was an attention-getter and would have interested even students who were not Hispanic. But the Mayan example would have had little effect without the teacher's insistence that the class study hard for a difficult examination.

Ethnic educators have seized upon the Mayan contribution to mathematics as the key to simultaneously boosting the ethnic pride of Hispanic children and attacking Eurocentrism. One proposal claims that Mexican-American children will be attracted to science and mathematics if they study Mayan mathematics, the Mayan calendar, and Mayan astronomy. Children in primary grades are to be taught that the Mayans were first to discover the zero and that Europeans learned it long afterwards from the Arabs, who had learned it in India. This will help them see that Europeans were latecomers in the discovery of great ideas. Botany is to be learned by study of the agricultural techniques of the Aztecs, a subject of somewhat limited relevance to children in urban areas. Furthermore, "ethnobotanical" classifications of plants are to be substituted for the Eurocentric Linnaean system. At first glance, it may seem curious that Hispanic children are deemed to have no cultural affinity with Spain; but to acknowledge the cultural tie would confuse the ideological assault on Eurocentrism.

This proposal suggests some questions: Is there any evidence that the teaching of "culturally relevant" science and mathematics will draw Mexican-American children to the study of these subjects? Will Mexican-American children lose interest or self-esteem if they discover that their ancestors were Aztecs or Spaniards, rather than Mayans? Are children who learn in this way prepared to study the science and mathematics that are taught in American colleges and universities and that are needed for advanced study in these fields? Are they even prepared to study the science and mathematics taught in *Mexican* universities? If the class is half Mexican-American and half something else, will only the Mexican-American children study in a Mayan and Aztec mode or will all the children? But shouldn't all children study what is culturally relevant for them? How will we train teachers who have command of so many different systems of mathematics and science?

The efficacy of particularist proposals seems to be less important to their sponsors than their value as ideological weapons with which to criticize existing disciplines for their alleged Eurocentric bias. In a recent article titled "The Ethnocentric Basis of Social Science Knowledge Production" in the *Review of Research in Education*, John

Stanfield of Yale University argues that neither social science nor science are objective studies, that both instead are "Euro-American" knowledge systems which reproduce "hegemonic racial domination." The claim that science and reason are somehow superior to magic and witchcraft, he writes, is the product of Euro-American ethnocentrism. According to Stanfield, current fears about the misuse of science (for instance, "the nuclear arms race, global pollution") and "the power-plays of Third World nations (the Arab oil boycott and the American-Iranian hostage crisis) have made Western people more aware of nonscientific cognitive styles. These last events are beginning to demonstrate politically that which has begun to be understood in intellectual circles: namely, that modes of social knowledge such as theology, science, and magic are different, not inferior or superior. They represent different ways of perceiving, defining, and organizing knowledge of life experiences." One wonders: If Professor Stanfield broke his leg, would he go to a theologian, a doctor, or a magician?

Every field of study, it seems, has been tainted by Eurocentrism, which was defined by a professor at Manchester University, George Ghevarughese Joseph, in *Race and Class* in 1987, as "intellectual racism." Professor Joseph argues that the history of science and technology—and in particular, of mathematics—in non-European societies was distorted by racist Europeans who wanted to establish the dominance of European forms of knowledge. The racists, he writes, traditionally traced mathematics to the Greeks, then claimed that it reached its full development in Europe. These are simply Eurocentric myths to sustain an "imperialist/racist ideology," says Professor Joseph, since mathematics was found in Egypt, Babylonia, Mesopotamia, and India long before the Greeks were supposed to have developed it. Professor Joseph points out too that Arab scientists should be credited with major discoveries traditionally attributed to William Harvey, Isaac Newton, Charles Darwin, and Sir Francis Bacon. But he is not concerned only to argue historical issues; his purpose is to bring all of these different mathematical traditions into the school classroom so that children might study, for example, "traditional African designs, Indian *rangoli* patterns, and Islamic art" and "the language and counting systems found across the world."

This interesting proposal to teach ethnomathematics comes at a time when American mathematics educators are trying to overhaul present practices, because of the poor performance of American children on national and international assessments. Mathematics educators are attempting to change the teaching of their subject so that children can see its uses in everyday life. There would seem to be an incipient conflict between those who want to introduce real-life applications of mathematics and those who want to teach the mathematical systems used by ancient cultures. I suspect that most mathematics teachers would enjoy doing a bit of both, if there were time or student interest. But any widespread movement to replace modern mathematics with ancient ethnic mathematics runs the risk of disaster in a field that is struggling to update existing curricula. If, as seems likely, ancient mathematics is taught mainly to minority children, the gap between them and middle-class white children is apt to grow. It is worth noting that children in Korea, who score highest in mathematics on international assessments, do not study ancient Korean mathematics.

Particularism is akin to cultural Lysenkoism, for it takes as its premise the spurious notion that cultural traits are inherited. It implies a dubious, dangerous form of cultural predestination. Children are taught that if their ancestors could do it, so could they. But what happens if a child is from a cultural group that made no significant contribution to science or mathematics? Does this mean that children from that background must find a culturally appropriate field in which to strive? How does a teacher find the right cultural buttons for children of mixed heritage? And how in the world will teachers use this technique when the children in their classes are drawn from many different cultures, as is usually the case? By the time that every culture gets its due, there may be no time left to teach the subject itself. This explosion of filiopietism (which, we should remember, comes from adults, not from students) is reminiscent of the period some years ago when the Russians claimed that they had invented everything first; as we now know, this nationalistic braggadocio did little for their self-esteem and nothing for their economic development. We might reflect, too, on how little social prestige has been accorded in this country to immigrants from Greece and Italy, even though the achievements of their ancestors were at the heart of the classical curriculum.

Filiopietism and ethnic boosterism lead to all sorts of odd practices. In New York State, for example, the curriculum guide for eleventh grade American history lists three "foundations" for the United States Constitution, as follows:

A. Foundations
  1. 17th and 18th century Enlightenment thought
  2. Haudenosaunee political system
     a. Influence upon colonial leadership and European intellectuals (Locke, Montesquieu, Voltaire, Rousseau)
     b. Impact on Albany Plan of Union, Articles of Confederation, and U.S. Constitution
  3. Colonial experience

Those who are unfamiliar with the Haudenosaunee political system might wonder what it is, particularly since educational authorities in New York State rank it as equal in importance to the European Enlightenment and suggest that it strongly influenced not only colonial leaders but the leading intellectuals of Europe. The Haudenosaunee political system was the Iroquois confederation of five (later six) Indian tribes in upper New York State, which conducted war and civil affairs through a council of chiefs, each with one vote. In 1754, Benjamin Franklin proposed a colonial union at a conference in Albany; his plan, said to be inspired by the Iroquois Confederation, was rejected by the other colonies. Today, Indian activists believe that the Iroquois Confederation was the model for the American Constitution, and the New York State Department of Education has decided that they are right. That no other state sees fit to give the American Indians equal billing with the European Enlightenment may be owing to the fact that the Indians in New York State (numbering less than forty thousand) have been more politically effective than elsewhere or that other states have not yet learned about this method of reducing "Eurocentrism" in their American history classes.

Particularism can easily be carried to extremes. Students of Fredonian descent must hear that their ancestors were seminal in the development of all human civilization and that without the Fredonian contribution, we would all be living in caves or trees, bereft of art, technology, and culture. To explain why Fredonians today are in modest circumstances, given their historic eminence, children are taught that somewhere, long ago, another culture stole the Fredonians' achievements, palmed them off as their own, and then oppressed the Fredonians.

I first encountered this argument almost twenty years ago, when I was a graduate student. I shared a small office with a young professor, and I listened as she patiently explained to a student why she had given him a D on a term paper. In his paper, he argued that the Arabs had stolen mathematics from the Nubians in the desert long ago (I forget in which century this theft allegedly occurred). She tried to explain to him about the necessity of historical evidence. He was unconvinced, since he believed that he had uncovered a great truth that was beyond proof. The part I couldn't understand was how anyone could lose knowledge by sharing it. After all, cultures are constantly influencing one another, exchanging ideas and art and technology, and the exchange usually is enriching, not depleting.

Today, there are a number of books and articles advancing controversial theories about the origins of civilization. An important work, *The African Origin of Civilization: Myth or Reality*, by Senegalese scholar Cheikh Anta Diop, argues that ancient Egypt was a black civilization, that all races are descended from the black race, and that the achievements of "western" civilization originated in Egypt. The views of Diop and other Africanists have been condensed into an everyman's paperback titled *What They Never Told You in History Class* by Indus Khamit Kush. This latter book claims that Moses, Jesus, Buddha, Mohammed, and Vishnu were Africans; that the first Indians, Chinese, Hebrews, Greeks, Romans, Britains, and Americans were Africans; and that the first mathematicians, scientists, astronomers, and physicians were Africans. A debate currently raging among some classicists is whether the Greeks "stole" the philosophy, art, and religion of the ancient Egyptians and whether the ancient Egyptians were black Africans. George G. M. James's *Stolen Legacy* insists that the Greeks "stole the Legacy of the African Continent and called it their own." James argues that the civilization of Greece, the vaunted foundation of European culture, owed everything it knew and did to its African predecessors. Thus, the roots of western civilization lie not in Greece and Rome but in Egypt and, ultimately, in black Africa.

Similar speculation was fueled by the publication in 1987 of Martin Bernal's *Black Athena: The Afroasiatic Roots of Classical Civilization*, Volume 1, *The Fabrication of Ancient Greece, 1785–1985,* although the controversy predates Bernal's book. In a fascinating foray into the politics of knowledge, Bernal attributes the preference of Western European scholars for Greece over Egypt as the fount of knowledge to nearly two centuries of racism and "Europocentrism," but he is uncertain about the color of the ancient Egyptians. However, a review of Bernal's book last year in the *Village Voice* began, "What color were the ancient Egyptians? Blacker than Mubarak, baby." The same article claimed that white racist archeologists chiseled the noses off ancient Egyptian statues so that future generations would not see the typically African facial characteristics. The debate reached the pages of the *Biblical Archeology Review* last year in an article titled "Were the Ancient Egyptians Black or White?" The author, classicist Frank J. Yurco, argues that some Egyptian rulers were black, others were not, and that "the ancient Egyptians did not think in these terms." The issue, wrote Yurco, "is a chimera, cultural baggage from our own society that can only be imposed artificially on ancient Egyptian society."

Most educationists are not even aware of the debate about whether the ancient Egyptians were black or white, but they are very sensitive to charges that the schools' curricula are Eurocentric, and they are eager to rid the schools of the taint of Eurocentrism. It is hardly surprising that America's schools would recognize strong cultural ties with Europe since our nation's political, religious, educational, and economic institutions were created chiefly by people of European descent, our government was shaped by European ideas, and nearly 80 percent of the people who live here are of European descent. The particularists treat all of this history as a racist bias toward Europe, rather than as the matter-of-fact consequences of European immigration. Even so, American education is not centered on Europe. American education, if it is centered on anything, is centered on itself. It is "Americentric." Most American students today have never studied any world history; they know very little about Europe, and even less about the rest of the world. Their minds are rooted solidly in the here and now. When the Berlin Wall was opened in the fall of 1989, journalists discovered that most American teenagers had no idea what it was, nor why its opening was such a big deal. Nonetheless, Eurocentrism provides a better target than Americentrism.

In school districts where most children are black and Hispanic, there has been a growing tendency to embrace particularism rather than pluralism. Many of the children in these districts perform poorly in academic classes and leave school without graduating. They would fare better in school if they had well-educated and well-paid teachers, small classes, good materials, encouragement at home and school, summer academic programs, protection from the drugs and crime that ravage their neighborhoods, and higher expectations of satisfying careers upon graduation. These are expensive and time-consuming remedies that must also engage the larger society beyond the school. The lure of particularism is that it offers a less complicated anodyne, one in which the children's academic deficiencies may be addressed—or set aside—by inflating their racial pride. The danger of this remedy is that it will detract attention from the real needs of schools and the real interests of children, while simultaneously arousing distorted race pride in children of all races, increasing racial antagonism and producing fresh recruits for white and black racist groups.

The particularist critique gained a major forum in New York in 1989, with the release of a report called "A Curriculum of Inclusion," produced by a task force created by the State Commissioner of Education, Thomas Sobol. In 1987, soon after his appointment, Sobol appointed a Task Force on Minorities to review the state's curriculum for instances of bias. He did this not because there had been complaints about bias in the curriculum, but because—as a newly appointed state commissioner whose previous job had been to superintend the public schools of a wealthy suburb, Scarsdale—he wanted to demonstrate his sensitivity to minority concerns. The Sobol task force was composed of representatives of African-American, Hispanic, Asian-American, and American Indian groups.

The task force engaged four consultants, one from each of the aforementioned racial or ethnic minorities, to review nearly one hundred teachers' guides prepared by the state. These guides define the state's curriculum, usually as a list of facts and concepts to be taught, along with model activities. The primary focus of the consultants, not surprisingly, was the history and social studies curriculum. As it happened, the history curriculum had been extensively revised in 1987 to make it multicultural, in both American and world history. In the 1987 revision the time given to Western Europe was reduced to one-quarter of one year, as part of a two-year global studies sequence in which equal time was allotted to seven major world regions, including Africa and Latin America.

As a result of the 1987 revisions in American and world history, New York State had one of the most advanced multicultural history-social studies curricula in the country. Dozens of social studies teachers and consultants had participated, and the final draft was reviewed by such historians as Eric Foner of Columbia University, the late Hazel Hertzberg of Teachers College, Columbia University, and Christopher Lasch of the University of Rochester. The curriculum was overloaded with facts, almost to the point of numbing students with details and trivia, but it was not insensitive to ethnicity in American history or unduly devoted to European history.

But the Sobol task force decided that this curriculum was biased and Eurocentric. The first sentence of the task force report summarizes its major thesis: "African-Americans, Asian-Americans, Puerto Ricans/Latinos, and Native Americans have all been the victims of an intellectual and educational oppression that has characterized the culture and institutions of the United States and the European American world for centuries."

The task force report was remarkable in that it vigorously denounced bias without identifying a single instance of bias in the curricular guides under review. Instead, the consultants employed harsh, sometimes inflammatory, rhetoric to treat every difference of opinion or interpretation as an example of racial bias. The African-American consultant, for example, excoriates the curriculum for its "White Anglo-Saxon (Wasp) value system and norms," its "deep-seated pathologies of racial hatred," and its "white nationalism"; he decries as bias the fact that children study Egypt as part of the Middle East instead of as part of Africa. Perhaps Egypt should be studied as part of the African unit (geographically, it is located on the African continent); but placing it in one region rather than the other is not what most people think of as racism or bias. The "Latino" consultant criticizes the use of the term "Spanish-American War" instead of "Spanish-Cuban-American War." The Native American consultant complains that tribal languages are classified as "foreign languages."

The report is consistently Europhobic. It repeatedly

expresses negative judgments on "European-Americans" and on everything Western and European. All people with a white skin are referred to as "Anglo-Saxons" and "WASPs." Europe, says the report, is uniquely responsible for producing aggressive individuals who "were ready to 'discover, invade, and conquer' foreign land because of greed, racism, and national egoism." All white people are held collectively guilty for the historical crimes of slavery and racism. There is no mention of the "Anglo-Saxons" who opposed slavery and racism. Nor does the report acknowledge that some whites have been victims of discrimination and oppression. The African-American consultant writes of the Constitution, "There is something vulgar and revolting in glorifying a process that heaped undeserved rewards on a segment of the population while oppressing the majority."

The New York task force proposal is not merely about the reconstruction of what is taught. It goes a step further to suggest that the history curriculum may be used to ensure that "children from Native American, Puerto Rican/ Latino, Asian-American, and African-American cultures will have higher self-esteem and self-respect, while children from European cultures will have a less arrogant perspective of being part of the group that has 'done it all.' "

In February 1990, Commissioner Sobol asked the New York Board of Regents to endorse a sweeping revision of the history curriculum to make it more multicultural. His recommendations were couched in measured tones, not in the angry rhetoric of his task force. The board supported his request unanimously. It remains to be seen whether New York pursues the particularist path marked out by the Commissioner's advisory group or finds its way to the concept of pluralism within a democratic tradition.

The rising tide of particularism encourages the politicization of all curricula in the schools. If education bureaucrats bend to the political and ideological winds, as is their wont, we can anticipate a generation of struggle over the content of the curriculum in mathematics, science, literature, and history. Demands for "culturally relevant" studies, for ethnostudies of all kinds, will open the classroom to unending battles over whose version is taught, who gets credit for what, and which ethno-interpretation is appropriate. Only recently have districts begun to resist the demands of fundamentalist groups to censor textbooks and library books (and some have not yet begun to do so).

The spread of particularism throws into question the very idea of American public education. Public schools exist to teach children the general skills and knowledge that they need to succeed in American society, and the specific skills and knowledge that they need in order to function as American citizens. They receive public support because they have a public function. Historically, the public schools were known as "common schools" because they were schools for all, even if the children of all the people did not attend them. Over the years, the courts have found that it was unconstitutional to teach religion in the common schools or to separate children on the basis of their race in the common schools. In their curriculum, their hiring practices, and their general philosophy, the public schools must not discriminate against or give preference to any racial or ethnic group. Yet they are permitted to accommodate cultural diversity by, for example, serving food that is culturally appropriate or providing library collections that emphasize the interests of the local community. However, they should not be expected to teach children to view the world through an ethnocentric perspective that rejects or ignores the common culture. For generations, those groups that wanted to inculcate their religion or their ethnic heri-

tage have instituted private schools—after school, on week-
ends, or on a full-time basis. There, children learn with
lovers of the same group—Greeks, Poles, Germans, Japanese, Chinese, Jews, Lutherans, Catholics, and so on—and
are taught by people from the same group. Valuable as this
exclusive experience has been for those who choose it, this
has not been the role of public education. One of the
primary purposes of public education has been to create a
national community, a definition of citizenship and culture
that is both expansive and *inclusive*.

The curriculum in public schools must be based on
whatever knowledge and practices have been determined
to be best by professionals—experienced teachers and
scholars—who are competent to make these judgments.
Professional societies must be prepared to defend the integrity of their disciplines. When called upon, they should
establish review committees to examine disputes over curriculum and to render judgment, in order to help school
officials fend off improper political pressure. Where genuine controversies exist, they should be taught and debated
in the classroom. Was Egypt a black civilization? Why not
raise the question, read the arguments of the different
sides in the debate, show slides of Egyptian pharoahs and
queens, read books about life in ancient Egypt, invite guest
scholars from the local university, and visit museums with
Egyptian collections? If scholars disagree, students should
know it. One great advantage of this approach is that
students will see that history is a lively study, that textbooks are fallible, that historians disagree, that the writing
of history is influenced by the historian's politics and
ideology, that history is written by people who make
choices among alternative facts and interpretations, and
that history changes as new facts are uncovered and new
interpretations win adherents. They will also learn that
cultures and civilizations constantly interact, exchange

ideas, and influence one another, and that the idea of racial or ethnic purity is a myth. Another advantage is that students might once again study ancient history, which has all but disappeared from the curricula of American schools. (California recently introduced a required sixth grade course in ancient civilizations, but ancient history is otherwise *terra incognita* in American education.)

The multicultural controversy may do wonders for the study of history, which has been neglected for years in American schools. At this time, only half of our high school graduates ever study any world history. Any serious attempt to broaden students' knowledge of Africa, Europe, Asia, and Latin America will require at least two, and possibly three years of world history (a requirement thus far only in California). American history, too, will need more time than the one-year high-school survey course. Those of us who have insisted for years on the importance of history in the curriculum may not be ready to assent to its redemptive power, but hope that our new allies will ultimately join a constructive dialogue that strengthens the place of history in the schools.

As cultural controversies arise, educators must adhere to the principle of "E Pluribus Unum." That is, they must maintain a balance between the demands of the one—the nation of which we are common citizens—and the many— the varied histories of the American people. It is not necessary to denigrate either the one or the many. Pluralism is a positive value, but it is also important that we preserve a sense of an American community—a society and a culture to which we all belong. If there is no overall community with an agreed-upon vision of liberty and justice, if all we have is a collection of racial and ethnic cultures, lacking any common bonds, then we have no means to mobilize public opinion on behalf of people who are not members of our particular group. We have, for example, no reason to support public education. If there is no larger community, then each group will want to teach its own children in its own way, and public education ceases to exist.

History should not be confused with filiopietism. History gives no grounds for race pride. No race has a monopoly on virtue. If anything, a study of history should inspire humility, rather than pride. People of every racial group have committed terrible crimes, often against others of the same group. Whether one looks at the history of Europe or Africa or Latin America or Asia, every continent offers examples of inhumanity. Slavery has existed in civilizations around the world for centuries. Examples of genocide can be found around the world, throughout history, from ancient times right through to our own day. Governments and cultures, sometimes by edict, sometimes simply following tradition, have practiced not only slavery but human sacrifice, infanticide, cliterodectomy, and mass murder. If we teach children this, they might recognize how absurd both racial hatred and racial chauvinism are.

What must be preserved in the study of history is the spirit of inquiry, the readiness to open new questions and to pursue new understandings. History, at its best, is a search for truth. The best way to portray this search is through debate and controversy, rather than through imposition of fixed beliefs and immutable facts. Perhaps the most dangerous aspect of school history is its tendency to become Official History, a sanctified version of the Truth taught by the state to captive audiences and embedded in beautiful mass-market textbooks as holy writ. When Official History is written by committees responding to political pressures, rather than by scholars synthesizing the best available research, then the errors of the past are replaced by the politically fashionable errors of the present. It may be difficult to teach children that history is both important and uncertain, and that even the best historians never have all the pieces of the jigsaw puzzle, but it is necessary to do so. If state education departments permit the revision of their history courses and textbooks to become an exercise in power politics, then the entire process of state-level curriculum-making becomes suspect, as does public education itself.

The question of self-esteem is extraordinarily complex, and it goes well beyond the content of the curriculum. Most of what we call self-esteem is formed in the home and in a variety of life experiences, not only in school. Nonetheless, it has been important for blacks—and for other racial groups—to learn about the history of slavery and of the civil rights movement; it has been important for blacks to know that their ancestors actively resisted enslavement and actively pursued equality; and it has been important for blacks and others to learn about black men and women who fought courageously against racism and who provide models of courage, persistence, and intellect. These are instances where the content of the curriculum reflects sound scholarship, and at the same time probably lessens racial prejudice and provides inspiration for those who are descendants of slaves. But knowing about the travails and triumphs of one's forebears does not necessarily translate into either self-esteem or personal accomplishment. For most children, self-esteem—the self-confidence that grows out of having reached a goal—comes not from hearing about the monuments of their ancestors but as a consequence of what they are able to do and accomplish through their own efforts.

As I reflected on these issues, I recalled reading an interview a few years ago with a talented black runner. She said that her model is Mikhail Baryshnikov. She admires him because he is a magnificent athlete. He is not black; he is not female; he is not American-born; he is not even a runner. But he inspires her because of the way he trained and used his body. When I read this, I thought how narrow-minded it is to believe that people can be inspired *only* by those who are exactly like them in race and ethnicity.

MULTICULTURALISM:
AN EXCHANGE

Molefi Kete Asante

Molefi Kete Asante is chairman of the African-American
Studies department at Temple University, the editor of
the *Journal of Black Studies,* and the author of, among
other books, *Kemet, Afrocentricity and Knowledge.* His
curriculum proposals have been adopted by several major
school districts. His response to Diane Ravitch appeared
in *The American Scholar,* Spring 1991. Her counterres-
ponse can be found in the same issue.

We are all implicated in the positions we hold about society,
culture, and education. Although the implications may take
quite different forms in some fields and with some scholars, such as the consequences and our methods and
inquiry on our systems of values, we are nevertheless
captives of the positions we take, that is, if we take those
positions honestly.

In a recent article in *The American Scholar* (Summer
1990), Diane Ravitch reveals the tensions between scholarship and ideological perpectives in an exceedingly clear

manner. The position taken in her article "Multicultural-ism: E. Pluribus Plures" accurately demonstrates the the-sis that those of us who write are implicated in what we choose to write. This is not a profound announcement since most fields of inquiry recognize that a researcher's presence must be accounted for in research or a historian's relationship to data must be examined in seeking to estab-lish the validity of conclusions. This is not to say that the judgment will be invalid because of the intimacy of the scholar with the information but rather that in accounting for the scholar's or researcher's presence we are likely to know better how to assess the information presented. Just as a researcher may be considered an intrusive presence in an experiment, the biases of a scholar may be just as intrusive in interpreting data or making analysis. The fact that a writer seeks to establish a persona of a noninterested observer means that such a writer wants the reader to assume that an unbiased position is being taken on a subject. However, we know that as soon as a writer states a proposition, the writer is implicated and such implication holds minor or extreme consequences.

The remarkable advantage of stating aims and objec-tives prior to delivering an argument is that the reader knows precisely to what the author is driving. Unfortu-nately, too many writers on education either do not know the point they are making or lose sight of their point in the making. Such regrettably is the case with Diane Ravitch's article on multicultural education.

Among writers who have written on educational mat-ters in the last few years, Professor Ravitch of Columbia University's Teacher's College is considered highly quota-ble and therefore, in the context of American educational policy, influential. This is precisely why her views on multiculturalism must not remain unchallenged. Many of the positions taken by Professor Ravitch are similar to the

positions taken against the Freedmen's Bureau's establishment of black schools in the South during the 1860s. Then,
the white conservative education policymakers felt that it
was necessary to control the content of education so that
the recently freed Africans would not become self-assured.
An analysis of Ravitch's arguments will reveal what Martin
Bernal calls in *Black Athena* "the neo-Aryan" model of
history. Her version of multiculturalism is not multiculturalism at all, but rather a new form of Eurocentric hegemon-
ism.

People tend to do the best they can with the information
at their disposal. The problem in most cases where intellectual distortions arise is ignorance rather than malice. Unlike in the political arena where oratory goes a long way, in
education, sooner or later the truth must come out. The
proof of the theory is in the practice. What we have seen in
the past twenty-five years is the gradual dismantling of the
educational kingdom built to accompany the era of white
supremacy. What is being contested is the speed of its
dismantling. In many ways, the South African regime is a
good parallel to what is going on in American education.
No longer can the structure of knowledge which supported
white hegemony be defended; whites must take their
place, not above or below, but alongside the rest of humanity. This is a significantly different reality than we have
experienced in American education and there are several
reasons for this turn of events.

The first reason is the accelerating explosion in the
world of knowledge about cultures, histories, and events
seldom mentioned in American education. Names of individuals and their achievements, views of historiography
and alternatives to European perspectives have proliferated
due to international interaction, trade, and computer technology. People from other cultures, particularly non-Western people, have added new elements into the educational

equation. A second reason is the rather recent intellectual liberation of large numbers of African-descended scholars. While there have always been African scholars in every era, the European hegemony, since the 1480s, in knowledge about the world, including Africa, was fairly complete. The domination of information, the naming of things, the propagation of concepts, and the dissemination of interpretations were, and still are in most cases in the West, a Eurocentric hegemony. During the twentieth century, African scholars led by W. E. B. Du Bois began to break from the intellectual shackles of Europe and make independent inquiries into history, science, origins, and Europe itself. For the first time in five hundred years, a cadre of scholars, trained in the West, but largely liberated from the hegemonic European thinking began to expose numerous distortions, often elevated to "truth" in the works of Eurocentric authors. A third reason for the current assault on the misinformation spread by white hegemonic thinkers is the conceptual inadequacy of simply valorizing Europe. Few whites have ever examined their culture critically. Those who have done so have often been severely criticized by their peers: the cases of Sidney Willhelm, Joe Feagin, Michael Bradley, and Basil Davidson are well known.

As part of the Eurocentric tradition, there seems to be silence on questions of hegemony, that is, the inability to admit the mutual conspiracy between race doctrine and educational doctrine in America. Professor Ravitch and others would maintain the facade of reasonableness even in the face of arguments demonstrating the irrationality of both white supremacist ideas on race and white hegemonic ideas in education. They are corollary and both are untenable on genetic and intellectual grounds.

Eurocentric Hegemonism

Let us examine the argument of the defenders of the Eurocentric hegemony in education more closely. The status quo always finds its best defense in territoriality. Thus, it is one of the first weapons used by the defenders of the white hegemonic education. Soon after my book *The Afrocentric Idea* was published, I was interviewed on "The Today Show" along with Herb London, the New York University professor/politician who is one of the founders of the National Association of Scholars. When I suggested the possibility of schools weaving information about other cultures into the fabric of the teaching-learning process, Professor London interrupted that "there is not enough *time* in the school year for what Asante wants." Of course there is, if there is enough for the Eurocentric information, there is enough time for cultural information from other groups. Professor Ravitch uses the same argument. Her strategy is to cast serious examinations of the curriculum as pressure groups, much like creationists in biology. Of course, the issue is neither irrational nor sensational; it is pre-eminently a question of racial dominance, the maintenance of which, in any form, I oppose. On the contrary, the status quo defenders, like the South African Boers, believe that it is possible to defend what is fundamentally anti-intellectual and immoral: the dominance and hegemony of the Eurocentric view of reality on a multicultural society. There is space for Eurocentrism in a multicultural enterprise so long as it does not parade as universal. No one wants to banish the Eurocentric view. It is a valid view of reality where it does not force its way. Afrocentricity does not seek to replace Eurocentricity in its arrogant disregard for other cultures.

The Principal Contradictions

A considerable number of white educators and some blacks have paraded in single file and sometimes in concert to take aim at multiculturalism. In her article Professor Ravitch attempts to defend the indefensible. Believing, I suspect, that the best defense of the status quo is to attack, she attacks diversity, and those that support it, with gusto, painting straw fellows along the way. Her claim to support multiculturalism is revealed to be nothing more than an attempt to apologize for white cultural supremacy in the curriculum by using the same logic as white racial supremacists used in trying to defend white racism in previous years. She assumes falsely that there is little to say about the rest of the world, particularly about Africa and African-Americans. Indeed, she is willing to assert, as Herbert London has claimed, that the school systems do not have enough time to teach all that Afrocentrists believe ought to be taught. Nevertheless, she assumes that all that is not taught about the European experience is valid and necessary. There are some serious flaws in her line of reasoning. I shall attempt to locate the major flaws and ferret them out.

Lip service is paid to the evolution of American education from the days of racial segregation to the present when "new social historians" routinely incorporate the experiences of other than white males. Nowhere does Professor Ravitch demonstrate an appreciation for the role played by the African-American community in overcoming the harshest elements of racial segregation in the educational system. Consequently, she is unable to understand that more fundamental than eliminating racial segregation has to be the removal of racist thinking, assumptions, symbols, and materials in the curriculum.

However, there is no indication that Professor Ravitch is willing to grant an audience to this reasoning because she plods deeper into the same quagmire by attempting to conceptualize multiculturalism, a simple concept in educational jargon. She posits a *pluralist* multiculturalism—a redundancy—then suggests a *particularistic* multiculturalism—an oxymoron—in order to beat a dead horse. The ideas are nonstarters because they have no reality in fact. I wrote the first book in this country on transracial communication and edited the first handbook on intercultural communication, and I am aware of the categories Professor Ravitch seeks to forge. She claims that the pluralist multiculturalist believes in pluralism and the particularistic multiculturalist believes in particularism. Well, multiculturalism in education is almost self-defining. It is simply the idea that the educational experience should reflect the diverse cultural heritage of our system of knowledge. I have contended that such is not the case and cannot be the case until teachers know more about the African-American, Native American, Latino, and Asian experiences. This position obviously excites Professor Ravitch to the point that she feels obliged to make a case for "mainstream Americans."

The Myth of Mainstream

The idea of "mainstream American" is nothing more than an additional myth meant to maintain Eurocentric hegemony. When Professor Ravitch speaks of mainstream, she does not have Spike Lee, Aretha Franklin, or John Coltrane in mind. Bluntly put, "mainstream" is a code word for "white." When a dean of a college says to a faculty member, as one recently said, "You ought to publish in mainstream journals," the dean is not meaning *Journal of Black Studies* or *Black Scholar*. As a participant in the racist system of education, the dean is merely carrying out the traditional function of enlarging the white hegemony over scholarship. Thus, when the status quo defenders use terms like "mainstream," they normally mean "white." In fact, one merely has to substitute the words "white-controlled" to get at the real meaning behind the code.

Misunderstanding Multiculturalism

Misunderstanding the African-American struggle for education in the United States, Professor Ravitch thinks that the call to multiculturalism is a matter of anecdotal references to outstanding individuals or descriptions of civil rights. But neither acknowledgment of achievements per se, nor descriptive accounts of the African experience adequately conveys the aims of the Afrocentric restructuring, as we shall see. From the establishment of widespread public education to the current emphasis on massaging the curriculum toward an organic and systemic recognition of cultural pluralism, the African-American concept of nationhood has been always central. In terms of Afrocentricity, it is the same. We do not seek segments or modules in the classroom but rather the infusion of African-American studies in every segment and in every module. The difference is between "incorporating the experiences" and "infusing the curriculum with an entirely new life." The real unity of the curriculum comes from infusion, not from including African-Americans in what Ravitch would like to remain a white contextual hegemony she calls mainstream. No true mainstream can ever exist until there is knowledge, understanding, and acceptance of the role Africans have played in American history. One reason the issue is debated by white scholars such as Ravitch is because they do not believe there is substantial or significant African information to infuse. Thus, ignorance becomes the reason for the strenuous denials of space for the cultural infusion. If she knew or believed that it was possible to have missed something, she would not argue against it. What is at issue is her own educational background. Does she know classical Africa? Did she take courses in African-American studies from qualified professors? Those who know do not question the importance of Afrocentric or Latino infusion into the educational process.

The Misuse of Self-Esteem

Professor Ravitch's main critique of the Afrocentric, Latin-ocentric, or Americentric (Native American) project is that it seeks to raise "self-esteem and self-respect" among Africans, Latinos, and Native Americans. It is important to understand that this is not only a self-serving argument, but a false argument. In the first place, I know of no Afrocentric curriculum planner—Asa Hilliard, Wade Nobles, Leonard Jeffries, Don McNeely being the principal ones—who insists that the primary aim is to raise self-esteem. The argument is a false lead to nowhere because the curriculum planners I am familiar with insist that the fundamental objective is to provide *accurate* information. A secondary effect of accuracy and truth might be the adjustment of attitudes by both black and white students. In several surveys of college students, research has demonstrated that new information changes attitudes in both African-American and white students. Whites are not so apt to take a superior attitude when they are aware of the achievements of other cultures. They do not lose their self-esteem, they adjust their views. On the other hand, African-Americans who are often as ignorant as whites about African achievements adjust their attitudes about themselves once they are exposed to new information. There is no great secret in this type of transformation. Ravitch, writing from the point of view of those whose cultural knowledge is reinforced every hour, not just in the curriculum, but in every media, smugly contends that she cannot see the value of self-esteem. Since truth and accuracy will yield by-products of attitude adjustments, the Afrocentrists have always argued for the accurate representation of information.

Afrocentricity does not seek an ethnocentric curriculum. Unfortunately, Diane Ravitch chose to ignore two books that explain why views on this subject, *The Afrocentric Idea* (1987) and *Kemet, Afrocentricity and Knowledge* (1990) and instead quotes from *Afrocentricity* (1980), which was not about education but about personal and social transformation. Had she read the later works she would have understood that Afrocentricity is not an ethnocentric view in two senses. In the first place, it does not valorize the African view while downgrading others. In this sense, it is unlike the Eurocentric view, which is an ethnocentric view because it valorizes itself and parades as universal. It becomes racist when the rules, customs, and/or authority of law or force dictate it as the proper view. This is what often happens in school curricula. In the second place, as to method, Afrocentricity is not a naive racial theory. It is a systematic approach to presenting the African as subject rather than object. Even Ravitch might be taught the Afrocentric Method!

American Culture

There is no common American culture as is claimed by the defenders of the status quo. There is a hegemonic culture to be sure, pushed as if it were a common culture. Perhaps Ravitch is confusing concepts here. There is a common American *society*, which is quite different from a common American culture. Certain cultural characteristics are shared by those within the society but the meaning of *multicultural* is "many cultures." To believe in multicultural education is to assume that there are many cultures. The reason Ravitch finds confusion is because the only way she can reconcile the "many cultures" is to insist on many "little" cultures under the hegemony of the "big" white culture. Thus, what she means by multiculturalism is precisely what I criticized in *The Afrocentric Idea,* the acceptance of other cultures within a European framework.

In the end, the neat separation of pluralist multicultural-ists and particularistic multiculturalists breaks down be-cause it is a false, straw separation developed primarily for the sake of argument and not for clarity. The real division on the question of multiculturalism is between those who truly seek to maintain a Eurocentric hegemony over the curriculum and those who truly believe in cultural plural-ism without hierarchy. Ravitch defends the former posi-tion.

Professor Ravitch's ideological position is implicated in her mis-reading of several scholars' works. When Professor John Stanfield writes that modes of social knowledge such as theology, science, and magic are different, not inferior or superior, Ravitch asks, "If Professor Stanfield broke his leg, would he go to a theologian, a doctor, or a magician?" clearly she does not understand the simple statement Stan-field is making. He is not writing about *uses* of knowledge, but about *ranking* of knowledge. To confuse the point by providing an answer for a question never raised is the key rhetorical strategy in Ravitch's case. Thus, she implies that because Professor George Ghevarughese Joseph argues that mathematics was developed in Egypt, Babylonia, Mes-opotamia, and India long before it came to Europe, he seeks to replace modern math with "ancient ethnic math-ematics." This is a deliberate misunderstanding of the professor's point: Mathematics in its modern form owes debts to Africans and Asians.

Another attempt to befuddle issues is Ravitch's gratui-tous comment that Koreans "do not study ancient mathe-matics" and yet they have high scores. There are probably several variables for the Koreans making the highest scores "in mathematics on international assessments." Surely one element would have to be the linkage of Korean traditions in mathematics to present mathematical problems. Kore-ans do not study European theorists prior to their own;

indeed they are taught to honor and respect the ancestral mathematicians. This is true for Indians, Chinese, and Japanese. In African traditions, the *European* slave trade broke the linkage, and the work of scholars such as Ahmed Baba and Hypathia remains unknown to the African-American and thus does not take its place in the family of world mathematics.

Before Professor Ravitch ends her assault on ethnic cultures, she fires a volley against the Haudenosaunee political system of Native Americans. As a New Yorker, she does not like the fact that the state's curriculum guide lists the Haudenosaunee Confederation as an inspiration for the United States Constitution alongside the Enlightenment. She says readers "might wonder what it is." Bluntly put, a proper education would acquaint students with the Haudenosaunee Confederation, and in that case Professor Ravitch's readers would know the Haudenosaunee as a part of the conceptual discussion that went into the development of the American political systems. Only a commitment to white hegemony would lead a writer to assume that whites could not obtain political ideas from others.

Finally, she raises a "controversy" that is no longer a controversy among reputable scholars: Who were the Egyptians? Most scholars accept a simple answer: They were Africans. The question of whether or not they were black was initially raised by Eurocentric scholars in the nineteenth century seeking to explain the testimony of the ancient Greeks, particularly Herodotus and Diodorus Siculus, who said that Egyptians were "Black with woolly hair." White hegemonic studies that sought to maintain the false notion of white racial supremacy during the nineteenth century fabricated the idea of a European or an Asian Egyptian to deny Africa its classical past and to continue the Aryan myth. It is shocking to see Professor Ravitch raise this issue in the 1990s. It is neither a controversial issue nor should it be to those familiar with the evidence.

The debate over the curriculum is really over a vision of the future of the United States. Keepers of the status quo, such as Professor Ravitch, want to maintain a "white framework" for multiculturalism because they have no faith in cultural pluralism without hierarchy. A common culture does not exist, but this nation is on the path toward it. Granting all the difficulties we face in attaining this common culture, we are more likely to reach it when we allow the full participation of all ethnic groups in a quest for a usable curriculum. In the end, we will find that such a curriculum, like inspiration, will not come from this or that individual model but from integrity and accuracy.

PART SIX

DIVERSE VIEWS

THE PROSPECT BEFORE US

Hilton Kramer

Hilton Kramer, the former art critic of *The New York Times* and presently the editor of *The New Criterion*, published this article about the new trends and the art world in *The New Criterion*, September 1990.

We are aware that a civilization has the same fragility as a life. The circumstances that send the works of Keats and Baudelaire to join the works of Menander are no longer inconceivable; they are in the newspapers.
—Paul Valéry

As this first year in the last decade of the twentieth century draws to a close, there can be no question but that our culture is in deep and terrible trouble. The engines of publicity—in the arts no less than in politics, if one may still make such a distinction—continue to produce their preposterous claims, and there is no shortage of people eager, if not indeed desperate, to embrace them even in the absence of any real conviction about their truth. But these empty rituals of celebration can no longer disguise the profound and enduring malaise that now pervades virtually every sphere of cultural life. The feeling that the arts have been captured by the enemies of art is more widespread than ever before. So is the sense that the standards that once guided us in matters of artistic accomplishment, intellectual analysis, and moral inquiry have now been supplanted by attitudes and ideologies that, in regard to both art and life, are transparently corrupt and corrupting. In the atmosphere of cynicism and opportunism that encloses so many aspects of our culture today, the very idea of stringent judgment and rigorous distinction, without which the life of art and the life of the mind are nothing but a sham, is openly and proudly disavowed. When the concept of quality in art was recently stigmatized in a lengthy article in *The New York Times* as little more than an instrument of racism and repression, the pronouncement of this pernicious doctrine merely confirmed in principle what the new barbarians had already established as a standard practice: the imposition of politics—above all, the politics of race, gender, and multiculturalism—as the only acceptable criterion of value in every realm of culture and life.

This barbarian element—so hostile to the fundamental tenets of our civilization, and so heedless of the wreckage it leaves in its wake—can no longer be regarded as constituting a marginal component of contemporary cultural life. Far from representing a radical fringe, which was once the case, it now commands an immense following in our mainstream institutions. It has already radically transformed the teaching of the arts and the humanities in our colleges and universities, and this has had the effect—among much else—of alienating some of the best intellectual talent from these fields of study. Many gifted teachers have left academic life because of the ideological tests that have come to dominate these fields; and many gifted students who might, in other cultural circumstances, have happily entered these fields are now permanently lost to them. The extent to which academic life, especially in the arts and the humanities, has become the arena of a fierce ideological orthodoxy—all in the name of "liberal" values, of course—is now an open scandal. Yet the situation gets worse even as it is more and more talked about. Its real cost will not be fully calculated until, a generation or more hence, the time will come when we shall be obliged to recognize how few first-rate minds chose to seek their intellectual fortunes in the academy.

Outside the universities, the situation is not much better. It was inevitable, perhaps, that as money and politics emerged as the dominant issues in the arts—as they overwhelmingly did in the 1980s—the whole level of discussion of artistic matters, not only in the press but in the institutions concerned with the arts, would be lowered and coarsened, if not irreversibly corrupted. Yet even expecting the worst, there was still something shocking about the hysteria and irresponsible hyperbole, often descending to outright demogoguery, that characterized the response of our arts institutions this summer to the debate in Congress over the re-authorization legislation for the National Endowment for the Arts. And here we are not talking primarily about the so-called "alternative space" groups. These are themselves the creation and the permanent wards of the government patronage system and could naturally be expected to fight for their right to remain licensed rebels at the taxpayers' expense. Licensed rebels: that is what they were created to be in the heyday of our national prosperity—a sort of negative cultural luxury that a thriving economy could easily afford—and it should have come as no surprise that its beneficiaries truly believed their annual government grant had become as much of an entitlement as the check from the Unemployment Office.

That was what the policy of our government arts agencies had given them to believe.

What was really shocking was the response of our major museums and other mainstream organizations—those that are supposed to represent what is finest and most enduring in our civilization—that went into action like any other special-interest political group, clearly prepared to conduct a cutthroat lobbying campaign at the behest of all those professional arts lobbies that now loom so large on the national cultural scene. (Make no mistake about it: the business of getting hold of the government's money for the arts is now itself big business.) The scene was the same the country over. All those frenzied petition-signing stations set up in the lobbies of our art museums, their tables draped with black crepe as a sign of mourning for the death of our civilization; all those leaflets, with their simple-minded slogans and misleading "facts"; the whole atmosphere of drummed-up fear and paranoia designed to suggest that our culture, if not the country itself, was on the verge of something like a fascist coup—all of this was not only damaging to the institutional probity of the museums and to their reputation (or what was left of it) for disinterested judgment, but is certain to bring them in the future the kind of unfriendly public scrutiny they will have every reason to regret. The truth is, our museums have become spendthrift institutions, lavishing immense sums of money on expanded facilities, expanded programs, and expensive acquisitions guaranteed to cause even greater fiscal problems in the future. They have also shown themselves to be unreliable guardians of their own collections, selling off treasured art works for easy cash and short-term goals. By entering the political arena as they have now done, museums have hastened the day when a public reckoning of their affairs will be insisted upon. This is not a happy development.

What was most appalling about this summer's display of political hysteria in the museums, however, was the sheer hypocrisy that surrounded it. Every museum curator in the country knows very well that our artists today enjoy a greater degree of freedom of expression than has probably been true of artists at any time, anywhere, in the past. Yet the entire curatorial profession agreed to participate in this well-organized charade that had as its premise the notion that we are living under some sort of McCarthyite terror in the arts. The names of Hitler and Stalin were bandied about by people—not only in the museums but in the media as well—who plainly hadn't the foggiest understanding of the realities of life under a totalitarian regime. It was an unlovely spectacle—irnorance and self-interest combining to obscure the truth.

If there was indeed any reason to fear the imposition of a McCarthyite prohibition on freedom of speech in this situation, the real threat was coming from the liberals themselves, who were so quick and so unashamed in denouncing anyone who disagreed with them—about the Mapplethorpe case, for example—as an enemy of democracy and freedom, perhaps even a fascist (the polite name for which in the media just now is "right-wing fundamentalist"). In all of this there was the added hypocrisy of pretending—which the museums and their allies in the arts lobbying organizations routinely did—that the entire debate about the National Endowment for the Arts came down to a simple choice between a total, unquestioned endorsement of the Mapplethorpe pictures and a total, unquestioned acceptance of the views of Senator Helms. That there was to be no place in this discussion for the concerns of ordinary citizens about the declining standards of public decency in our society was, incredibly, the position—the public position, anyway—of virtually every representative of a major cultural institution who spoke out on this issue. Privately, to be sure, one often heard otherwise. After I published a long article on the subject in *The New York Times* in July 1989—well before Senator Helms introduced his notorious amendment on the Senate floor—more than one museum director confided to me privately that he completely agreed with the position I had taken, which was that the public did indeed have a legitimate concern about the way the allocation of tax dollars might affect standards of public decency and amenity. The *Times* received an avalanche of letters in response to that article, but none of the museum directors who had spoken to me was heard from. One told me frankly that if he spoke up publicly on this issue, his entire staff might resign in protest and his own job might be in jeopardy. It went without saying that a job in another museum would be out of the question. He would be tainted. This is the real McCarthyism of our time—liberal McCarthyism.

Where the new barbarism manifests itself most insidiously, of course, is in its adamant insistence that it is now the primary function of the arts—and of arts institutions—to serve the cause of redressing every social, political, sexual, ethnic, and even regional grievance that one or another "minority," or self-proclaimed victim group, may wish to bring as an indictment against our society. To this deadly doctrine the universities have totally surrendered, and they are not alone. The foundations faithfully abide by it, the museums are rapidly capitulating to it, our theater long ago placed itself completely at its service, and the media more and more endorse and advance its every claim. What is most glaringly obvious is the leveling effect of this political program, for the implementation of which quotas based on race, gender, etc., are mandatory and aesthetic distinctions must be abandoned, if not indeed declared to be obsolete—this, after all, was the point of that article in

The New York Times condemning the idea of quality in art. In other words, distinctions of quality must be jettisoned in the interest of affirmative action.

What may not, at first glance, be quite so apparent are the destructive consequences that this program guarantees for the minorities it is ostensibly intended to benefit. We shall soon find ourselves, as the influence of this political gospel makes itself felt, in a situation in which no artists belonging to a minority group will ever be able to believe that their work has been singled out on the basis of merit. This is a terrible fate for an artist: never to know if one's work has been acclaimed on the grounds of its achievement or, as it is now more likely to be the case, simply because its producer belongs to the requisite racial, sexual, ethnic, etc., category. What this program will amount to in practice is the creation of a special class of "artists," who will be seen—by themselves as well as others—as the art world's counterpart to welfare clients, an artist-underclass entirely lacking in artistic legitimacy or credibility and sustained solely by bureaucratic fiat and a government dole. It is a grim prospect—and grim, most of all, for artists of talent and accomplishment who belong to the minorities in question.

For this development, terrible as it undoubtedly is, is not going to destroy the life of art in our society. But it is going to drive more and more art of real quality and distinction out of the public arena, and make it once again—as it was in the age of the avant-garde in the late nineteenth and early twentieth centuries—a more or less coterie experience, its access limited to the few who know and care. This, if it should happen, will be a real loss for our democratic culture—but it is a denouement that is being forced upon us by the fanatic partisans of a political movement that insists that all distinctions of quality in art be abandoned in the name of democracy.

P. C. RIDER

Enrique Fernández

Enrique Fernández is the editor of *Más*, a national Spanish-language magazine, and a columnist for *The Village Voice*, where this brief commentary appeared in the issue of June 18, 1991.

O tempora, o mores. Western culture, we're being warned, is under siege by a new wave of barbarians: the multiculturalists. Sound the alarm! I agree that some of what passes for multiculturalism in American universities is illiteracy mixed with the "good consciences" of the left, which is the same pesky nonsense as illiteracy mixed with the bad consciences of the right. In the end, the debate over political correctness—a term originally appropriated by political progressives to mock the assholes in their own ranks—winds up as a pathetic exchange of rancors between bands of the unlettered. For who, in this day and age, would argue over such a sloppy term as "Western culture"?

If what was meant was the culture of the American West, we could talk—damnedest most interesting chunk of American life I know, and let's not leave out the Chicanos, who were there first. But what is really meant is Anglo-American culture as the heir to some grand European tradition. Anglo-American culture? That would have been a good laugh to José Enrique Rodó. The influential fin-de-siècle Uruguayan essayist, soul brother in spite of himself to today's gringo neocons doing righteous battle for the values of the West, argued in his *Ariel* that Latin-American culture was the heir to the grand European tradition and that the natural enemies of these values were the Anglo Americans. Rodó's argument had history on its side: Latins, after all, are descended from Rome; the Anglos, as everyone knows, were barbarians. Chauvinistic nonsense? You betcha.

Still, one hears the righteous critics of multiculturalism condescend to allowing certain Hispanic authors into the canon, while the rads promote Latin letters as some sort of critique of the West. *Necios hombres!* to quote Sor Juana out of context. Whatever "Western" means, one thing should be obvious: Latin-American and Anglo-American letters are either in it or out of it together. I must admit, however, the left is responsible for this confusion.

"The Third World." That's a category of politics and economics, not culture. "The South" is trendier, but perhaps the Poor World is the only real category. Because most poor people today live in Africa, Asia, and among the nonwhite communities of Latin America (and Anglo America, but never mind), it's common to locate the Third/South/Poor World outside the West and outside Western culture. The left—or a loose cluster of progressives, visionaries, and *artistas*, as far back as the European modernists of the late 19th century—has glorified the Third World, has seen its values and attitudes as alternatives to the worst of the West. Thus, the revolutionary drive of Latin America seemed like a good idea a while ago, and the notion of Latin-American literature as Third World and, mutatis mutandis, non-Western, was born. Blame it on Fidel Castro.

No kidding. The Cuban revolution had a cultural agenda and through its own prestigious venues it promoted the politicized edge of what was a cultural revolution shaking Latin America. No one stopped to think, I'm afraid, that Cuba's literary acumen came from its own, very Western, very elitist, very politically incorrect literary tradition. It was the Cuban influence on Latin letters, for example, that promoted the engagé genre of testimonial narrative, an influence born out of generation after generation of a vanguardism that often wallowed, quite gloriously, in decadence. Which means that the same force that gave life to such a rarefied cultural artifact as Lezama Lima's *Paradiso* also begat, in a screwy way, *I, Rigoberta Menchú*.

But I'm here neither to bury Castro nor to praise him. The point is that if García Márquez is non-Western, so is Faulkner. Borges? Yes, if his favorite sources, cabalistic philosophy, Norse mythology, and Chesterton's fiction, are also. Rulfo, who was at least non-Western by blood, was a strict formalist in the European tradition, even if his subject matter was the mestizo peasantry, no less Western than Vargas Llosa, whose white face cost him a presidential election last year. And let's not forget Carpentier and Cortázar: their thick French accents would've gotten them lynched by partisans had they lived in Goya's Spain.

Latin America is populated by non-Western peoples, as is this America, and like this America, its culture has been and still is firmly in the hands of the dreaded White Male. Oh, I know a certain Anglo tendency thinks of Hispanics (in the original sense: people of Spanish culture and blood) as nonwhite, but that, like the Black Legend, is a residue from the days when our parent empires were warring. It's a European (Western?) hangover. You're in America, act like a *criollo*, for chrissakes.

Multiculturalism has a separatist current (if I'm Latino and you're not, you can't use my secret handshake), and some of it is, alas, necessary for survival—literally, in some streets: culturally, in some salons. It also has an integrationist current. And that means enlarging the scope of culture by breaking down the artificial barriers erected by chauvinism. In that current, culture is no one's hegemony: not one nationality's, not one class's, not one gender's, not one race's, no one's. It's culture as integration, instead of submission and assimilation. It's culture defined in that most generous of old-fashioned concepts: the humanities. If it's human, it's yours. Take it. Share it. Mix it. Rock it.

DIVERSE NEW WORLD

Cornel West

Cornel West, professor of religion and director of the Afro-American Studies Program at Princeton, is the author of, among other works, *The American Evasion of Philosophy* and *The Ethical Dimensions of Marxist Thought*. This article was originally a talk at the Socialist Scholars Conference and was published in the July/August 1991 issue of *Democratic Left,* the organ of the Democratic Socialists of America.

We are grappling with the repercussions and implications of what it means to live now forty-six years after the end of the age of Europe. This age began in 1492, with the encounter between Europeans and those who were in the new world, with the massive expulsion of Jews in Spain, and with the publication of the first Indo-European grammar books in 1492. It continued through World War II, the concentration camps, and the shaking of the then fragile European maritime empires. Forty-six years later is not a long time for that kind of fundamental glacier shift in civilizations that once dominated the world.

Analyzing multiculturalism from a contemporary philosophical perspective, and looking at its roots especially among the professional managerial strata, in museums, in galleries, in universities and so forth, it is an attempt to come to terms with how we think of universality when it has been used as a smokescreen for a particular group. How do we preserve notions of universality given the fact that various other particularities—traditions, heritages, communities, voices and what have you—are moving closer to the center of the historical stage, pushing off those few voices which had served as the centering voices between 1492 and 1945.

The United States has become the land of hybridity, heterogeneity, and ambiguity. It lacks the ability to generate national identity and has an inferiority complex vis-a-vis Europe, and the U.S. must deal with indigenous people's culture, including the scars and the dead bodies left from its history. Expansion across the American continent trampled the culture and heritages of degraded, hated, haunted, despised African peoples, upon whose backs would constitute one fundamental pillar for the building of the United States and for the larger industrializing processes in Europe.

Within the milticulturalist debate, leading Afrocentric and Africanist thinkers Leonard Jeffries and Molefi Asante articulate a critical perspective that says they are tired of the degradation of things African. On this particular point, they're absolutely right. However, they don't have a subtle enough sense of history, so they can't recognize ambiguous legacies of traditions and civilizations. They refuse to recognize the thoroughly hybrid culture of almost every culture we have ever discovered. In the case of Jeffries, this lack of subtlety slides down an ugly xenophobic slope—a mirror image of the Eurocentric racism he condemns.

We need to see history as in part the cross-fertilization of a variety of different cultures, usually under conditions of hierarchy. That's thoroughly so for the U.S. For example, jazz is the great symbol of American culture, but there's no jazz without European instruments or African poly-rhythms. To talk about hybrid culture means you give up all quest for pure traditions and pristine heritages.

Yes, black folk must come up with means of affirming black humanity. Don't just read Voltaire's great essays on the light of reason—read the "Peoples of America," in which he compares indigenous peoples and Africans to dogs and cattle. Don't read just Kant's *Critique of Pure Reason*, read the moments in *The Observations of the Sublime*, in which he refers to Negroes as inherently stupid. It's not a trashing of Kant. It's a situating of Kant within eighteenth century Germany, at a time of rampant xeno-phobia, along with tremendous breakthroughs in other spheres. An effective multicultural critique recognizes both the crimes against humanity and the contributions to hu-manity from the particular cultures in Europe.

We have to demystify this notion of Europe and Euro-centrism. Europe has always been multicultural. Shake-speare borrowed from Italian narratives and pre-European narratives. When we think of multiculturalism, we're so deeply shaped by the American discourse of positively valued whiteness and negatively valued blackness, that somehow it's only when black and white folk interact that real multiculturalism's going on. The gradation of hybridity and heterogeneity is not the same between the Italians and the British, and the West Africans and the British. But "Europe" is an ideological construct. It doesn't exist other than in the minds of elites who tried to constitute a homogeneous tradition that could bring together heterogeneous populations—that's all it is.

In looking at history with a subtle historical sense, I also have in mind the fundamental question: What do we have in common? By history, I mean the human responses to a variety of different processes over time and space— various social structures that all human beings must respond to. In responding to these circumstances, the problem has been that most of us function by a kind of self-referential altruism, in which we're altruistic to those nearest to us, and those more distant, we tend to view as pictures rather than human beings. Yet, as historical beings, as fallen and fallible historical beings, we do have a common humanity. We must not forget our long historical backdrop. The present is history—that continues to inform and shape and mold our perceptions and orientations.

On the political level, multiculturalism has much to do with our present-day racial polarization—which is in many ways gender polarization, especially given the vicious violence against women, and sexual-orientation polarization with increased attacks on gays and lesbians. These conflicts, mediated or not mediated, reverberate within bureaucratic structures, and within the larger society.

Certain varieties of multiculturalism do have a politics. Afrocentrism is an academic instance of a longer black nationalist tradition, and it does have a politics and a history. Black nationalism is not monolithic—there's a variety of different versions of black nationalism. In so many slices of the black community, with the escalation of the discourse of whiteness and blackness, racism escalates, both in terms of the life of the mind as well as in practices. We're getting a mentality of closing of ranks. This has happened many, many times in the black community; and it takes a nationalist form in terms of its politics. Black nationalism politics is something that has to be called for what it is, understood symptomatically, and criticized openly. It's a question of, if you're really interested in black freedom, I am too—will your black nationalist view in education, will your black nationalist view in politics deliver the black freedom that you and I are interested in? You're upset with racism in Western scholarship. I am too, and some white folk are too.

As democratic socialists, we have to look at society in a way that cuts across race, gender, region, and nation. For most people in the world, their backs are against the wall. When your back is against the wall, you're looking for weaponry: intellectual and existential weaponry to sustain yourself and your self-confidence and your self-affirmation in conditions that seemingly undermine your sense of possibility; political weaponry to organize, mobilize, to bring your power to bear on the status quo.

If you're Afro-American and you're a victim of the rule of capital, and a European Jewish figure who was born in the Catholic Rhineland and grew up as a Lutheran, by the name of Karl Marx, provides certain analytical tools, then you go there. You can't find too many insightful formulations in Marx about what it is to be black; you don't go to Marx for that. You go to Marx to keep track of the rule of capital, interlocking elites, political, banking, financial, that's one crucial source of your weaponry. You don't care where you get it from, you just want to get people off of your back.

If you want to know what it means to be black, to be African in Western civilization and to deal with issues of identity, with bombardment of degrading images, you go to the blues, you go to literature, you go to Du Bois's analysis of race, you go to Anna Julia Cooper's analysis of race. For what it means to be politically marginalized, you go to a particular tradition that deals with that.

To gain a universal perspective, the left must have a

moral focus on suffering. Once you lose that focus, then you're presupposing a certain level of luxury that is all too common among the professional managerial strata in their debates. Their debates begin to focus on who's going to get what slice of what bureaucratic turf for their bid for the mainstream, for middle class status. Now, that for me is one slice of the struggle, but it's just a slice. The center of the struggle is a deeper intellectual and political set of issues: understanding the larger historical scope, the post-European age, the struggles of Third World persons as they attempt to deal with their identity, their sense of economic and political victimization. We need to not only understand but also to assist people trying to forge some kinds of more democratic regimes, which is so thoroughly difficult.

Let's not package the debate in static categories that predetermine the conclusion that reinforces polarization— that's the worst thing that could happen. Polarization paralyzes all of us—and we go on our middle class ways, and the folk we're concerned about continue to go down the drain.

The political challenge is to articulate universality in a way that is not a mere smokescreen for someone else's particularity. We must preserve the possibility of universal connection. That's the fundamental challenge. Let's dig deep enough within our heritage to make that connection to others.

We're not naive, we know that argument and critical exchange are not the major means by which social change takes place in the world. But we recognize it has to have a role, has to have a funciton. Therefore, we will trash older notions of objectivity, and not act as if one group or community or one nation has a god's eye view of the world. Instead we will utilize forms of intersubjectivity that facilitate critical exchange even as we recognize that none of us are free of presuppositions and prejudgments. We will put our arguments on the table and allow them to be interrogated and contested. The quest for knowledge without presuppositions, the quest for certainty, the quest for dogmatism and orthodoxy and ridigity is over.

THE CHALLENGE FOR THE LEFT

Barbara Ehrenreich

Barbara Ehrenreich, the social critic, *Time* magazine columnist, and author of *The Worst Years of Our Lives* and
other books, gave this talk at the Socialist Scholars Conference. It was published in *Democratic Left*, July/August
1991.

When Communism collapsed in the Soviet Union and
Eastern Europe, I knew there would have to be a replacement for it—because the American right requires an evil,
all-powerful ideological enemy. And so I waited, wondering
what would replace the international Communist conspiracy.

An answer came with the media assault on multiculturalism. It started with a *Newsweek* cover story which used
words like "totalitarianism" and "new fundamentalism."
New York Magazine, Time, and many others, have all devoted major attention to the issue of multiculturalism—

which I believe most of their readers had never heard of until they read it in the magazines.

The attack on multiculturalism originated in places like *Commentary, Partisan Review,* and *The New Republic,* which is increasingly a journal of the right. The U.S. right itself, in its less intellectual manifestations, has been going through a subtle shift away from the pro-family focus of the eighties toward a greater focus on race, immigration, and ethnic diversity. This shift is reflected in the English-only movement and in the relative success of David Duke—who did not play up issues like abortion but stuck to "white empowerment." Even Jesse Helms's successful campaign has been attributed mostly to his anti-affirmative action commercial, rather than the traditional issues of school prayer and abortion.

The American new right is becoming more and more like the new right in Europe—which has always focused on nativist and racist issues. This is a predictable sort of response to the internationalization of capital and labor—a racist, nativist backlash. The drive against multicultural-ism in education is ultimately only the intellectual expres-sion of this ugly development on the right.

People on the left should defend multiculturalism from the right's campaign. The most pragmatic defense is that, in the face of an increasingly global economy, in the face of our own society, which is now more than 20 percent so called minorities, the old *monocultural* education will not do. Monoculturalism represents a retreat into parochialism, and in a practical sense, is not a good preparation for living in this world. I should explain that when I say multicultur-alism, I do not mean African-American students studying only African-American subjects; I mean African-Ameri-cans studying Shakespeare (perhaps taught by African-American professors). I mean Caucasian students studying

African-American history, Asian-American history, and so on. That is my idea of a genuine multicultural education.

However, we're not going to be able to defend multiculturalism without addressing its silly and obnoxious side, the phenomenon of political correctness. I have seen P.C. culture on college campuses, chiefly among relatively elite college students and on relatively elite college campuses. It amounts to a form of snobbery that is easily made fun of by the right and even by students who are not on the right. P.C. culture, as far as I can tell, is a limited phenomenon. The major problems on American campuses are racial and sexual harassment, alcoholism, and the anti-intellectualism of young white Republican males. Interestingly, there were no cover stories about the wave of racist incidents that occurred on college campuses a couple of years ago. The emphasis in the media is all wrong here: P.C.-ness has been blown out of all proportion.

Nevertheless, it is worth talking about some problems with P.C. culture among students. First, there's a tendency to rely on administration-enforced rules to stop offensive speech and to enforce a new, and quite admirable, kind of civility. Quite aside from the free speech issue, the problem is: Rules don't work. If you outlaw the use of the term "girl" instead of "woman," you're not going to do a thing about the sexist attitudes underneath. Changing sexist, racist, and homophobic attitudes is a challenge for those of us who believe in a multicultural, just, and equal world. It is not a problem you turn over to the police, to the administration, or anybody else. The only route is through persuasion, education, and organizing.

Secondly, there is a tendency to confuse verbal purification with real social change. I've noticed students that I would characterize as P.C. who get very worked up about imagined or real verbal slights, but you don't see them running en masse to support campus workers when they're organizing or striking. I've sat in meetings with students who agonized at great length about the way they were going to work against the war, and agonized about the coaltion they would need to get together, and about how they couldn't possibly make a move until they had every one of sixteen different constituencies involved. All this agonizing was a lot easier of course, than getting out in the community to talk to as many citizens as possible about the terrible things that were done in our name in the Middle East.

Now, I'm all for verbal uplift. I like being called Ms. I don't want people saying "man" when they mean me, too. I'm willing to make an issue of these things. But I know that even when all women are Ms., we'll still get sixty-five cents for every dollar earned by a man. Minorities by any other name—people of color, or whatever—will still bear a huge burden of poverty, discrimination, and racial harassment. Verbal uplift is not the revolution.

Finally, I worry about the paralysis of the P.C. subculture on some campuses, and its unattractiveness to potential radicals. I've seen former high school radicals get turned off by the P.C. environment on some college campuses. Why would you want to join a group just to be criticized and "corrected"? Remember that the expression "politically correct" was crafted by people on the left, some time in the seventies, I believe, as a form of self-mockery. We have to regain that sense of humor and perspective.

To return to multiculturalism: I am alarmed that there has been so little response to the media fuss over multiculturalism from intellectuals of the left. In our defense, of multiculturalism, we should not make the mistake that many conservatives make of confusing multiculturalism with the left itself. First, for the somewhat embarrassing reason that the left is not sufficiently multicultural to deserve being confused with multiculturalism, at least not yet. The left is very Balkanized. There's an African-American left, there are feminist lefts, and so forth. In most quarters, multiculturalism would be a big step upward on the left, something to strive for.

Second, multiculturalism does not, so far as I can see, define a moral or political outlook. It is at best pluralism, which is a big step up from *mon-ism*. Too often, however, it leads to the notion of politics as a list. Political "theory" becomes a list of all the groups, issues, and concerns that you must remember to check off lest you offend somebody with no larger perspective connecting them. But a list does not define a political outlook.

Multiculturalism as pluralism leads to a moral slackness, the slackness of cultural relativism. As an example, consider the arguments that some of us had during the Gulf crisis, about how to criticize gender relations in Saudi Arabia. One of the positions was that you can't criticize gender relations in Saudi Arabia, because that's "their" culture. But I'm not comfortable with a political outlook that says I can't criticize what looks to me like gender apartheid. As Cornel West has said, there has to be some way that the different perspectives can begin to interpenetrate, so that in a debate like this for example, I can learn something about Arab culture, but I can also make my criticism of its gender relations.

At a deeper level, though, any possibility of a moral perspective gets erased by a position fashionable among some of our post-modernist academics, that there can be no absolutes, no truths, and hence, no grounds for moral judgments. There can't be a left if there's no basis for moral judgment, including judgments that will cut across group or gender or ethnic lines. There can be no left where the only politics is narrow politics of identity. We have to defend multiculturalism, but let's remember always that at its intellectual and moral core, the left isn't multi-anything.

Yes, the left should be diverse in its representation and its constituencies, but the left always has to be an attempt to find, in the rich diversity of the human world, some point of moral unity that brings us all together.

PAUL BERMAN, a 1991 recipient of the prestigious MacArthur Fellowship, is regarded as one of America's top political and cultural commentators. His essays on the American Left, the Nicaraguan Revolution, the Rushdie affair, and other topics are well known to the readers of *The Village Voice, The New Republic, The New York Times Book Review, Dissent,* and other magazines. He served as drama critic of *The Nation,* 1984–86, and is now a fellow of the New York Institute for the Humanities at New York University. He is currently working on a history of the American left.